Small Business Marketing

FOR

DUMMIES®

2ND EDITION

Praise for "Small Business Marketing For Dummies"

"Schenck writes with the authority of a woman who has been advising clients for 20 years. . . . Marketing issues are presented as real-world problems with real-world solutions. Entrepreneurs of all sizes should be able to identify strategies they can use immediately."

— *Business Week*

"Barbara Schenck's *Small Business Marketing For Dummies* threads the needle between sky-high strategy and ground-level tactics — the space every small business owner experiences daily and sometimes hourly. Most importantly, Barbara isn't afraid to drive stakes in the ground with business ratios, average costs, and response rates that deliver practical value at both levels."

— Gene Kinkaid, Instructor, Department of Advertising, University of Texas at Austin

"Barbara's book is like a 4-year degree in marketing packaged by a person who has been there, done that. Her understandable and realistically actionable advice gives you the street smart steps to do the right things. This book is a shining testimony to clarity, crispness, and advice you can remember and act on."

— Bob Boylan, Executive Presentation Consultant and Author, President/Owner of Successful Presentations

"Go ahead, clear your shelf of all other marketing books. From now on you only need one, and this is it! The accuracy and detail of this concise volume is remarkable. This book reads like you're getting the real scoop from a trusted friend — only this friend is a knowledgeable marketing pro. Give it to your marketing people and ad agency; they could use it as well."

— Robert L. Newhart II, CEO, Innovation Center

Small Business Marketing

FOR

DUMMIES®

2ND EDITION

by **Barbara Findlay Schenck**

Marketing Consultant

Wiley Publishing, Inc.

Small Business Marketing For Dummies, 2nd Edition

Published by
Wiley Publishing, Inc.
111 River St.
Hoboken, NJ 07030-5774
www.wiley.com

Copyright © 2005 by Wiley Publishing, Inc., Indianapolis, Indiana

Published simultaneously in Canada

For general information on our other products and services, please contact our Customer Care Department within the U.S. at 800-762-2974, outside the U.S. at 317-572-3993, or fax 317-572-4002.

For technical support, please visit www.wiley.com/techsupport.

Wiley also publishes its books in a variety of electronic formats. Some content that appears in print may not be available in electronic books.

Library of Congress Control Number: 2004117340

ISBN: 0-7645-7839-1

Manufactured in the United States of America

10   9   8   7   6   5   4   3

2O/RY/QR/QV/IN

WILEY

About the Author

Barbara Findlay Schenck built her career matching products to markets, which is what marketing — and what this book — is all about.

Her involvement in the field began in the University of Oregon public relations office, where she developed an interest in marketing that she has followed literally around the world. She graduated with a degree in English from Oregon State University and immediately moved to Hawaii, where she became director of admissions and instructor of writing at a small private college on Oahu before joining the staff of Honolulu's largest public relations firm.

In 1978 she and her husband, Peter, left Hawaii for a village on the South China Sea, where for two years they managed a development program for the Peace Corps in Malaysia.

In 1980, they returned to their home state of Oregon and founded an advertising agency, attracting a clientele that included ski and golf resorts, banks, apparel and equipment manufacturers, the state's tourism, lottery, and job training divisions, and a good number of small and larger-sized businesses that provided the wealth of hands-on experience reflected in this book.

In 1995, they sold the agency and moved with their son to Italy, where Barbara began work on several book projects. In 2000, she co-wrote *Portraits of Guilt*, the Edgar Award-nominated memoir of internationally recognized criminal investigative artist Jeanne Boylan. In 2001, she authored the first edition of *Small Business Marketing For Dummies*, which *Business Week* praised for presenting "marketing issues as real-world problems with real-world solutions."

Today, she's still forming her thoughts into headlines, news releases, and marketing plans, but on a more relaxed schedule. In addition to writing, she offers marketing presentations and workshops. Contact her by writing BFSchenck@aol.com.

Author's Acknowledgments

As I finish this second, updated edition of *Small Business Marketing For Dummies*, my gratitude reaches back to all those who helped bring the book into existence the first time round, and it spins forward to the current long list of those who helped me overhaul the contents to incorporate the rapid-fire changes that affect today's business world.

As in the first edition, my greatest thanks goes to Peter, my husband, collaborator, and best friend, and to our son Matthew, who bails me out with computer advice and, increasingly, with marketing wisdom gleaned from his own ascent in the business world.

My longtime and treasured business associates and friends Kathy DeGree and Meaghan Ryan Houska win heaps of appreciation for the resources, perspective, and enthusiasm they've shared throughout this and every other project we've undertaken together.

Revising this book to address the technical realities of today's world required current, hands-on expertise, and I am deeply indebted to our hometown newspaper, *The Bulletin*, for providing help without limit as I prepared the chapters on media buying and public relations. Likewise, I'm grateful to the team at Alpine Internet Solutions who shared hours reviewing the online marketing advice included in Chapter 16.

Brad Hill, author of *Building Your Business with Google For Dummies* didn't think twice before responding to my call for help. The same is doubly true for Jim Schell, author of *Small Business For Dummies,* with whom I'm fortunate to work on an ongoing basis.

In the first edition I wrote that my book's editorial team, led by editor Norm Crampton, "would make any author wish for an encore performance." This edition is proof that wishes come true. This time, thanks goes to Acquisitions Editor Kathy Cox (a champion), Project Editor Corbin Collins (I still can't believe my luck that someone with his talent edited this book), and Technical Reviewer Kimberly McCall, the Marketing Angel referred to us by the wonderful editors at *Entrepreneur* magazine.

Finally and most sincerely, my gratitude in life begins and ends with my parents, Walt and Julie Findlay, and the best three sisters ever put on this earth. Thank you all.

Publisher's Acknowledgments

We're proud of this book; please send us your comments through our Dummies online registration form located at www.dummies.com/register/.

Some of the people who helped bring this book to market include the following:

Acquisitions, Editorial, and Media Development

Project Editor: Corbin Collins

(Previous Edition: Norm Crampton)

Acquisitions Editor: Kathy Cox

Copy Editor: Corbin Collins

Assistant Editor: Holly Gastineau-Grimes

Technical Editor: Kimberly L. McCall

Editorial Manager: Carmen Krikorian

Editorial Assistants: Courtney Allen, Nadine Bell

Cartoons: Rich Tennant, www.the5thwave.com

Composition

Project Coordinator: Adrienne Martinez

Layout and Graphics: Lauren Goddard, Barry Offringa, Lynsey Osborn, Melanee Prendergast, Jacque Roth, Julie Trippetti, Mary Gillot Virgin

Proofreaders: Leeann Harney, Jessica Kramer, Carl William Pierce, TECHBOOKS Production Services

Indexer: TECHBOOKS Production Services

Publishing and Editorial for Consumer Dummies

Diane Graves Steele, Vice President and Publisher, Consumer Dummies

Joyce Pepple, Acquisitions Director, Consumer Dummies

Kristin A. Cocks, Product Development Director, Consumer Dummies

Michael Spring, Vice President and Publisher, Travel

Brice Gosnell, Associate Publisher, Travel

Kelly Regan, Editorial Director, Travel

Publishing for Technology Dummies

Andy Cummings, Vice President and Publisher, Dummies Technology/General User

Composition Services

Gerry Fahey, Vice President of Production Services

Debbie Stailey, Director of Composition Services

Contents at a Glance

Table of Contents

Introduction

Welcome to the 2nd edition of *Small Business Marketing For Dummies,* updated for faster and easier use by the millions of small businesses that comprise the vast heart and soul of today's business world.

Since *Small Business Marketing For Dummies* first hit bookshelves in 2001, I've visited with hundreds of small business owners to learn how they've used the book, what they've found most useful, and which marketing issues they continue to find most pressing. Again and again I've heard that the needs of small businesses are far more immediate than those of their big-budget corporate cousins. You don't want to know *why* as much as you want to know *how.* You are constantly in search of solutions to put to work — right *now.*

In response to requests for more guerrilla-style tactics, you'll find more bull's-eye Tip icons in the margins throughout this edition. Each flags a cost-effective, do-it-now idea to act upon.

In response to the reality that small businesses either use advertising or alternative means to get the word out, you'll find the contents of this edition are arranged so that all information on advertising is consolidated into Part III, and all information on how to get the word out *without* advertising — using direct mail, publicity, Internet communications, and promotional literature — is in Part IV. This way you can flip right to the part featuring approaches that fit best with your business.

Finally, in response to the fact that today's consumers are wooed by competitive alternatives as never before, this edition includes an all-new Part V, with advice for converting prospects to customers, making sales, developing customer satisfaction, and cultivating loyalty.

Whether you're running a home office, a small firm, a family business, or a nonprofit organization, winning and keeping customers is your key to success. This book shows you how.

How to Know That This Book Is for You

Are you just starting out in business? Or are you so busy trying to run your business that you barely have time for marketing? For that matter, do the words *marketing, advertising,* and *sales* seem interchangeable or confusing? Do you wish some marketing guru would step in to help you out?

Small Business Marketing For Dummies, 2nd Edition, is especially for businesses like yours that operate without the benefit — or the expense — of a high-powered marketing vice-president, an award-winning ad agency, or even a staff person dedicated full-time to the task of managing your marketing program.

Every example is directed at the businessperson who wears all the hats and markets in whatever time remains. If that person sounds a lot like you, keep reading!

How to Use This Book

You have a business to run, customers to serve, product issues to address, and a lineup of deadlines and decisions looming. If you fit the small business mold, you're strapped for time and need quick answers, rapid-fire advice, and street-smart solutions that you can put to work immediately.

Hit the Table of Contents or Index and you can dart straight to the pages that hold the advice you need right now.

Or become the marketing genius for your business by reading this book from cover to cover. It will walk you through the full marketing process and help you tailor your own marketing program, create your marketing messages, and produce marketing communications that work. For the cover price of this book, you can get what big businesses pay big dollars for: a self-tailored marketing "consultation."

How This Book Is Organized

Each part of *Small Business Marketing For Dummies,* 2nd Edition, tackles a different aspect of your marketing program. From marketing terms to marketing plans to nitty-gritty details for getting your marketing message into ads, promotions, and online — you'll find it all shoehorned into the pages of this book.

Part I: Getting Started in Marketing

Part I begins with a plain-language marketing overview that strips away the mystery and puts you in position to rev up your business and jumpstart your marketing program. Subsequent chapters help you analyze and define your customers, your product, and your competitors. A final chapter leads through the essential steps of setting your marketing goals, objectives, strategies, and budgets. In short, Part I helps you shape your business's future.

Part II: Sharpening Your Marketing Focus

This part takes an unbiased look at your marketing to help uncover gaps that may exist between what people believe about your business and what you think or wish they believed. Then it looks at what you've been saying (or not saying) to lead to misperceptions. With all that in mind, it steers you through the process of defining your business position and brand — including explanations of what those terms mean. Finally, it offers advice on when and how to bring in professionals to help you implement your marketing program.

Part III: Creating and Placing Ads

Part III takes you on a tour of the world of advertising, complete with a quick-reference guide to mass media, a glossary of advertising jargon, how-to's for creating print and broadcast ads that work, and step-by-step instructions for planning and buying ad space and time.

Part IV: Getting the Word Out without Advertising

Part IV is packed with information on the tactics small businesses use most, including direct mail, brochures, publicity, promotions, and online communications. In the first edition of this book, Part IV was dedicated to the then-new topic of online marketing. Over a few fast years, though, businesses have adopted Internet marketing so completely that in this edition you'll find online advice integrated throughout the book, along with a fact-filled Chapter 16 dedicated entirely to online marketing ideas and information.

Part V: Winning and Keeping Customers

A widely cited study by the U.S. Department of Commerce found that it takes five times more effort to get a new customer than it does to keep one. This part gives you priceless tips on how to do both. It begins with the process of capturing the interest of prospects and turning these prospects into customers through good sales techniques. Then it moves to the most important topic of all: developing customer loyalty by making customer service a cornerstone of your business.

Part VI: The Part of Tens

Chapter 20 leads you through the ten most important questions to ask and answer before naming or renaming your business or one of its products. Chapter 21 shares ten all-time best and ten all-time worst marketing ideas. Finally, Chapter 22 brings it all together by outlining the ten steps to follow as you build your own easy-to-assemble marketing plan.

Icons Used in This Book

Marketing is full of logos, seals of approval, and official stamps. In keeping with tradition, throughout the margins of this book you'll find symbols that spotlight important points, shortcuts, and warnings. Watch for these icons:

This icon highlights the golden rules for small business marketing. Write them down, memorize them, and use the cheat sheet in the front of this book to remember them.

Remember the line, "Don't tell me, show me"? This icon pops up when an example shows you what the surrounding text is talking about.

Not every idea is a good idea. This icon alerts you to situations that deserve your cautious evaluation. Consider it a flashing yellow light.

The bull's-eye marks tried-and-true approaches for stretching budgets, short-cutting processes, and seizing low-cost, low-effort marketing opportunities.

It's not all Greek, but marketing certainly has its own jargon. When things get a little technical, this icon appears to help you through the translation.

Ready, Set, Go!

The role of marketing is to attract and maintain enough highly satisfied customers to keep your business not just *in* business but on an upward curve. That's what this book is all about.

Part I

Getting Started in Marketing

The 5th Wave   By Rich Tennant

In this part . . .

Whether you're running a do-it-yourself sole proprietorship, a family business, a professional practice, a retail establishment, a non-profit organization, or, for that matter, a multimillion-dollar corporation, Part I helps you focus on the plain-and-simple marketing truths that will fuel your business success.

The chapters in this part offer clear-cut definitions and lead you on your own fact-finding marketing mission, helping you analyze your customer, your product, and your competition before setting goals and objectives that will shape your business future.

If you're in business, you're a marketer. This part gets you well-introduced to your job!

Chapter 1

A Helicopter View of the Marketing Process

In This Chapter

▶ Understanding the meaning and role of marketing

▶ Differentiating small business marketing from big business marketing

▶ Jumpstarting your marketing program

*Y*ou're not alone if you opened this book in part to find the answer to the question: "What is marketing anyway?" Everyone seems to know that marketing is an essential ingredient for business success, but when it comes time to say exactly what it is, certainty takes a nose dive.

If you pick up the phone and call any number of marketing professors, marketing vice presidents, or marketing experts and ask them to define marketing, odds are you won't get the same answer twice. In fact, if you look the word up in different dictionaries, you'll find many different definitions.

To settle the matter right up front, here is a plain-language description of what marketing — and what this book — is all about.

Marketing is the process through which you create — and keep — customers.

- ✔ Marketing is the matchmaker between what your business is selling and what your customers are buying.

- ✔ Marketing covers all the steps that are involved to tailor your products, messages, distribution, customer service, and all other business actions to meet the desires of your most important business asset: your customer.

- ✔ Marketing is a win-win partnership between your business and its market.

Marketing isn't about talking *to* your customers; it's about talking *with* them. Marketing relies on two-way communication between your business and your buyer.

Seeing the Big Picture

If you could get an aerial view of the marketing process, it would look like Figure 1-1. Marketing is a nonstop cycle. It begins with customer knowledge and goes round to customer service before it begins all over again. Along the way, it involves product development, pricing, packaging, distribution, advertising and promotion, and all the steps involved in making the sale and serving the customer well.

The marketing wheel of fortune

Every successful marketing program — whether for a billion-dollar business or a hardworking individual — follows the marketing cycle illustrated in Figure 1-1. The process is exactly the same whether yours is a start-up or an existing business, whether your budget is large or small, whether your market is local or global, and whether you sell through the Internet, via direct mail, or through a bricks and mortar location.

Just start at the top of the wheel and circle round clockwise in a never-ending process to win and keep customers and to build a strong business in the process.

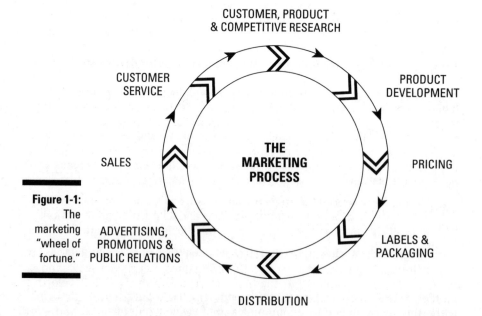

Figure 1-1:
The marketing "wheel of fortune."

CUSTOMER, PRODUCT & COMPETITIVE RESEARCH

CUSTOMER SERVICE

PRODUCT DEVELOPMENT

SALES

THE MARKETING PROCESS

PRICING

ADVERTISING, PROMOTIONS & PUBLIC RELATIONS

LABELS & PACKAGING

DISTRIBUTION

As you loop around the marketing wheel, here are the actions you take:

1. **Get to know your target customer and your marketing environment.**

2. **Tailor your product, pricing, packaging, and distribution strategies** to address your customers' needs, your market environment, and the competitive realities of your business.

3. **Create and project marketing messages** to grab attention, inspire interest, and move your prospects to buying decisions.

4. **Go for and close the sale — but don't stop there.**

5. **Once the sale is made, begin the customer-service phase.** Work to ensure customer satisfaction so that you convert the initial sale into repeat business and word-of-mouth advertising for your business.

6. **Talk with customers to gain input about their wants and needs and your products and services.** Combine what you learn with other research about your market and competitive environment and use your findings to fine-tune your product, pricing, packaging, distribution, promotional messages, sales, and service.

And so the marketing process goes round and round.

In marketing, there are no shortcuts. You can't just jump to the sale, or even to the advertising stage. To build a successful business, you need to follow every step in the marketing cycle, and that's what the rest of the chapters are all about.

Marketing and sales are not synonymous

People confuse the terms *marketing* and *sales*. They think that *marketing* is a high-powered or dressed-up way to say *sales*. Or they mesh the two words together into a single solution that they call *marketing and sales*.

Selling is one of the ways you communicate your marketing message. Sales is the point at which the product is offered, the case is made, the purchasing decision occurs, and the business-to-customer exchange takes place.

Selling is an important part of the marketing process, but it is not and never can be a replacement for it.

Without all the steps that precede the sale — without all the tasks involved in fitting the product to the market in terms of features, price, packaging, and distribution (or availability), and without all the effort involved in developing awareness and interest through advertising, publicity, and promotions — without these, even the best sales effort stands only a fraction of a chance for success.

Marketing: The whole is greater than the parts

Advertising. Marketing. Sales. Promotions. What are the differences? The following story has circulated the marketing world for decades and offers some good answers for what's what in the field of marketing communications:

- If the circus is coming to town and you paint a sign saying "Circus Coming to the Fairground Saturday," that's *advertising*.

- If you put the sign on the back of an elephant and walk it into town, that's *promotion*.

- If the elephant walks through the mayor's flowerbed, that's *publicity*.

- And if you get the mayor to laugh about it, that's *public relations*.

- If the town's citizens go to the circus, and you show them the many entertainment booths, explain how much fun they'll have spending money there, and answer questions, ultimately, if they spend a lot of money at the circus, that's *sales*.

Because marketing involves way more than marketing communications, here's how the circus story might continue if it went on to show where research, product development, and the rest of the components of the marketing process fit in:

- If, before painting the sign that says "Circus Coming to the Fairground Saturday," you check community calendars to see whether conflicting events are scheduled, study who typically attends the circus, and figure out how much they're willing to pay and what kinds of services and activities they prefer, that's *market research*.

- If you invent elephant ears for people to eat while they're waiting for elephant rides, that's *product development*.

- If you create an offer that combines a circus ticket, an elephant ear, an elephant ride, and a memory-book elephant photo, that's *packaging*.

- If you get a restaurant named Elephants to sell your elephant package, that's *distribution*.

- If you ask everyone who took an elephant ride to participate in a survey, that's *customer research*.

- If you follow up by sending each survey participant a thank-you note along with a two-for-one coupon to next year's circus, that's *customer service*.

- And if you use the survey responses to develop new products, revise pricing, and enhance distribution, then you've started the *marketing process* all over again.

Jumpstarting Your Marketing Program

Business owners clear their calendars for the topic of marketing typically at three predictable moments:

- At the time of business start-up

- When it's time to accelerate business growth

- When there's a bump on the road to success, perhaps due to a loss of business because of economic or competitive threats

Your business is likely in the midst of one of those three situations right now. As you prepare to kick your marketing efforts into high gear, flip back a page or two and remind yourself that marketing isn't just about selling. It's about *attracting customers* with good products and strong marketing communications, and then it's about *keeping customers* with products and services that don't just meet but far exceed their expectations. As part of the reward, you win repeat business, loyalty, and new customer referrals.

Marketing a start-up business

If your business is just starting up, you face a set of decisions that existing businesses have already made. Existing companies have existing business images to build upon, whereas your start-up business has a clean slate upon which to write exactly the right story.

Before sending messages into the marketplace, know your answers to these questions:

- ✔ What kind of customer do you want to serve? (See Chapter 2.)
- ✔ How will your product compete with existing options available to your prospective customer? (See Chapter 3.)
- ✔ What kind of business image will you need to build in order to gain your prospect's attention, interest, and trust? (See Chapters 6 and 7.)

A business setting out to serve corporate clients would hardly want to announce itself by placing free flyers in the grocery store entrance. It needs to present a much more exclusive, professional image than that, probably introducing itself through personal presentations or via letters on high-quality stationery accompanied by a credibility-building business brochure.

On the other end of the spectrum, a start-up aiming to win business from cost-conscious customers probably wouldn't want to introduce itself using full-page, full-color ads, because prospects would likely interpret such an investment as an indication that the advertiser's fees are outside the range of their small budgets.

To get your business image started on a strong marketing footing, define your target customer's profile and then project communications capable of attracting that person's awareness and prompting the feeling that, "Hey, this sounds like something for *me*."

Pay special attention to the chapters in Part I of this book. They can help you identify your customers, determine price and present your product, size up your competition, set your goals and objectives, establish your market position and brand, and create marketing messages that talk to the right prospects with the right messages.

If you haven't already settled on your business name, see Chapter 20.

Marketing to grow your business

Established businesses grow their revenues by following one of two main routes:

- ✔ Grow market share by pulling business away from competitors. (See Chapter 4.)
- ✔ Grow customer share by increasing purchases made by existing customers, either by generating repeat business or by achieving larger sales volume at the time of each purchase. (See Chapter 19.)

Almost always, the smartest route is to look inside your business first, work to shore up your product and service offerings, and strengthen your existing customer satisfaction and spending levels *before* trying to win new prospects into your clientele. Part V of this book offers a complete game plan to follow.

Scaling your program to meet your goal

Whether you're launching a new business or accelerating growth of an existing enterprise, start by defining what you're trying to achieve.

Too often, small business owners feel overwhelmed by uncertainty over the scope of the marketing task. They aren't sure how much money they should dedicate to the effort, whether they need to hire marketing professionals, and whether to create ads, brochures, and Web sites. They may have all kinds of other questions that get in the way of forward motion. And they delay launching their marketing efforts as a result.

Here's the solution: Rather than worry about the tools you need to do the job, first put the task in perspective by focusing on what it is you're trying to accomplish. Ask yourself:

- ✔ How much business are we trying to gain?
- ✔ How many clients do we want to add?

A social service agency might set a goal to raise $100,000 in donor funds. An accounting firm might want to attract six corporate clients. A retailer might want to build an additional $50,000 in sales. A doctor might want to attract 100 patients for a particular new service. A weekly newspaper might want to gain 500 new subscribers.

By setting your goal first (more on this important step in Chapter 5), the process of creating your marketing plan (see Chapter 22 for how to write a plan in ten easy steps) becomes a focused, goal-oriented, and vastly easier activity.

How Small Business Marketing Is Different

All marketing programs need to follow the same marketing process, but the similarities between big business and small business marketing stop there. Budgets, staffing, creative approaches, and communication techniques vary hugely between an international mega-marketer like, say, Coca-Cola, and a comparatively micro-budget marketer like, well, like you.

This book is for *you*. Here's why.

Dollar differences

As a small business, you already know one difference between your marketing program and those of the corporate behemoths that loom over you in all directions: The big guys have the big budgets. They talk about a couple hundred thousand dollars as a discretionary line-item issue. You talk about a couple hundred dollars as an amount worthy of careful consideration. The advice in this book is scaled to your budget, not to the million-dollar jackpots you see referenced in most other marketing books.

Staffing differences

Look at the organization chart of any major corporation. Nearly always, you find a marketing vice president. Under that position you see a bunch of other professionals, including advertising directors, sales managers, online marketing managers, research directors, customer service specialists, and so on. In contrast, strong small businesses blend marketing with the leadership function. The small business organization chart puts responsibility for marketing in the very top box, where the owner, in the essential role, oversees the process as a hands-on task.

Creative differences

The top-name marketers routinely spend six figures to create ads with the sole purpose of building name recognition and market preference for their brands — often without a single word about a specific product or price.

Small businesses take a dramatically different approach. They want to develop name recognition just like the biggest advertisers, but their ads have to do double duty. You know firsthand that each and every small business marketing investment has to deliver immediate and measurable market action. Each effort has to stir enough purchasing activity to offset the cost involved in creating and running the ad in the first place. The balancing act, discussed in Part III of this book, is to create consistency in your marketing communications so that they build a clear brand identity while at the same time inspiring the necessary consumer action to deliver sales — *now*.

Strategic differences

In big businesses, bound copies of business plans grace every bookshelf, whereas in many small businesses, the very term *marketing plan* provokes a guilt pang. If you just felt this typical reaction, turn to Chapter 22 for the antidote. It provides an outline for putting your plan in writing — without any mysterious jargon and with advice and examples scaled specifically to small businesses like yours.

Truth is, creating a marketing plan is pretty straightforward and reasonably manageable. It's one of those pay-a-little-now-or-pay-a-lot-more-later propositions. If you invest a bit of time up front to plan your annual marketing program, then implementation of the plan becomes the easy part. But without a plan, you'll spend the year racing around in response to competitive actions, market conditions, and media opportunities that may or may not fit your business needs.

The small business marketing advantage

As a small business owner, you may envy the dollars, people, and organizations of your big-business counterparts, but you have some advantages they envy as well.

The heads of Fortune 500 firms allocate budgets equal to the gross national products of small countries to fund research into getting to know and understand their customers. Meanwhile, you can talk with your customers face to face, day after day, at virtually no additional cost at all.

Because the whole point of marketing is to build and maintain customer relationships, it stands to reason that no business is better configured to excel at the marketing task than the very small business.

Making Marketing Your Key to Success

How many times have you heard small-business people say that they just don't have time for marketing?

Think of it this way. It's the simple truth that without customers, a business is out of business. Because marketing is the process by which your business gets and keeps customers, that means marketing is the key to keeping your business in business.

Put in terms like that, marketing is the single most important activity in any business — including yours. The fact that you're holding this book means you've made a commitment, and that gives you an edge over many of your competitors. Go for it!

Chapter 2

All About Customers

In This Chapter

▶ Getting to know who buys from you

▶ Charting your customer *graphics:* geographics, demographics, and psychographics

▶ Mapping when, how, and why your customers buy

*E*very marketer mulls the same questions: Who are my customers? How did they hear about me? Why do they buy from me? How can I reach more people like them?

Successful businesses use the answers to these questions to influence every product design, pricing, distribution, and communication decision they make.

✔ If your business is going great guns, use this chapter to create a profile of your best customers so that you can attract more just like them.

✔ If your business feels busy, but your sales and profits are weak, this chapter can help you differentiate between the customers who are costing you time and money and the ones who are making you money. Once you know the difference between the two, you can direct your marketing efforts at the moneymakers.

✔ If your business has hit a frustrating plateau — or worse, if your sales are sliding downhill — you need to get and keep more customers, period. That means knowing everything you can about who is buying products or services like the ones you're selling and what it will take to make those people buy from you.

Business owners don't work for themselves; they work for their customers.

This chapter places your perspective on the only boss that really matters in business: that person over there with an open billfold.

Anatomy of a Customer

An important part of knowing your customer is differentiating who's who among your clientele. It's called *market segmentation* — the process of breaking your customers down into segments that share distinct similarities.

Here are some common market segmentation terms and what they mean:

- **Geographics:** Segmenting customers by regions, counties, states, countries, ZIP codes, and census tracts.

- **Demographics:** Segmenting customers into groups based on aspects such as age, sex, race, religion, education, marital status, income, and household size.

- **Psychographics:** Segmenting customers by lifestyle characteristics, behavioral patterns, beliefs, values, and attitudes about themselves, their families, and society.

- **Geodemographics:** A combination of geographics, demographics, *and* psychographics. Geodemographics, also called *cluster marketing* or *lifestyle marketing,* is based on the age-old idea that birds of a feather flock together — that people who live in the same area tend to have similar backgrounds and consuming patterns. Geodemographics helps you to target your marketing efforts by pinpointing neighborhoods or geographic areas where residents share the age, income, lifestyle characteristics, and buying patterns of your prospective customers.

Collecting information about your customer

People with the profile of your current customers are apt to become customers as well. That's why target marketing starts with customer knowledge. By knowing everything you possibly can about the person who currently buys from your business, you can direct your marketing efforts toward others who match that same profile.

Do-it-yourself fact-finding

You can get a good start on conducting customer research without ever walking out the front door of your business.

- **Collect addresses from shipping labels and invoices and group them into areas of geographic concentration.** For example, you can group customers into those living within a certain number of miles of your business, customers living within various regions of your state and within neighboring states, customers living in other countries, and so on.

- **Follow the data trail from credit card transactions to see where customers live.**

✔ **Request ZIP code information at the beginning of cash register transactions.**

✔ **Survey customers.** If your business generates substantial foot traffic, find places where customers naturally pause and be there to conduct formal or informal research — depending on your business environment. Whether you survey all customers or limit your effort to every *n*th customer (every tenth one, for example), keep the question period short and maintain a log of the answers. Spread your interviews over a span of time so that your findings reflect responses from customers during various days and weeks. (Obviously, you don't want to end up with results based only on customers who visit your business at noon on Thursdays!)

One other important reminder: Be sure to respect and protect the privacy of information you collect from customers. Establish and share your company's privacy policy. If you collect information online, visit the Web site of the Online Privacy Alliance (`http://privacyalliance.org`) and click on "Business Resources" for policy guidelines.

A cardinal sin in small business is to treat a long-standing customer like a stranger. As you interview customers, instead of asking, "Is this your first visit?" try to get at the answer indirectly, as shown in these examples:

- The front desk staff can ask, "Have you been here since we moved the reception area?"

- Hotel clerks can ask, "Have you stayed with us since we started our evening wine reception?"

- Savvy restaurateurs don't have to ask at all. They know that if a customer asks for directions to the restroom, that person is likely to be a first-time patron. On the other hand, a waiter who overhears a customer recommending a certain menu item to a tablemate can assume that the patron is a repeat guest.

The important thing is to find ways to treat your loyalists like the very important business insiders they are.

✔ **Observe your customers.** What kinds of cars do they drive? How long do they spend during each visit to your business? Do they arrive by themselves or with friends or family members? Do those who arrive alone account for more sales or fewer sales than those who arrive accompanied by others? Where do they pause or stop in your business? Your observations will help you define your customer profile while also leading to product decisions, as shown in these examples:

- A small theme park may find that most visitors stay for 2 hours and 15 minutes, which is long enough to want something to eat or drink. This could lead to the decision to open a café or restaurant.

- A retailer may realize that women who shop with other women spend more time and money in the store, which may lead to a promotion that offers lunch for two after shopping on certain days of the week.

- A motel may decide to post a restaurant display at a hallway entry where guests consistently pause.

✔ **Use contests to collect information.** Create a postcard-sized survey and use it as a contest entry form. For the cost of a nice prize, you'll collect information that will help you develop your customer profile.

✔ **Monitor the origin of incoming phone calls.** When prospects call for information about your business, find out where they're from and how they found you.

Callers will tolerate only a certain number of questions. Remember that they're calling to *receive* information, not to become research subjects.

- If you use a caller identification phone feature, use it to collect the incoming phone number prefix and area code, which will enable you to create an incoming call geographic origin report.

- Your phone service providers may be able to furnish lists of incoming call area codes or dialing prefixes for your reference.

✔ **Track response to ads and direct mailers.** Include an offer for a brochure, a product sample, or some other incentive to inspire a reaction to your ads. As prospects respond, collect their addresses and other information to build an inquiry profile.

Be sure to deliver the promised item promptly upon request so that the value of your research effort isn't offset by a bad impression generated by slow follow-through.

✔ **Study Web reports to learn about prospects who visit you online.** Work with your Web site hosting and management firm to discuss available reports and how to mine the information you collect.

Research methods

Consider the information in Table 2-1 as you make research decisions.

Table 2-1	Research Approaches		
Method	*Purpose*	*Advantages*	*Challenges*
Questionnaires and surveys	Obtain general information	Anonymous. Inexpensive. Easy to analyze. Easy to format and conduct.	Impersonal.Feedback may not be accurate. Wording can skew results.
Interviews	Obtain information and probe answers	Develops customer relationships. Adaptable to each situation. Accesses fuller range of information.	Time-consuming. Reliant on good interviewers. Difficult to analyze.

Method	Purpose	Advantages	Challenges
Observation	Document actual buyer behavior	Anonymous. Immediate findings. Relatively easy to implement.	Can be difficult to interpret findings. Can be difficult to target which behaviors to monitor. Can be expensive.
Documentation review	Study factual history of clients and transactions	Readily available. Not disruptive to operations. Not subject to interpretation.	Time-consuming. May be incomplete. Research is limited to previously collected data.
Focus groups	Learn about and compare customer experiences and reactions	Convey information to customers. Collect customer impressions.	Requires expert facilitation. Requires advance scheduling. Difficult to analyze findings.

When to call in the pros

Doing it yourself doesn't mean doing it all on your own. Here are places where an investment in professional advice pays off:

- ✔ **Questionnaires:** Figure out what you want to learn and create a list of questions. Retain a trained marketer or market researcher to review the wording, sequence, and format for you. Then have a member of your staff or a freelance designer prepare the handout or mailer so that it makes a good visual impression on your business's behalf. Include a letter or introductory paragraph explaining why you're conducting research and presenting your business as a strong, forward-thinking organization that cares about its customers' opinions and experiences.

- ✔ **Phone or in-person surveys:** Employ an outside group to do the questioning on your behalf. When you ask the questions yourself, it's easy to let your biases, preconceptions, and business pressures leak through and sway your customers. Posing questions so that they don't skew the results is a real art. Plus, customers are more apt to be candid with third parties. (If you need proof, think of all the things people are willing to say behind someone's back that they'd never say to the person's face. The same premise applies in customer research.)

- ✔ **Focus groups:** If you're assembling a group of favorite clients to talk casually about a new product idea, you're fine to go it alone. But if you're trying to elicit helpful information from outsiders or if you want to learn opinions about such delicate areas as customer service or pricing, use a professional facilitator who is experienced in managing group dynamics so that a single dominant participant doesn't steer the group outcome.

To seek outside assistance, contact research firms, advertising agencies, marketing firms, and public-relations companies. Explain what you're trying to accomplish and ask whether they can either do the research for you or direct you toward the right resources.

Another good starting point is your Small Business Development Center, often located at a community college or university. To find a nearby center, visit the Small Business Association Web site at `www.sba.gov/sbdc` and click on the "Your Nearest SBDC" button.

Geographics: Locating your market areas

The fact that you can be located in Rome, Georgia, and serve customers in Rome, Italy, doesn't necessarily make the Eternal City a target market for your business. To target your market geographically, you need to ask, "Where am I most likely to find potential customers, and where am I most apt to inspire enough sales to offset my marketing investment?" To help you answer these questions, here's some advice:

- ✔ **Start with the addresses of your existing customers:** Wherever you have a concentration of existing customers, you also have a concentration of *potential* customers. Those are the areas where you should direct your advertising efforts and money.

- ✔ **Follow your inquiries:** Inquiries are customers waiting to happen. They are consumers whose interest you've aroused and whose radar screens you have managed to pop onto, even though they haven't yet made the decision to purchase your product or service. The addresses of your inquiries will define target geographic areas where people have demonstrated interest in the products and services you offer. Your first objective should be to convert inquiry interest into buying action (see Chapter 17 for inquiry-to-customer conversion information). At the very least, your inquiry follow-up efforts will help you find out why prospects *didn't* buy, and that information may help you retool your product, pricing, distribution, or communications.

- ✔ **Locate your noncustomers:** Identify geographic areas with concentrations of people who have the attributes of your current customers but who don't yet buy from you. These are noncustomers who are also *potential* customers. By discovering regions where these prospects live, you also discover areas for potential market expansion.

- Start with calls to advertising representatives at the leading publications that serve your business sector. Media outlets conduct and purchase research, and often they will share information as a way to convince you of their ability to carry your marketing message to the right prospects. Ask for information regarding geographic areas with a concentration of people who fit your customer profile.

- Contact your industry association. Inquire about industry market analyses that detail geographic areas with concentrated interest in your offerings. If your offering is one that can be exported beyond your regional marketplace, you may discover national or international market opportunities that you otherwise wouldn't have considered.

- Visit your library reference desk. Study the *SRDS Lifestyle Market Analyst,* a rich source of market-by-market demographic and lifestyle information, and the *CACI Sourcebook of ZIP Code Demographics,* which details the population profiles of 150 U.S. ZIP codes and county areas. Through these resources, you can find and target areas that have a concentration of residents with lifestyle interests ranging from sewing to golfing to crossword puzzles — and everything in between. If your business offers, for example, a product for pets, these books can lead you to the market areas with concentrations of pet owners. (See the Appendix for additional information about these and other resources.)

Each time you discover a geographic area with easy access to your business and with a concentration of residents who fit your buyer profile, you've uncovered an area that should be on your list of geographic target markets.

Demographics: Collecting data to define your market

After you've determined *where* your customers are, the next step is to define *who* they are so that you can target your marketing decisions directly at people who fit your customer profile.

Sometimes business owners want to think that their products have such wide appeal that everyone is part of their market. That's a costly mistake, though, because if you try to market to *everyone,* you'll have to place ads *everywhere,* which is a budget-breaking proposition. The answer is to narrow your customer definition by using demographic facts to zero in on exactly whom you serve. Follow these steps:

1. **Start with your own general impressions** to define your customers in broad terms based on age, education level, ethnic background, income, marital status, profession, sex, and household size. Answer these questions about your customers:

   - Are they mostly male or female?

   - Are they mostly children, teens, young adults, early retirees, or senior citizens?

   - Are they students, college grads, or PhDs?

   - What do they do — are they homemakers, teachers, young professionals, or doctors?

   - Are they mostly single, couples with no children at home, heads of families, grandparents, or recent empty nesters?

2. **Break your market into subgroups,** perhaps categorized by the kinds of products purchased or the time of year they do business with you.

   A restaurant that analyzes its weekday lunchtime clientele and patrons of its dinner business might learn that the products draw customers with dramatically different demographic profiles. As a result, the restaurant may realize that its weekday lunch hour clientele is comprised mostly of businesspeople from the nearby area, whereas the dinner traffic is largely tourist families. This may lead to development of two very different and highly targeted promotions: a *50 minutes or it's free* lunchtime offer aimed at the nearby business community and promoted through the chamber of commerce newsletter or some other low-cost local business publication; and a *Kids under 7 eat free* offer aimed at tourists and promoted through hotel desk clerks and local visitor publications.

3. **Verify your answers by asking your customers.**

   You can incorporate questions into information conversations you have during inquiry and sales contacts. Table 2-1, earlier in this chapter, outlines a list of information-collection options.

Psychographics: Customer buying behaviors

Knowing *where* your customer is and the statistical facts about *who* your customer is give you the information you need to select the right communication vehicles to carry your marketing messages. As you decide *what* to say and *how* to present your message, you also want to know as much as you can about the attitudes, beliefs, purchasing patterns, and behaviors of your customers. This information helps you form marketing messages that interest your prospects and motivate them to buy from you.

Start by defining who isn't a prospect for your product

Sometimes the easiest way to start your customer profiling is to think about who *isn't* likely to buy from your business.

- ✔ A manufacturer of swing sets knows that its customers aren't young professional couples living in urban lofts. It needs to talk to families whose homes have backyards.

- ✔ A landscape and nursery business knows that it won't find many customers in downtown high-rise apartments.

- ✔ A manufacturer of architectural siding may decide that its buyer isn't the end user — or homeowner — at all. Rather, the customer is the architect who specifies the product in the first place.

- ✔ A homebuilder specializing in custom-built family houses with price tags starting at $300,000 can be pretty certain that its customers aren't young families getting ready to dive into home ownership for the first time; nor are they families currently living in neighborhoods full of million-dollar homes. Instead, the builder might narrow its focus to 30- to 40-year-old individuals or couples with at least one child, who currently live in homes they own but who are seeking to move to nicer residences in areas with higher prestige than those provided by their current addresses.

Look at what your customers have in common

Particularly, study the tendencies of your best customers — the ones who account for the fewest service problems and the greatest profits. Make a list of their common traits by answering the following questions:

- ✔ Do they buy on impulse or after careful consideration?

- ✔ Are they cost-conscious or more interested in the quality and prestige of the purchase?

- ✔ Are they loyal shoppers who buy from you on a frequent basis or are they one-time buyers?

- ✔ Do they buy from your business exclusively or do they also patronize your competitors?

- ✔ Do they reach you through a certain channel — for example, your satellite office or your Web site — or do they contact you via referrals from other businesses or professionals?

A retailer in a vacation destination area might categorize its customers into the following subgroups:

- ✔ **Geographic origin:** Local residents, in-state visitors, out-of-state visitors, international visitors

- ✔ **Activity interest:** Golfers, skiers, campers, business travelers/convention guests

By creating customer subgroups, the retailer can begin to chart which kinds of guests purchase which kinds of products or respond to which kinds of offers.

You'll see patterns emerge. Certain customer groups account for higher sales volume or more frequent purchases. Or perhaps some subgroups purchase certain types of products from you. Once you know the tendencies of your various market segments, you know what to say to each target group.

Using customer profiles to guide marketing decisions

Customer knowledge leads to strong marketing decisions, including decisions that affect product development, media selections, and the creation of marketing messages. The following two examples show how businesses use customer knowledge to steer their marketing efforts.

✔ A downtown dry-cleaning and laundry business determines that its market is comprised primarily of affluent professionals who live and work in the nearby area. Knowing this, the business decides to remain open from 6:30 a.m. until 7:00 p.m. so that its customers, who work full-time during the day, can drop in before and after work. Additionally, when placing ads, the business avoids airing broadcast messages during daytime hours when its prospects are at work. Instead, it schedules ads during evening and weekend financial, news, and sports programs.

✔ A life-insurance representative finds that her clients are primarily young, newly married couples. Knowing this, she rejects a half-price offer to run an ad in an upcoming special section of the local newspaper focusing on senior citizens. Instead, she approves a schedule that includes ads in the newspaper's entertainment section, where her prospects may be looking for information about things to do over the weekend. And she asks the media advertising representatives to let her know when they're publishing special sections on home improvements or do-it-yourself money-saving remodeling — or any other opportunities that would correlate with the lifestyles and interests of her market.

Determining Which Customers Buy What

Especially for small businesses, marketing is a matter of resource allocation. It's about figuring out who's buying what and then weighting your marketing efforts behind the products and markets apt to give you the best return on your marketing investment.

No budget — not even those of mega-brands like General Motors or McDonald's — is big enough to do it all. At some point, every marketer has to decide to throw its dollars into the markets and products that have the best chance of delivering results.

Viewing your sales by market segment

Break your sales down by product categories to determine what kind of buyers your products attract. Then define the customer for each line.

✔ A furniture manufacturer might divide its products into office, dining, and children's lines — each meeting the demands of a different market segment and even employing a different distribution and retailing strategy. When planning marketing communications, the manufacturer would follow three separate strategies, placing primary emphasis (and budget allocation) on the line that research shows is most apt to deliver top sales volume over the upcoming period.

✔ An accounting firm might sort its clientele both by type of service purchased and by client profile. It might target individual clients for tax-return business during the first quarter of the year, high-net worth clients for estate- and tax-planning right after the shell shock of the April 15 tax-filing deadline, and business clients for strategic planning services in early fall, when those customers are thinking about their business plans for the upcoming year.

After you know where your target markets are located, try to determine the kind of products that are of greatest interest in each area. This information can help you target your product promotions.

A motel owner may find that customers from a particular market area stay predominantly at the hotel for only one night at a time and usually only over weekends, but guests from another area tend to stay three nights and usually arrive mid-week.

Knowing this, the motel might choose to promote quick getaway offers to the weekend travel group, perhaps offering incentives to get guests to stay a second night. But the motel wouldn't likely promote three-night stays to this market segment, as that offer wouldn't fit the market's proven interests. Similarly, the motel would be wasting money if it marketed one-night offers in the three-night market, because customers in that area are interested in booking longer stays.

Table 2-2 shows how a motel might categorize its market geographically so that it can learn the travel tendencies of each area and respond with appropriate promotional offers.

Table 2-2	Geographic Market Distribution Analysis: Mountain Valley Motel			
	Hometown	Rest of Home State	Neighboring States	Other Natl./ Internatl.
Total Sales				
$712,000	$56,960	$462,800	$128,160	$6,080
	8%	65%	18%	9%
Sales by Length of Stay				
1-night stay	$48,416	$83,304	$19,224	$3,204
2-night stay	$2,848	$231,400	$70,488	$32,448
3–5 night stay	none	$101,816	$32,040	$28,428
6+ night stay	$5,696	$46,280	$6,408	none
Sales by Season				
Summer	$5,696	$277,680	$96,120	$54,468
Fall	$11,962	$55,536	$12,816	$6,408
Winter	$4,557	$37,024	$6,408	none
Holiday	$22,783	$23,140	none	none
Spring	$11,962	$69,420	$12,816	$3,204

With detailed market knowledge, a business can make market-sensitive decisions that lead to promotions tailored specifically to consumer patterns and demands. The following examples show how the motel featured in Table 2-2 might use its findings to make future marketing decisions:

- ✔ **Local market guests** primarily stay for a single night, and mostly during the holiday season. This tendency provides some good local area promotion opportunities. Additionally, 10 percent of local guests stay for six nights or longer, likely while they are going through household renovations or lifestyle changes. This long-stay business tends to occur during nonsummer periods when the motel occupancy is low, so the motel may want to consider special rates to attract more of this low-season business.

- ✔ **Within the home state market area** half of the guests spend two nights per stay, although nearly a third spend three to six nights, which proves that the motel is capable of drawing statewide guests for longer stays. This information might lead to an add-a-day promotion idea. Three-quarters of home state guests visit during the peak-season summer months. The motel would be wise to offer summer guests special incentives that encourage them to return in the spring and fall to build year-round business.

✔ **National and international guests** account for approximately one-quarter of the motel's business. Because these guests are a far-flung group, the cost of trying to reach them in their home market areas via advertising would be staggering. Instead, the motel managers might research how they found out about the motel in the first place. If they booked following advice from travel agents or tour group operators, the managers might cultivate those sources for more bookings. Or, if they made their decisions while driving through town, the motel would benefit from a few well-placed billboard ads to inspire more such spur-of-the-moment stays.

Conduct a similar analysis for your own business:

✔ How do your products break down into product lines? (See Chapter 3 for more information about this important topic.)

✔ What kind of customer is the most prevalent buyer for each line?

If you determine that one of your product lines attracts customers who are highly discerning and prestige-oriented, you probably won't want to employ a strategy that relies on coupons, for example. Likewise, if you know that a certain product line appeals to a particularly athletic or health-conscious group, you can forget about trying to prompt purchases by offering such things as all-you-can-eat dinners.

Tracing your distribution channels

Distribution is the means by which you get your product to the customer. A good distribution system blends knowledge about your customer (from the first half of this chapter, that part should be clear) with knowledge of how that person ended up with your product (that's what distribution is about). It's often a surprisingly roundabout route.

To demonstrate, take a look at how visitors might arrive at a local museum or cultural attraction.

Say that 50,000 visitors walk through the turnstiles every year. Suppose that 10,000 of those visitors are school groups who arrive on school buses, 5,000 arrive as part of tour groups, 5,000 arrive with tickets prepurchased through local motels and hotels, 5,000 prepurchased their tickets online through the Web sites of the museum and the regional visitor bureau, 5,000 arrive with tickets distributed by partner businesses as part of special promotional programs, and 20,000 arrive at the museum's entry gate as either museum members or independent visitors.

Based on these numbers, the museum is distributing its tickets through the following channels:

- ✔ Educators (possibly influenced by curriculum directors)
- ✔ Tour companies (possibly influenced by state or local travel bureaus)
- ✔ Lodging establishment front desks (probably influenced by hotel and motel marketing departments)
- ✔ The Internet (possibly influenced by state or local travel bureaus)
- ✔ Partner businesses (through museum promotional efforts)
- ✔ The museum entrance gate (influenced by museum marketing efforts)

This method results in channels of distribution as shown in Table 2-3.

Table 2-3	Channel Distribution Analysis		
Distribution Channel	**Ticket Revenue**	**# of Guests/% of Total**	**Sales Revenue/% of Total**
Educators	$5	10,000/20%	$50,000/16%
Tour companies	$6	5,000/10%	$30,000/10%
Motels/hotels	$6.50	5,000/10%	$32,500/11%
Internet			
Museum Web site	$8	3,000/6%	$24,000/8%
Visitor Bureau Web site	$6.50	2,000/4%	$13,000/4%
Museum entry gate			
Museum members	$3	5,000/10%	$15,000/5%
Independent visitors	$8	15,000/30%	$120,000/39%
Partnering businesses	$4	5,000/10%	$20,000/7%

Study the channels through which your business generates customers and the levels of business that come through each one.

1. **Track changes by distribution channel.**

   If you start to see one distribution channel decline radically, either you need to give that channel more marketing attention or enhance another channel to replace the distribution loss.

2. **Compare percentage of sales to percentage of revenue from each channel.**

   You can see which channels deliver higher-than-average and lower-than-average income per unit sold. Channels that deliver lower-than-average income per unit should involve lower-than-average marketing investment or they should deliver some alternative benefit to your business. For example, in the case of the museum in Table 2-3, the tickets distributed through partnering businesses deliver lower-than-average revenue and likely require a substantial marketing investment. Yet they introduce new people to the museum and therefore cultivate membership sales, donations, and word-of-mouth support.

3. **Communicate with the decision makers in each distribution channel.**

   Once you know your channels and who influences each one, you know exactly whom to contact with special promotional offers or marketing information. For example, if school groups arrive at a museum because the museum is on an approved list at the state's education office, that office is the decision point and it is where the museum would want to direct marketing efforts. If they arrive because art or history teachers make the choice, the museum would want to get information to art or history teachers.

There's an old, self-evident saying: "Without customers, a business is out of business."

When in doubt, spend more — not less — time defining, communicating with, and nurturing your customers. The more you know about who they are, where they are, and what motivates their buying decisions, the easier it is to make marketing decisions that deliver positive results.

Chapter 3

Seeing Your Product through Your Customers' Eyes

*T*he best products aren't *sold* — they're *bought*.

Yet you'll never hear a customer say he *bought* a lemon at the used car lot. Nope, someone *sold* him that lemon — but hopefully not you or your business. If you're a good marketer, when it comes time for the purchase, you aren't *selling* anyone anything. Instead, you're helping customers to select the right products to solve their problems, address their needs, or fulfill their desires. You're helping them *buy.*

As a result, you devote the bulk of your marketing efforts to the steps that take place long before money changes hands. These efforts involve targeting customers, designing the right product line, and communicating your offerings in terms that address the customer's wants and needs. Then when the customer is ready to make the purchase, all you have to do is facilitate a pleasant exchange and make sure he or she feels good about trading money for the right product.

Chapter 2 focuses on your customers — who they are, where they are, and what needs they have. This chapter puts the spotlight on everything there is to know about your products and, even more so, on all the reasons your customers would want to buy those products from you.

In a Service Business, Service Is the Product

If your business is among the great number of companies that sell services rather than three-dimensional or packaged goods, from here on when you see the word *product*, think *service*. In your case, service *is* your product.

Today, nearly 80 percent of all Americans work in service companies. Services — preparing tax returns, writing wills, creating Web sites, unclogging kitchen drains, styling hair, or designing house plans, to name a few — aren't things that you can hold in your hands. In fact, the difference between services and tangible products is that customers can see and touch the tangible product *before* making the purchase, whereas when they buy a service they need to commit to the purchase before seeing the outcome of their decisions.

Even nonprofit organizations have products. Look at a Boys and Girls Club. One of its products is the service it provides to young people. Another is the recognition and satisfaction it provides to benefactors who contribute funds to keep the club in business. If it rents the club facility to other groups to use during off-hours, the rental activity represents yet a third "product."

If you generate revenue, then you're selling *something* — your product.

Telling "Just the Facts" about What You Sell

Freeze-frame your business to study the products you offer your customers.

To get started, consider the products of a lakeside resort as an example. The owners would list the number of cabins, seats in the restaurant, and rowboats for rent. Then they'd include the shopping opportunities provided by the resort's Barefoot Bait Shop. Their list might also include summer youth camps, winter cross-country ski packages, and all-inclusive corporate retreats.

A law office might describe its product offerings by listing the number of wills, estate plans, incorporations, bankruptcies, divorces, adoptions, and lawsuits it handles annually. And if it's well managed, the lawyers will know which of those product lines are profitable and which services are performed at a loss in return for the promise of future business or a larger customer relationship.

What about your business?

- ✔ What do you sell? How much? How many? What times of year or week or day do your products sell best?
- ✔ What does your product or service do for your customers? How do they use it? How does it make them feel?
- ✔ How is your offering different and better than your competitors'?
- ✔ How is it better than it was even a year ago?
- ✔ What does it cost?
- ✔ What do customers do if they're displeased or if something goes wrong?

The faster you can answer these questions, the better you understand your business. And the better you understand your business, the more able you are to steer its future.

Tallying your sales by product line

Make a list of every kind of product you offer to your customers, along with the revenue generated by each offering. Concentrate only on the end products you deliver. For example, a law office provides clerical services, but those services are part of other products and are not the reason why a person does business with the attorneys in the first place — so they shouldn't show up on the attorney's product list.

To get you started, Table 3-1 shows products for a bookstore.

Table 3-1	Independent Bookstore Product Analysis	
Product	*Product Revenue*	*Percentage of Revenue*
Books	$250,000	44%
Magazines	$95,000	16%
Coffee and pastries	$95,000	16%
Greeting cards and gift items	$55,000	9%
Audio books	$45,000	8%
Audio book rentals	$18,500	3%
Pens and writing supplies	$18,000	3%

Using the cash register to steer your business

Your product analysis will detail exactly which products your customers are buying. You can put this information to work as you prioritize and manage your product line.

✔ **Sell what people want to buy:** Study your list for surprises. You may find products that are performing better than you imagined. This knowledge will alert you to changes in customer interests that you can ride to higher revenues. As an example, the bookstore owners in Table 3-1 realized when they scoured their product analysis that nearly a third of all revenues were coming from the combined activity of beverage/pastry and magazine sales. This finding led to the decision to move the magazine display nearer to the café, giving each area a greater sense of space and bringing consumers of either offering into nearer proximity, and therefore buying convenience, of the complementary offering.

✔ **Promote the products that you've hidden from your customers:** You may have a product line that is lagging simply because your customers aren't aware of it. When the bookstore in Table 3-1 realized that only 3 percent of revenues were coming from sales of pens and writing supplies, they decided to try boosting the line by enhancing and moving the display to a more prominent store location. Sales increased. Had the line continued to lag, though, the owners were ready to replace it with one capable of drawing greater customer response.

✔ **Back your winners:** Use your product analysis to track which lines are increasing or decreasing in sales and respond accordingly. If the bookstore in Table 3-1 is fighting a decline in book sales (perhaps due to sales erosion by deep discounters and online booksellers) while sales of cards and gifts are growing, the owners might decide to capitalize on the trend by adding an array of reading accessories, including lamps, bookshelves, and even reading glasses.

✔ **Bet on product lines that have adequate growth potential:** Before committing increased marketing dollars to a product line, use your product analysis to project your potential return on investment. For example, a glance over the bookstore revenues shows that 3 percent of sales result from audio book rentals. If the store could *double* this business, it would increase annual revenues by only $18,000. Realizing this, the owners need to ask themselves: What is the likelihood that we're going to double this business — and at what cost? On the other hand, if the bookstore could increase café sales by just 20 percent, it would realize $19,000 of additional revenue, which the owners might decide is a safer marketing bet and a stronger strategic move.

Illogical, Irrational, and Real Reasons People Buy What You Sell

When you can buy bread for under a dollar at the grocery store, why would anyone pay nearly $5 to pick up a loaf at the out-of-the-way Italian bakery?

Why pay nearly double for a Lexus instead of a Toyota, when some models of both are built on the same chassis with many of the same components?

For that matter, why would people seek cost estimates from three different service providers and then choose the most expensive bid when all three offer nearly the same proposed solution?

Why? Because people rarely buy what you think you are selling.

People don't buy your *product*. They buy the promises, the hopes, or the satisfaction that they believe your product will deliver.

They buy the $5 loaf of salt-crusted rosemary bread because it satisfies their sense of worldliness and self-indulgence. They opt for the high-end sedan for the feeling of prestige and luxury it delivers. They pay top price for legal, advertising, or accounting services because they like having their name on a prestigious client roster — or maybe they simply like or trust the attorneys, advertisers, or CPAs more than they do the people who provided the lower cost estimates.

People may choose to buy from your business over another simply because you make them feel better when they walk through your door.

Don't fool yourself into thinking that you can win your competitor's customers simply by matching features or price.

People decide to buy for all kinds of illogical reasons, and then they justify and rationalize their purchases by pointing out product features, services, or even the price tag. They buy because they see some intangible and often impossible-to-define value that makes them believe the product is a fair trade for the asking price. Often that value has to do with the simple fact that they like the people they're dealing with. Never underestimate the power of a personal relationship.

Buying Decisions Are Rarely about Price, Always about Value

Whatever you charge for your product, that price must accurately reflect the way your customer values your offering.

If a customer thinks your price is too high, expect one of the following:

- The customer won't buy.

- The customer *will* buy but won't feel satisfied about the value, meaning you win the transaction but sacrifice the customer's goodwill and, possibly, the chance for repeat business.

- The customer will tell others that your products are overpriced.

Before you panic over being called high-priced by a customer, remember that it is only bad news if others respect this particular person's opinions regarding price and value. It's often better to let a cherry-picking bargain hunter go than to sacrifice your profit margins trying to price to that person's demanding standards. If your prices are on the high end, though, just be certain that the quality, prestige, and service — the *value* — that you offer is commensurate with your pricing.

Then again, if a prospect thinks your product is worth more than its price tag

- You may sacrifice the sale if the prospect interprets the low price as a reflection of a second-rate offering.

- You may make the sale, but at a lower price (and lower profit margin) than the customer was willing to pay, leaving money in her billfold and possibly a question mark in her mind.

- The customer may leave with the impression that you are a discounter. That perception will steer the kinds of purchases he chooses to make from you in the future.

Unless you really want to try to own the bargain basement position in your market (a dangerous strategy because some other business can always beat you by a penny), you're better off providing excellent value and setting your prices accordingly.

The value formula

During the split second that customers rate the value of your product, they weigh a range of attributes (see Figure 3-1):

✔ What does it cost?

✔ What is the quality?

✔ What features are included?

✔ Is it convenient?

✔ Is it reliable?

✔ Can they trust your expertise?

✔ How is the product supported?

✔ What guarantee, promise, or ongoing relationship can they count on?

Figure 3-1:
Many
attributes
besides
price
contribute
to a
customer's
perception
of value.

The Value Formula

How Customers Compute Value

Price
Quality
Features
Convenience
Reliability
Expertise
+   Support
_____
V A L U E

These considerations start an invisible mental juggling act to determine what, in the customer's mind, is the value of your offering.

If your product's quality and features are only average, then they'll expect a low price to tip the deal in your favor.

On the other hand, if customers place a premium on your promise of reliability (think Federal Express), they'll likely cut you some slack when it comes to low price or convenience.

Have you heard the old chestnut, "Price, Quality, and Speed — choose any two"? Well, for successful 21st-century small businesses, those days are gone. Your customer expects you to be the best at one and competitive in all *three* areas. Not the *best* in all three areas — but at least competitive.

Here are some well-known examples:

✔ Costco = Best price

✔ Nordstrom = Best service

✔ Starbucks = Best product

- Federal Express = Best reliability
- BMW = Best performance
- Rolex = Best quality

Riding the price/value teeter-totter

Price emphasizes the dollars spent. Value emphasizes what is received in exchange for the dollars spent.

Pricing truths

When sales are down or customers seem dissatisfied, small businesses turn too quickly to their pricing in their search for a quick-fix solution.

Before you reduce your prices to increase sales or satisfaction levels, think first about other ways to increase the value you deliver. Consider the following points:

- Your customer must perceive the value of your product to be greater than the asking price. If you charge 99 cents, deliver at least a dollar in value.

- The less value customers equate with your product, the more emphasis they'll put on low price.

- The lower the price, the lower the perceived value.

- Customers like price reductions way better than they like price increases, so be sure when you reduce prices that you can live with the change, because reversing your decision — and upping your prices again later — may not settle well.

- Products that are desperately needed, rarely available, or one-of-a-kind are almost never price-sensitive.

The difference between penny-pinching and shooting the moon

What makes a product price-sensitive?

Tell a person he needs angioplasty surgery, and he'll pay whatever the cardiac surgeon charges — no questions asked. But tell him he's out of dishwasher detergent, and he'll comparison shop. Why? Because one product is more essential, harder to substitute, harder to evaluate, and needed far less often than the other. One is a matter of life and death, the other mundane.

See where your product fits by checking out Table 3-2.

Table 3-2	Price Sensitivity Factors
Price Matters Less if Products Are:	*Price Matters More if Products Are:*
Hard to come by	Readily available
Purchased rarely	Purchased frequently
Essential	Nonessential
Hard to substitute	Easy to substitute
Hard to evaluate and compare	Easy to evaluate and compare
Wanted or needed immediately	Easy to put off purchasing until later
Emotionally sensitive	Emotion-free
One-of-a-kind	A dime a dozen

Pricing considerations

Give your prices an annual checkup. Here are the factors to consider and the corresponding questions to ask:

- ✔ **Your price level:** What is the perceived value of this product compared with its price? What are the prices of competitive products? How easily can the customer find a substitute — or choose not to buy at all? (See Chapter 4.)

- ✔ **Your pricing structure:** How do you price for extra features/benefits? What features/benefits do you include at no extra charge? What promotions, discounts, rebates, or incentives do you offer? Do you offer quantity discounts?

- ✔ **Pricing timetable:** How often do you change your pricing? How often do your competitors change their pricing? Do you anticipate competitive actions or market shifts that will affect your pricing? Do you expect your costs to affect your prices in the near future? Are there looming market changes or buyer taste changes you need to consider?

Presenting prices

The way you present your prices can either inspire your prospects — or confuse or underwhelm them. Use Table 3-3 and the following list to show your prices in the most favorable light:

✔ Don't let your offer get too complex.

✔ Don't be misleading.

✔ Do present prices so they look visually attractive and straightforward.

✔ Do make the price compelling. In today's world of outlet malls, online bargains, and warehouse stores, "10 percent off" isn't considered an offer at all.

✔ Do support your pricing announcements with positive reasons and added benefits. Price alone is never reason enough to buy.

Table 3-3	Pricing Presentation Do's and Don'ts	
Don't	**Do**	**Why**
We've just cut our nightly rates — $89 mid-week. Some restrictions apply.	Announcing a new St. Louis number to remember — $89 per night	The second approach makes the deal sound noteworthy, whereas the first approach provides no positive rationale and implies that "small print applies."
Sofa and Loveseat $1,995.00	Sofa and Loveseat $1,995	When prices are more than $100, drop the decimal point and zeroes to lighten the effect.
25% off two or more	1/2 off second pair	Complicated discounts are uninspiring, plus "1/2 off" sounds like double the discount of 25% off when you buy two.
30% off	Regularly $995; now $695 while supplies last	1/3 off sounds more compelling than 30% off; but showing a $300 reduction is stronger yet. "While supplies last" adds incentive and urgency.

Don't	Do	Why
$6.99 each	$13.99 — Buy One, Get One Free	Sometimes a low price conveys low value. Consider doubling the price but making a powerful two-for-one limited-time offer.
$14.95 plus shipping/handling	$17.95. We pick up all shipping and handling	The word "plus" alerts the consumer that the price is only the beginning. Calculate and include shipping and handling to remove buyer concern and possible objection.
State and local taxes extra	State and local taxes apply	"Extra" goes into the same category as "plus" when it comes to pricing.

The Care and Feeding of Your Product Line

There are two ways to increase sales:

1. Sell more to existing customers.

2. Attract new customers.

Figure 3-2 presents questions to ask as you seek to build business from new and existing customers through new and existing products.

Figure 3-2: Questions to ask as you assess your sales growth options.

How can we sell more **Existing Products** to **Existing Customers**

How can we initiate sales of **Existing Products** to **New Customers**

What **New Products** would build business with **Existing Customers**

What **New Products** can we offer to attract **New Customers**

Enhancing the appeal of existing products

At least annually, small businesses need to assess whether their products still appeal to customers or whether it's time to adjust features, services, pricing, and product packaging — or make other changes to sustain or reignite buyer interest. Here are some of your options:

- **Same product, new use:** Start by looking for ways you can re-present your offerings.

  One of the best historic examples of re-presenting a product comes from Arm & Hammer baking soda. When people reduced the amount of baking they did, the amount of baking soda they needed tumbled into the basement. So, rather than stand by and watch sales slide, Arm & Hammer responded by reintroducing baking soda — this time not as a recipe ingredient but rather as a refrigerator deodorizer.

- **Same product, new promotional offer:** Examine ways to update how you offer your product to customers, including new customer-responsive pricing, new packages combining top-selling products with others your customers may not have tried, or other ways to help your customers see your offerings with a new appeal.

Be sure your new offerings are true improvements that address customer wants and needs. Before you offer a new "deal," be sure that you can say yes to the following question: Does this provide customers with a better, higher-value way to buy your products?

A Web designer may increase sales of consulting services by bundling quarterly site traffic reporting and analysis with site design, thereby delivering consulting services to customers who otherwise would have purchased only design expertise.

A landscape/nursery business may offer half-price terra cotta pots with all perennial purchases over $50 — thereby giving customers an incentive to buy higher volumes of flowers *and* increasing interest in the nursery's line of pottery.

Chapter 4 has more on winning a greater share of your customer's buying decisions and thereby increasing your sales to existing customers.

✔ **Same product, new customer:** Invite new customers into your business with a fairly risk-free introductory or trial offer or some other way to sample your product and service. Issue invitations to free seminars or guest lectures — or even host a community fundraiser that attracts the kinds of people you serve. For more information on how to build interest among new prospects, see Chapter 10.

Even products have life cycles

Products get old. They follow a life cycle (shown in Figure 3-3) that begins with product development and proceeds until the product reaches the point where it is old hat, at which time its growth rate halts and profits decrease.

Figure 3-3: Sales follow a predictable curve throughout the product life cycle.

Product Reaches Maturity

Increased Promotion Growth Rate Slows

Competitors Enter Similar Products Introduced

Repeat Purchase and New Sales Price Wars

New Product Sales Sales Decline

Development Product Withdrawal or Reinvention

Introduction Growth Maturity Saturation Decline

Product Life Cycle

Raising a healthy product

Sales follow a predictable pattern as a product moves through the life cycle illustrated in Figure 3-3. The following descriptions explain the marketing steps and sales expectations that accompany each phase of the product's life:

✔ **Introductory phase:** Build awareness, interest, and market acceptance while working to change existing market tendencies. Use introductory offers that motivate prospects to try the product. Drive sales to speed up your cost/investment recovery.

Though it is tempting to drive early sales through low pricing, be careful because that first impression will stick and limit your ability to increase price later. Set the price where it belongs relative to your product value and gain sales through introductory offers and heavy start-up advertising.

✔ **Growth phase:** The product enters this phase once it is adopted by the first 10 to 20 percent of the market, the market *innovators* or *early adopters*. The masses follow this pace-setting group, and when the masses start buying, growth takes off. At this point, competitors enter. Consider promotions and special offers to protect and build market share.

✔ **Maturity:** When the product reaches maturity, its sales are at their peak level and sales growth starts to wind down.

✔ **Saturation phase:** The market is now flooded with options. Sales come largely from replacement purchases. Pricing offers and other incentives are needed to recruit new customers and win them from competitors.

✔ **Declining phase:** When the product reaches the depth of its sales decline, a business has several choices. One is to abandon the product in favor of new opportunities, perhaps introducing phaseout pricing to hasten the cycle closure. Another is to let the product exist on its own with minor marketing support and, as a result, minor sales expectations. Yet a third option is to reinvent the product's usage, application, or distribution to gain appeal with a new market.

Developing new products

Whether it is to seize a new market opportunity or to offset shrinking sales with replacement products, one of the most exhilarating aspects of small business is introducing new products. It's also one of the most treacherous, because it involves betting your business resources on a new idea. Figure 3-4 shows the product development process. Follow it, without jumping over the important middle step, to minimize your risk.

The Chinese character for "crisis" combines characters representing "danger" and "opportunity." Proceed with caution to avert danger while you seize opportunity by adding new products to your line.

Figure 3-4:
Give special
attention to
the middle
step in the
product
development
sequence.

| IDEA | EVALUATION, RESEARCH, TESTING | LAUNCH |

As you pursue a new product idea, push yourself by asking these questions:

✔ What current product can we significantly update or enhance?

✔ What altogether new idea will satisfy the known wants and needs of our customers and prospective customers?

✔ What market trend can we ride via a new product?

Many new products are developed to address some hot new market trend. Before you consider riding a market trend, though, be sure you aren't entering too late. Take a second to review Figure 3-3, the product life cycle. If you enter when a product is already in the saturation phase, you have to offer pricing and other incentives to win business from the line-up of competitors already in the field. If you do decide to offer a product responsive to a market trend, have a marketing plan that allows you to get in *and get out* fast, so that you've realized success and moved on before the product idea reaches its end.

Here are questions to ask during the research stage of product development:

✔ Is it unique? Is it already being produced or offered by another business, and, if so, how will your product be different — and better?

✔ Does it deliver customer value? If this is an upgrade of an existing product, how is it different in a way that will matter to your customer?

✔ Does it have market potential? Will it appeal to a growing market? What is its customer profile? What do potential customers say about it?

✔ Is it feasible? What will it cost to produce or deliver, and how much can you charge for it?

✔ Is it credible? Does it fit with your company image? Is it consistent with what people already believe about you or does it require a leap of faith?

✔ Is it legal and safe? Does it conform to all laws? Does it infringe on any patents? Does it have safety concerns?

✔ Can you make and market it? Do you have the people and cash resources to back it? Can you get it to market? Is it easily feasible for success?

✔ Can you find a unique niche in the marketplace for it? The topic of positioning and branding products is a chapter unto itself, so turn to Chapter 7 for more information.

As you study new product ideas, beware of the following:

✔ Features that don't inspire your customer

✔ Features that don't deliver clear customer benefit

✔ Product enhancements that don't add significant product value

✔ "New" products that are really old products in some newfangled disguise that means nothing to customers

✔ Products that don't fit within your expertise and reputation

✔ Products that address fads or trends that are already starting to wane

Product line management isn't about what you're selling; it's about what the market is buying. Keep your focus on your customers — on what they value not just today, but tomorrow.

Chapter 4

Sizing Up Competitors and Staking Out Market Share

*N*o matter how unique your offering, no matter how much you think you play on a "field of one," even if you're the only hitching post in a one-horse town, you have competition.

Every business has competition.

When Alexander Graham Bell called to Mr. Watson through his newfangled invention in 1876, even he already had competition. He held in his hand the one and only such device in the whole wide world, yet from its very moment of inception, the idea of the telephone had to fight for market share. It had to compete with all the existing and more familiar means of message delivery — plus it was certain to spawn a crop of copycat products to vie for message delivery in the future.

Competition may not be obvious. It may not even be direct. But it is always there. The sooner you face it and plan for it, the better. This chapter shows you how.

Playing the Competitive Field

Competition is the driving force in nature and it's also the core of the free enterprise system as we're lucky to know it. Competition occurs whenever winning attention is necessary for selection and survival. In nature, the peacock's tail, the rose's scent, and the apple's sweetness are the marketing tools, while in business the battle is fought and won with marketing programs designed to attract customers to one business over another.

Thanks to the forces of competition, the free enterprise system is undergoing constant improvement. Here are a few examples:

- ✔ Competition prompts product upgrades and innovations.
- ✔ Competition leads to higher quality and lower prices.
- ✔ Competition enhances selection.
- ✔ Competition inspires business efficiencies.

Competition is the contest between businesses for customers and sales. The opposite of competition is a *monopoly,* where a single company has complete control of an industry or service offering.

The terminology of competition

Your sales figures provide your first indication of how you're doing in your competitive arena. If they are strong and growing, your business is on the right track. If they're sliding downhill, you have your work cut out for you. Either way, you can take control of your sales — and therefore of your business success — by using the information in this chapter to gauge and grow your "share" of business, as defined by your market share, share of customer, and share of opportunity.

Market share

Market share is your slice of the market pie — or your portion of all the sales of products like yours that are taking place in your market area. For example, say that you manage a movie theatre in a market with a dozen other movie theatres within a reasonable driving distance. Your market share would be the percentage that your theatre sells of all the movie tickets sold by all 13 movie theatres. See the "Calculating Your Market Share" section later in this chapter for tips on how to determine and grow your market share.

Share of customer

Share of customer is the percentage that you capture of all the possible purchases that your customer *could* make at your business. Continuing with the movie theatre example, in addition to tickets, the theatre sells popcorn, soda, candy, movie posters, "movie money" gift certificates, and who knows what else. Every customer who purchases just a movie ticket — nothing else — represents lots of room for growth in terms of share of customer, also known as *share of billfold.* For tips on calculating and growing your share of customer, see Chapter 19.

Share of opportunity

Share of opportunity looks beyond existing customers and competitors to consider who is *not* buying products like the ones you're selling — and what it might take to get those people to see your product as a solution to their needs.

Years ago, Coca-Cola released research documenting that nearly six billion people in the world were consuming, on average, 64 ounces of fluid a day. Of that total intake, only two ounces of the liquid consumed was in the form of Coca-Cola. Coca-Cola officials used this information as the basis of an effort to increase what they termed their *share of stomach.*

This kind of planning goes beyond market share (how much of all soft drink purchases are captured by Coke), and even beyond share of customers (how much of each Coke drinker's total soft drink purchases are captured by Coke). It moves into the arena of market development by capturing sales by *likely* customers who are currently opting for alternatives rather than purchasing cola products.

Find a "stomach share" analogy for your business. What satisfaction does your product address? What solution does your business provide? Then think about how you can present your products to grab a greater share of that total opportunity. Here are a couple more examples:

- ✔ A roller rink sells skating, of course, but it also provides a solution for youth and teen recreation. Its opportunity reaches to include all kids who spend money to fill out-of-school hours. When considering how to grow its share of the total market opportunity, the roller rink owners might think in terms of *birthday party share* or *youth leisure time share.*

- ✔ An insurance brokerage sells life insurance, which provides a solution for peace of mind. Its competition comes from competing insurers and all the other ways people address their desire for financial security — including everything from investing in stocks to stashing money under the mattress to buying lottery tickets. The insurance brokerage might want to think in terms of how to increase its *nest egg share.*

Knowing what you're up against

Your business faces three kinds of competition, as illustrated in Table 4-1.

Direct competitors

These businesses offer the same kinds of products or services you do and appeal to customers in the same geographic markets where you do business. To increase your market share, think about how you can woo business away from your direct competitors and over to your business.

Indirect competitors

You're either losing sales to or splitting sales with these businesses. For instance, if you're selling paint, and your customer is buying the paintbrush somewhere else, that brush seller is an indirect competitor of your paint store, because it is capturing the secondary sale. To increase your share of customer, figure out what kind of business is being won by your indirect competitors. Then find a way to serve as a one-stop solution for your customers by offering your primary product and also the secondary, complementary, or add-on products that your customers currently leave your business to obtain elsewhere.

Phantom competitors

No one *has* to buy what you're selling. In fact, one of the biggest obstacles to the purchase — and therefore the biggest phantom competition — is your customer's inclination to do nothing at all or to find some alternative or do-it-yourself solution instead of buying what you're selling. Taking the paint store example a step further, if you're offering the choice between enamel and latex paint, and your customers are opting for never-need-paint vinyl siding, that siding outlet is a phantom competitor capable of roadblocking your business. For that matter, if your customers decide that their houses can go another year without a paint job, the option to do nothing is your phantom competitor. To increase your share of opportunity, think about where your phantom competitors are hiding. Then find ways to make your product an easier, more gratifying, more satisfying, and more valuable alternative.

Table 4-1	Examples of Competition		
The Product	*Direct Competitors*	*Indirect Competitors*	*Phantom Competitors*
Log home construction	Other log homebuilders	Traditional housing contractors, kit homes, manufactured housing	Remodeling, motor coaches, time-share offers, doing nothing

The Product	Direct Competitors	Indirect Competitors	Phantom Competitors
Movie theatre	Other movie theatres	Movie rentals, cable TV, satellite services	Other leisure activities such as attending sporting events, listening to live music, bowling, watching TV, doing nothing
Life insurance	Other life insurance brokers	savings bonds, investment accounts, IRAs	Paying bills, paying tuition, buying lottery tickets, gambling, stashing money under the mattress, doing nothing

How businesses compete

When everything else is equal, most customers opt for the product with the lowest price. If you want to charge more, make sure that everything else _isn't_ equal between you and your lower-priced competitor. Most competitors fall into one of the following two categories:

- **Price competitors:** These businesses emphasize price as their competitive advantage. They must be prepared to offset lower profit margins with higher sales volume. They also have to be prepared for some other business to beat their price and therefore take away their one-and-only competitive edge.

- **Nonprice competitors:** These businesses charge a higher price than their competitors. They must be prepared to compete and win based on superior quality, prestige, service, location, reputation, uniqueness of offering, and customer convenience. In other words, they must offer an overall value that customers perceive to be worth a higher price tag. (See "The value formula" section in Chapter 3.)

Winning Your Share of the Market

You win market share by taking business from your direct competitors, therefore reducing their slice of the market pie while increasing your own. To advance in the market share game, here's what you must do:

1. **Know your direct competition.** If prospects decide to buy from some other place than your business, where do they go instead?

2. **Learn why your customers are choosing those competing businesses over yours.**

3. **Analyze how you can beef up the value that the market equates with your business and products** so that buyers will opt for your offerings rather than the competing alternatives available to them.

Defining your direct competition

On an annual or regular basis, ask yourself these questions:

✔ **Whom does your business really compete with?**

When your prospect considers buying your product or service, what other businesses does that person think of at the same time?

Be realistic as you answer this question. Just because a retailer sells jewelry in New York City, that business doesn't necessarily compete with Tiffany's. List the businesses that actually swipe your customers' business away from you.

If you have a service business, list the competitors against whom you regularly go up against head-to-head as you try to win contracts or jobs. If you're a retailer, list the businesses whose shopping bags your customers tote into your store, or the business names you overhear while they deliberate whether to buy your product or some other alternative. Investigate further by conducting customer research (see Chapter 2).

✔ **How does your business rate against the businesses that your prospects also consider when they consider your offerings?**

Create a list with the name of every business with which you regularly and actually compete. For each competing business, assess the following three factors:

- What are this competitor's strengths when compared to your business?

- What are this competitor's weaknesses when compared to your business?

- What could your business do differently to draw this competitor's customers over to your business?

As you evaluate your business in comparison with your competitors, use the Customer Satisfaction Analysis in Chapter 19. It presents a list of the attributes and values that prospects consider when choosing between competing businesses.

✔ **Where does your business rank among your competitors?**

Avis knew where it fit in the rental car competitive hierarchy back when it began advertising that Avis was #2 and trying harder. The company built a successful strategy and marketing plan around an honest assessment of how it ranked competitively. What about your business?

- Evaluate your sales revenues in comparison to those of your competitors to get a feel for how you rank based on size alone.

- Estimate your market share compared to that of your competitors. (See the following section for market share calculation advice.)

- Evaluate your *top of mind* ranking — sometimes called your *mind share*. When prospects are asked to name three to five businesses in your field, does your name consistently pop up as one of their answers? If so, you can be pretty sure that you rank in the top-tier competitive level for your business arena. Keep listening and you'll gain a great indication of what other dominant businesses your prospects think you're up against. And if you don't hear your business name, listen anyway, because once you know which businesses *are* in the top-of-mind category, you can begin to analyze what they're doing differently to achieve the prominence you seek.

Moving up the competitive ladder

Most businesses misdirect their time and energy by tackling the wrong competitors. They shoot too high — taking on the biggest names in their market area rather than the biggest threats to their business. As you develop your competitive plan of attack, follow these steps:

1. **Start by winning market share from the businesses you're actually losing customers to *today*.** Do this even if it involves facing the harsh reality that your customers consider your business among a less prestigious group than you wish they did.

2. **Make a list of the companies you *wish* you were running with.** Evaluate why you're not in that group. Is it because of the physical look or location of your business? Or might the nature of your clientele mark you as a lower-level player? Or do your product line and pricing hold you back from your desire to compete with the biggest names in your business arena?

3. **Consider whether changing competitive levels would be advantageous.** Assess whether your business is more apt to be successful at its current competitive level (think of the big-fish-in-a-small-pond concept) or at the next competitive level (where perhaps you can compete for bigger and more lucrative business).

4. **Change competitive levels if necessary.** If you decide that your business would be better off competing with more visible and prestigious businesses in your arena, commit to making the changes necessary to get the market to see you through new eyes. See Chapter 7 for information on influencing market perceptions and winning your chosen place in your marketplace.

Calculating Your Market Share

Having a sense of your market share gives you a good indication of your competitive rank. It also provides a way to monitor the growth of your business within your target market.

Sizing up your target market

To calculate your share of the market, first define the size of the market in which you compete.

The *total* market includes the entire nation or world — a market area that matters enormously to such major marketers as Nike, Levi's, General Motors, Citibank, or other internationally known brand names.

But to a small business like yours, what matters is your *target* market — the one within the sphere of your business's influence. You can assess the size of your target market by using the following criteria:

✔ **Geographic targeting:** Where are your customers? For example, a retailer may determine that its geographic target market consists primarily of people who live or vacation within a two-hour drive of the retailer's place of business. An accountant may determine that her geographic target market is concentrated within the city limits.

✔ **Customer targeting:** Rather than consider the full market (or world) population as your potential market, determine which people actually fit your customer profile. (See Chapter 2 for profiling information.) A golf course community developer, for instance, may determine that its target market includes only high-income golfers aged 50 and over who live in the surrounding three-state region. An office furniture manufacturer may target all of the nation's office-furnishing retail establishments, along with architects and interior designers who specify office furnishings. An online florist may focus exclusively on wedding planners and brides-to-be. (See Chapter 16 for tips on defining Web customers.)

✔ **Product-oriented targeting:** Sometimes the most effective way to measure the size of your target market is through an analysis of how many sales of products like yours are taking place. For instance, a microbrewery might measure its share of the market as a percentage of all premium beer sold in its geographic target area. (The microbrewery wouldn't try to measure its sales against *all* beer sales but rather it would focus on premium beer sales, because that is the microbrewery's sphere of business influence.) Likewise, an attorney specializing in land-use planning would assess the number of land-use cases in his statewide area before trying to calculate market share.

Doing the math

Once you have a good sense of the size of your total target market, you can use several approaches to calculate your share.

✔ **Unit sales:** Some businesses can easily figure out the total number of products like theirs sold each year. A motel manager, for instance, could estimate the size of the target market by multiplying the number of motel rooms that exist in the target market area by the region's approximate occupancy rate. If there are 2,000 rooms and a 75-percent occupancy rate, then the market area experiences rental of 547,500 room rentals a year. If the motel manager knows that her 100-room motel books 24,000 room rentals a year, she can figure that her share of local market motel business is approximately 4.5 percent.

A real estate agent may do a similar calculation, checking assessor office records to determine the total number of residential house sales over the previous year and comparing that total figure with the number of houses the agent sold personally.

✔ **The number of potential customers:** If you know that 30,000 adults are in your target market area, and if you can make an educated guess that one in ten of them — or 10 percent of the total — is a consumer of services like yours, you can assume that your business has a total potential market of 3,000 adults. If you're serving 300 of those adults, then you have a 10-percent share of your target market.

To aid in your guesswork, visit the reference area of your local library and flip through the Standard Rate and Data Service (SRDS) *Lifestyle Market Analyst* to learn valuable information about consumers in your market area.

For instance, imagine a fabric and sewing supply store in Albany, Georgia, that serves a geographic area that includes 7,000 homes located within a 15-minute drive of the store. The owners could turn to the *Lifestyle Market Analyst* profile for consumers who participate in "Sewing" and see that 18.5 percent of the households in the Albany area participate in home sewing. Armed with this fact, they could multiply their 7,000-household market area by 18.5 percent to learn that they have 1,295 potential customers in their geographic market area. If the owners currently serve 250 of these potential customers, then they have a market share of just less than 20 percent — meaning plenty of opportunity for growth.

✔ **Based on total sales volume:** Another way to estimate market share is to arrive at a total estimate of how much people are spending at businesses like yours in your market area each year and divide that figure by your own sales revenue. For example, if you determine that total annual sales in your market area are $5 million and your business does $500,000, you can estimate that your business has 10-percent market share ($500,000 divided by $5,000,000 total market sales).

Regional business journals and newspapers compile "Top 25" lists ranking businesses in industries or service sectors ranging from architects to zoos. Businesses submit their revenues (often slightly inflated, so read them with a realistic eye) as a basis for appearing in these lists. Within the lists for your industry, you'll find clues to regional sales revenues in your field.

Market share: Sample calculation

Suppose that Green Gardens, a residential landscaping business, serves a market area that includes 20,000 houses, of which approximately 10 percent use landscape services. This creates a total potential residential landscape service market of 2,000 homes. If Green Gardens has a client roster that includes 200 homes, then it has a 10-percent market share based on the total number of potential customers in the area (200 divided by 2,000).

Another way to look at market share is by dollar volume. Green Gardens could estimate the revenues of each of its competitors and then add those figures to the Green Gardens revenue figure. That would produce an estimate of the total amount being spent on residential landscape services in the given market area annually. If the estimated total sales volume is $4 million, and if Green Gardens has annual sales of $600,000, then Green Gardens has a 15-percent market share ($600,000 divided by $4 million).

If Green Gardens analyzed its market share based on unit sales (number of houses served) *and* based on dollar volume, its owners could conclude that although they have only a 10-percent share of the houses served, they have 15 percent of the total dollar volume. This finding could lead them to conclude that they are serving larger-sized accounts than some of their competitors. And based on that, they should have a small celebration!

Increasing Your Market Share

As you work to increase market share, don't get intimidated by the refrain, "no one has ever heard of us." The comment usually follows an encounter with a new prospect who admitted having no knowledge of your business.

Rest assured, if you are in business and ringing up sales, you enjoy at least some level of market awareness. But you can be equally certain that not everyone knows about or buys from your business. The biggest advertisers spent hundreds of millions on marketing every year, and yet no brand in the world has 100-percent brand awareness, let alone 100-percent market share.

The moral of the story is: Be reasonable as you set your market share goals and growth expectations.

Also, as you seek to increase market share, steer clear of these landmines:

- ✔ **Avoid "buying" market share through price reductions.** Don't sacrifice your bottom line as you prepare to welcome new customers through the door. Before you go the price-slashing route, glance through the pricing advice in Chapter 3.

- ✔ **Be ready before issuing an invitation to new customers.** Don't procrastinate, but at the same time give yourself time to be sure you're ready to make a great first impression. Run through the following checklist before launching a new business development effort:

  - **Current customer satisfaction levels:** Are your current customers happy with your product? Are they happy with your business in general? Do they return to your business again and again, or do you have a high turnover rate? Do customers speak well on your behalf? Do you rank well on the customer satisfaction attributes detailed in Chapter 19?

  - **Customer-service adjustments:** Before working to draw in more customers, consider changes that will enhance your customer service levels (see Chapter 18) so that customers — new and old — will want to stay once they arrive. Do you need to fine-tune your product offering — how you price it, how you package and present it, even how you guarantee it? Do you need to dust off your environment? This could include everything from enhancing the appearance of your office space to revising your on-hold message to improving the speed and accuracy of your Web site. And definitely review your customer conveniences — ranging from public restrooms to payment policies. Have you received legitimate customer complaints about your product or services, and have you done all you can to address them positively and effectively?

- **Business readiness:** Are you ready to issue an invitation for new customers to try out your business? Do you have the inventory (or for a service business, the staff and talent and capacity) to deliver what you're offering? Is your staff informed of the offer and ready to help prospects become buyers once they respond to your offer? (How many times have you called in response to an ad only to have a sales associate say, "What? I don't know about that offer. Let me ask my supervisor." And how many times have you hung up after being placed on hold? *That's* wasted advertising!)

When market share means market saturation

The common rule is that 25-percent market share is considered a dominant market position. As you calculate your share within your target market area, watch closely as it reaches a dominant position. When it gets there, take time to celebrate, for sure, but then be aware that as your share edges still upward, it will near a level called market saturation.

Market saturation occurs when a business captures the sales of close to a majority of the potential customers within the target market. Usually that figure is pegged at about 40 percent. Once a business is doing that well, one of several things tends to happen:

- Competition enters the market area. Take a second to review the Product Life Cycle (Figure 3-3 in Chapter 3). Saturation happens sometime after a new business or product reaches its maturity in the marketplace. By then others realize that market opportunity exists, which brings on a line-up of Johnny-come-lately competitors.

- Your business gets complacent, quality gets lax, and customers begin to stray.

- Your customers have bought the products they need from you. Other than replacements, their purchases are few and far between.

- It's time for change. Look for new markets to open, and new products to offer within your current market. And most of all, it's time to restore emphasis on customer service and satisfaction — the very thing that made the business a success in the first place.

Market dominance is the dream of every business. But keep your eye on the road in front of you so that should you near saturation, you have a plan for where you'll go next to grow your business. Don't turn from a growing market too soon, and don't cling exclusively to a saturated market too long. Use market share knowledge as your navigating device.

Chapter 5

Goals, Objectives, Strategies, and Budgets

In This Chapter

▶ Defining your business mission and vision

▶ Setting goals and objectives — and knowing the difference between the two

▶ Funding your marketing program

*T*oo many small business leaders feel paralyzed by the marketing process for the simple reason that they don't know where to start. They ask, "Should we hire a marketing director?" or "How much should we spend?" before they ask, "What are we trying to achieve?"

Once they get around to setting their goals, though, most small businesses find that they face a pretty reasonable marketing task. An accounting firm might determine that it wants to add three new corporate clients. A retail establishment might want to gain $20,000 in new sales. A commercial cleaning business might want to take on five more business contracts.

Knowing the goal simplifies everything.

What's more, when small business owners are clear about where they want to go, they nearly always get there. In huge companies, the process of getting all the departments focused on the same end point is like herding cats. But in small businesses there are fewer people to orchestrate, and the owner's will can more clearly impact the actions of the full business team. As a small business marketer, if you start with a goal, a plan, and a reasonable budget for achieving your desired outcome, chances are you'll get where you want to go.

Where Are You Going, Anyway?

Mission. Vision. Goals. Objectives. What's what?

Some consultants do nothing except lead corporations and organizations through the *visioning* process, helping them clarify why they exist, what they hope to achieve, and how they intend to get where they want to be.

Small companies rarely have the funds to dedicate to this kind of a strategic process. For that matter, they rarely have time to stop and think about what they're trying to accomplish beyond the survival objective of bringing in enough revenue to cover the expenses. That's why your business will have an edge — and a greater chance for success — if you devote some time up front to setting your sights and aiming yourself and your business.

The "vision" thing

Well-run businesses set annual goals that are supported by the foundation of a business vision and mission. The terms *mission* and *vision* are often used interchangeably, but there is a fine-line difference. Your *vision* is a statement of what your company *strives to be*. It defines your desired future. Your *mission* is a statement of how to create your vision. It defines your core purpose and the approach you will take to achieve your objectives.

Your company vision is the big picture of where you're going, whereas your mission is the path you plan to follow to achieve success.

A hallmark example of clearly defined vision and mission statements comes from the Oregon Trail, the 19th-century trek from Missouri to Oregon. If ever an organization needed a vision to overshadow the rigor of the mission and to guide all goals and objectives, it was this 2,200-mile journey across America.

> **Oregon Trail Vision:** To find a better life
>
> **Oregon Trail Mission:** To travel by wagon to Oregon

Even if your own challenges pale in comparison to those of America's pioneers (and with any luck, they do!), your organization will still benefit from clear statements that define your direction, focus your organization, and rally your employees, associates, and customers behind a common purpose.

A more modern example of vision and mission comes from the Habitat for Humanity program, which now reaches around the globe to provide housing for people in lower-income groups.

Habitat for Humanity Vision: To eliminate poverty housing and home-lessness from the world, and to make decent shelter a matter of conscience and action.

Habitat for Humanity Mission: To build and rehabilitate simple, decent, affordable homes in partnership with those who lack adequate shelter.

Developing your statement of purpose

Some companies combine mission and vision into a single statement of purpose that defines their purpose, long-range goals, and core values.

It's up to you whether to create statements of mission and vision or whether to write an overall statement of purpose. Either way, your business will be stronger if you put into writing the ultimate reason that you come to work every day. Consider these questions as you work on your reason for being:

✔ Why did you get into this business in the first place?

✔ What need did you see that you felt you could fulfill better than anyone else could?

✔ What makes your business different from others?

✔ What commitment do you make to those you deal with — from employees to suppliers to customers?

✔ What is the ultimate reason for your work?

Turning a profit is a desired result of your success, but don't let the bottom line become your purpose. Instead, articulate what positive change you are trying to create through your business. This defines the heart and soul of your company and the driving force behind all the decisions that you make. From there, success — and profits — should flow.

Success stories

Most successful companies display their statements of purpose throughout their workplaces and in their written communications. Check annual reports and Web sites to find the statements of purpose from the business world's success stories. Here are some examples:

✔ **Intel:** To be the preeminent building block supplier to the worldwide Internet economy.

✔ **3M:** To solve unsolved problems innovatively.

✔ **Dell Computer:** To be the most successful computer company in the world by delivering the best customer experience in the markets we serve.

✔ **Microsoft:** To enable people throughout the world to realize their full potential.

Now it's your turn: Use the formula in Figure 5-1 to create a sentence that serves as the beacon for your business. As you develop your statement, think in terms of your vision (what positive change you are working to achieve) and your mission (what you will do to make your vision real).

Formula for a Purpose Statement

BEGIN WITH

A Verb that describes the change you want to make

THEN ADD

A clause summarizing the need your business addresses

AND YOU HAVE

The Purpose Statement for your company

Figure 5-1:
How to develop a statement of purpose.

Goals and Objectives Defined Simply

Following are definitions for the terms *goal, objective, strategy,* and *tactic*. To see how they fit together, see the planning pyramid in Figure 5-2.

✔ **Goal:** The overall sales or professional target that your marketing program seeks to achieve. Your goal is an expression of a realistic and clearly defined target, usually accompanied by a time frame.

✔ **Objective:** The measurable result that will be necessary to achieve the goal. A plan usually has several objectives that define the major means by which the goal will be met.

> ✔ **Strategy:** The plan for achieving each measurable objective.

> ✔ **Tactic:** An action you will take to enact your strategy.

Figure 5-2:
The planning pyramid.

THE ACTIONS WE WILL TAKE — Strategy

HOW WE WILL ACHIEVE IT — Objectives

WHAT WE WANT — Goals

WHY WE DO THIS — Vision, Mission and Core Values/Purpose

Setting goals and objectives

The line between goals and objectives is razor thin, and many marketers spend undue time trying to differentiate between the two. The truth is that you can run a perfectly successful company without drowning in goal-versus-objective details. Yet sure enough, the minute you decide to skip the whole drill, some banker or venture capitalist or major partner will ask you to define how you've set them, and you'll be left tongue-tied in the meeting. If that happens, the following descriptions will bail you out:

> ✔ **Your goal** is what you want to achieve during the upcoming marketing period to move toward the vision you've set for your company.

> A local newspaper may set an annual goal to increase readership by 5 percent in order to more fully achieve its vision to serve as the region's most trusted information vehicle. The goal defines *what* the newspaper wants to achieve, but not *how* it will achieve it.

> ✔ **Your objectives** define how your business will achieve its goal over the upcoming year. Table 5-1 shows a kind of X-ray of the objectives a newspaper might set to increase readership by 5 percent.

Table 5-1		Anatomy of an Objective
A Verb	*A Noun*	*A Precise Description of the Desired Change*
To introduce	a new section	aimed at young, affluent urban professionals
To gain	5 percent	market share from Competitor X
To improve	delivery time	by one hour daily

Setting strategies

Strategies are the plans for achieving business objectives. They are practical, achievable, and action-oriented. Strategies generally detail changes that a business intends to make to the four marketing functions called the *marketing mix:* pricing, product, promotion, and place (also known as distribution). These four marketing mix elements are easily remembered as *The Four Ps.*

- ✔ **Product:** What will you sell? How will you develop or alter your offering to meet your goal and objectives?

- ✔ **Pricing:** How will you set or change your pricing or payment options?

- ✔ **Promotion:** What will you say in your advertising and promotions? How will you communicate your product benefits?

- ✔ **Place:** Where will you make your product available to your customers? How will it be distributed?

Cast your goals and objectives in cement when you create your marketing plan each year. But your strategies must remain flexible so that you can adjust them in response to competitive forces, economic realities, or new opportunities that arise over the course of the year. As you alter your strategies, though, remember that the only strategy worth pursuing is one that directly supports your goals and objectives.

Goals, objectives, and strategies in action

Once you're clear about your annual goal, every action becomes a building block toward achieving that ultimate desired end.

Small businesses sometimes falter when asked to state their goals. Instead they say that they're going to open a new office, begin selling a new product, or increase prices in June. But those aren't goals — those are strategies. Knowing your strategies without being clear about the goal you're trying to reach is like wandering in the woods wearing a blindfold.

In Figure 5-3, you can see how all parts of the business program fit together in the plan for a housing developer.

Purpose: To create a vibrant urban core community featuring quality housing opportunities for a wide range of residents.

Annual Goal:
Increase gross revenues by 10%.

Objectives:
Increase prospect generation by 20%.
Achieve prospect-to-sale conversion rate of 5%, an 8% increase over current rate.
Increase number of units sold by 8%.
Increase revenue from ancillary services by 20%

Strategies:

Place or Distribution Strategy

- Redesign, reintroduce and increase visits to the development sales office.
- Establish an exclusive designated real estate broker relationship.
- Revise commission schedule to enhance incentive for regional realtor referrals.

Pricing Strategy

- Increase prices by 3-15%, depending on residential product, to adjust for inflation and enhanced appeal.
- Establish a 90% developer financing option.
- Add buyer incentive by offering a lifetime health club membership for second-quarter closings on new unit sales.

Product Strategy

- Announce and break ground on a 24-hour health club with swimming, tennis, exercise and social facilities.
- Announce and break ground on a new building featuring view units, private courtyards, garages, and other high-value attributes.
- Plan and open a design division to guide new owners through the selection of unit finishes and appliances, and to provide fee-based design consultation services.

Promotion Strategy

- Host and promote special events including urban-garden tours, a variety of classes and seminars, and Thursday night events featuring live music and cultural tie-ins to draw the target audience to the sales office arena.
- Include sales center travel directions, invitations and special event announcements in all advertisements and promotional material.
- Include call-to-action in all marketing communications and collect names into a data base.
- Institute a data base communication program that ensures meaningful and progressive prospect contact every two weeks

---

Figure 5-3:
An urban housing developer's business program.

The failsafe planning sequence

Successful business marketers follow the same lock-step marketing scenario:

1. **Conduct market research.** Doing so ensures that you know everything you can about your customer, your product, your competition, and your business environment. Follow the steps outlined in Chapters 2, 3, and 4.

2. **Establish marketing goals and objectives.** The previous portion of this chapter is full of instructions on this step.

3. **Set the marketing strategies and determine the marketing mix that you will employ to achieve your objectives.**

4. **Choose your marketing tools and tactics.** That's what the rest of this book is about.

Never, ever start with Step 4. In other words, never decide on your tactic — whether to run an ad or hire a new distributor or take on a new partner — until you know your strategies. Because when you know your strategies, you know your objectives, which means that you know your goals, which means that you know where you want your business to go.

Tactics *follow* strategies — not vice versa.

Budgeting to Reach Your Goals

To reach your goals and achieve your objectives, fuel your strategies with a marketing investment appropriate to the size of the task at hand.

Realistic talk about small business marketing budgets

Leaders of successful companies never say, "We'll see how much money is available and then spend it on advertising." They dedicate funds in advance because they know that without good marketing there won't be any left over!

The most important commitment you can make to your marketing program is to establish and stick to a budget. What is commitment? It has four parts:

- ✔ Establishing a marketing budget
- ✔ Spending the funds on a planned marketing program

✔ Viewing the allocation as an important business investment

✔ Managing the program well

When a business cuts back on marketing, it puts itself on a dangerous down-hill slide. Sure, you recoup some money at the time of the budget cut, but following that one-time savings, look at what happens. With less money for marketing, you can fund fewer communication efforts. With fewer communications, sales decline. Declining sales reduce your overall revenues, which means you have even less money to allocate for future marketing.

Think long and hard before trimming your marketing budget, because it's the one expense item designated specifically to attract and keep customers.

How much should you be spending?

It depends. Everyone wants a magic formula, but there isn't one. Mature businesses in established markets with low growth goals can get away with low marketing expenditures. Companies targeting high growth must spend far more. A business getting sales primarily as a subcontractor can spend practically zero on marketing, but a business trying to win a broad cross-section of retail customers must budget enough for media ads and promotions.

One industry survey finds that businesses that market primarily to other businesses spend an average of 3.49 percent of revenues on marketing. Other studies show that businesses that market to the public spend closer to 8 to 10 percent. There is no one answer. Consider the following budgeting methods:

✔ **The arbitrary method:** Best-guess budgeting, based on intuition and experience, often using the past year's budget as a benchmark.

✔ **Competitive parity:** This could be called "budgeting to keep up with the Joneses." The budget is based on how much your competitors are spending and how your business compares in terms of size and strength. In other words, if your volume is even with that of a particular competitor, then your budget should be at least even as well.

✔ **Goal-oriented budgeting:** This is a "spend what's necessary" approach. It involves taking a serious look at what you expect your business to accomplish and what level of marketing is necessary to accomplish the task. It is based on a calculation of the costs involved to implement a marketing program capable of achieving your business goals.

✔ **Percentage of sales budgeting:** Call it "name the magic number." Under this model, a business forecasts next year's sales and allocates a percentage of that to marketing. Though this is the most frequently cited way of establishing a budget, it is problematic because the percentages that businesses allocate to marketing vary from 1 percent to as much as 50 percent — depending on the industry, the product or service, the competitive arena, and the cost of media in the particular market area.

Budgeting considerations

As you determine how much to allocate for marketing, consider

- ✔ **The nature of your business and your market:** Businesses that market to other businesses — such as attorneys and accountants — tend to allocate a lower percentage of sales to marketing than do businesses that market to the public-at-large. It's the proverbial rifle versus shotgun difference. The business-to-business marketer can set its sites and reach its customers through direct sales efforts, whereas the business-to-consumer marketer must cover a wider range, usually involving more costly investments in mass-media advertising.

- ✔ **The maturity of your business:** Start-up businesses need to budget for the development of marketing materials and the implementation of programs, which are extraordinary one-time costs that existing businesses have behind them, to gain first-time prospect awareness.

- ✔ **The size of your market area:** A business that serves customers who are primarily located within a short drive or walk from the business location — a neighborhood coffee shop or a locals-only fitness center, for example — can target all its marketing into a concise market area. As a result, it can probably allocate a lower percentage of its sales to marketing than would be the case if the business had to purchase ads in statewide, national, or even international media to reach its market.

- ✔ **Your competition:** Another important budgeting consideration has to do with your competitive situation. If you've been the only game in town and you find out that several competitors are about to open their doors, you have to invest in a ramped-up marketing program if you intend to defend your business. Or if you've been the underdog and you want to take on the leaders, you have to spend accordingly.

- ✔ **Your objective and task:** The most important consideration in setting your budget is to understand what you want to accomplish. Look at your sales goals. The more aggressive they are, the more money you need to budget. For example, if you're planning to launch a new product or open a new location, you need to increase your marketing efforts to gain the awareness, interest, and action, and to fund the training, marketing support, and additional advertising required to make your plan possible.

Your money or your time? How companies decide

Some businesses decide *not* to invest significant dollars in marketing programs. Instead, they determine that they can best meet their goals by dedicating time to sales presentations, networking efforts, or charitable and social events where they meet prospects. That doesn't mean they aren't investing in marketing. They are investing time (plus dollars for entertainment, charitable contributions, and investments) rather than money on traditional advertising vehicles. Here are examples of relying on time investment rather than money:

✔ **A small ad agency** may set as its goal to add two accounts to its roster. It may decide that the best way to do this is by handling the campaign of a high-profile charity pro bono. It invests in industry creative contests to showcase its pro bono creative work to win industry accolades and, ultimately, the attention of potential clients. The agency's marketing investment involves a donation of time (pro bono) and checks to the creativity competitions.

✔ **An attorney** wanting to attract regional corporate clients may serve as board member and volunteer counsel for a community nonprofit organization, knowing that this will generate working relationships with fellow board members who fit the target client profile.

✔ **A regional ski resort** wishing to attract more families from the local market area might decide to offer free ski lessons and rentals to all fifth graders as a way to establish relationships directly rather than via marketing communications.

Why a static budget is headed downhill

Every year the cost of advertising, personnel, consultants, and virtually every other element of marketing go up by at least the cost of inflation. So if your budget remains static from year to year, your ability to market it is cut back by whatever percentage the rest of the business world moved forward.

You can cut your marketing budget and reap an extra $100, $1,000, $10,000, or even $100,000 in the bottom line. But you'll realize that savings only once.

But if you leave your wisely aimed marketing budget intact, it can positively impact your bottom line well into the future. Marketing investments keep delivering even after the ad is finished or the sales call has long since ended. If you wonder about the truth of that statement, finish this sentence: "Where's the —?" Wendy's hasn't run that campaign for years. But the company's investment in the slogan *Where's the beef?* still pays off all these years later.

You *must* dedicate time or money, or both, if you want to market your business from where it is to where you want it to be.

Part II

Sharpening Your Marketing Focus

The 5th Wave
By Rich Tennant

"Right here..., crimeorg.com. It says the well-run small-criminal concern should have no more than nine goons, six henchmen and four stooges. Right now, I think we're goon-heavy."

In this part . . .

Each encounter with your business affects whether a prospect decides to buy from you or take his business elsewhere.

Part II helps you fine-tune every contact point — from the indelible first impression to each subsequent communication — so that every marketing act is capable of building your name into a strong brand and moving market opinion in the direction that you want it to go.

Each impression you make is a priceless moment to convince — and amaze — those who deal with your business. This part shows you how.

Chapter 6

Projecting the Right Image

*R*ight now, your business is making an impression. Somewhere, some prospect is encountering your ad, seeing your logo, placing a call to your business, visiting your Web site, or walking through your door. Maybe someone is driving by the sign on your locked-up shop at night, or seeing your listing when the Yellow Pages fall open.

As a result, right now people are drawing conclusions about your business. Based on what they're seeing or hearing, they're making quick mental calculations about where you fit in the business pecking order, deciding whether your business looks like a top-tier player, an economical alternative, or a struggling start-up — all based on impressions that you may not even be aware that you're making.

This chapter is about where and when your business makes impressions and how you can align your communications so that people will form the opinion you want them to have.

Making First Impressions

You've heard the saying a thousand times: "You never get a second chance to make a first impression." The advice is self-evident and it sounds easy enough to follow until you realize that your business most often makes its first impressions when you're nowhere to be found. In your stead is your ad, your voice mail message, your direct mailing, your business sign, your employee, or maybe your logo on the back of some Little League player's uniform.

Most of the time, your marketing communications make your business impressions for you. Ask yourself the following questions as you assess whether your materials are representing you well:

- ✔ When people receive multiple impressions of your business, do they see evidence of a consistent, reliable, well-managed, successful enterprise?

- ✔ Do your communications look like they all represent the same company?

- ✔ Does your logo always look the same? What about your use of type styles and color selections?

- ✔ If you use a tag line or slogan, is it always the same, or does it change from one presentation to the next?

Ads, publicity, direct mailings, personal contacts, referrals from mutual friends, building signage — these are all make-it-or-break-it impression points.

To evaluate what kinds of messages you're sending — and what kinds of impressions you're making — begin by tracking the ways that customers approach your business. Then work backward to determine what marketing efforts led to their arrivals. And work forward to determine what kinds of impressions they form once they actually "meet" your business, whether that first contact is made in person, over the phone, by an ad, or online.

Arriving by telephone

Often, with no prompting at all, callers will tell you how they found your number. "John Jones suggested I call" or "I'm curious about the new whatchamacallits I see in your ad" or "I was on your Web site, but I couldn't tell whether your business is open Sundays." If the conversation doesn't naturally uncover how the person obtained your phone number, take a few seconds (but only a few seconds) to ask something like, "I'm glad you called us. We're always working to improve our communications and I'd love to note how you got our phone number."

The responses help you see what is and isn't working to generate phone calls. They also help you determine which first impression points are bringing you qualified prospects who are likely to become customers, and which ones are reeling in people who are "just looking." In the latter case, realize that the problem isn't with the caller; the problem is with the impression point.

A real estate brokerage specializing in high-end residential properties continuously fielded calls from shoppers trying to buy homes in a much lower price tier than those listed by the realty company. Upon questioning, the real estate agents learned that most of the dissatisfied callers found the phone number in the Yellow Pages, where the company's ad read, "We have your dream home." Although the agents thought that their tag line appropriately reflected the caliber of the brokerage offerings, upon study they realized that it appealed to the wrong target market. As a result, they amended their ad to include a discreet line reading "Specialists in fine properties and estate homes."

If you want the right prospects to call your business, help them understand what you offer, make your phone number appropriately large and bold, give them a reason to dial it, and then be ready to treat every call as a very valuable business opportunity — which it is.

The cost of phone book listings, Web sites, advertising placements, and other efforts that work to prompt a prospect's phone call mounts higher and faster than most small businesses realize. Then when the hard-won call comes, too often the phone rings and rings, or an outdated message clicks on. Just as bad, sometimes a coveted contact gets dropped into a costly phone silence after a harried person answers the phone with "Could you hold please?"

Here are some ways to make sure your phone calls don't get fumbled:

- ✔ **Answer calls promptly.** Pick up after the first or second ring whenever possible. Even if you have a receptionist, train others to serve as back-ups, answering if calls reach a third ring. When a phone rings on and on it sends a silent message: "We're too busy to talk to you right now."

- ✔ **Transfer calls as quickly as you answer them.** Be prompt about getting the caller to the appropriate person in your business. If that person isn't available, say so immediately. Offer to take a message, put the caller through to voice mail, or find someone else to help. On hold is a dangerous and costly place to leave valuable prospects.

- ✔ **Get everyone in your company to answer the phone in a consistent and professional manner — always starting with the business name.** In this age of personal lines on every desk, people too often answer all calls as if they were personal calls. "Hello, this is John" is not an appropriate business greeting unless you're a one-person business that receives calls only from people who know they want to talk with John.

- ✔ **Keep voice mail messages brief and friendly.** Use wording that conveys your business purpose and personality. Avoid long, overly programmed greetings. Offer a very limited number of menu choices (try to limit it to three — otherwise you'll lose callers in the confusion) that invite callers to jump quickly to the option they seek.

   "Thank you for calling 20/20 Vision. We're focusing on eye exams and frame selections right now, but please press 1 for our hours and location or press 2 to leave a message. We promise to call you back within the hour."

- ✔ **Ask your phone company to monitor and report on your hang-up rate.** Multiple rings, lengthy hold times, and voice mail responses are reasons for callers to abandon their efforts to reach your business.

Consider placing mirrors near the phones if your business relies heavily on telephone contact. The theory is that people instinctively smile at themselves in mirrors, simply because it makes them look more attractive. Beyond that, a smile also makes a voice more attractive — and more natural, friendly, and enthusiastic. You'll be able to hear the difference — and so will the person on the other end of the line.

Approaching your business in person

If a person walks into your business, looks around puzzled, and asks, "What kind of a business is this?" you can make an educated guess that the drop-in was unplanned and triggered only by a look at your signage or window displays. (Given the question, you may want to improve these impression points to better address this obvious question.)

Making your voice mail more personal

A personal greeting, a meaningful message, and a commitment to prompt personal follow-up are all it takes to turn voice mail from a personality-free automated and sometimes annoying fact of life to a pleasant and efficient means to present yourself and your message when you're otherwise unavailable. Follow these tips:

✔ Record a greeting that accurately reflects the image of your business, update it regularly, and check for messages faithfully.

✔ Make sure that your greeting includes your company name (or your own name if it is a desk line), gives an indication of when the call will be returned, and invites the caller to leave a message.

✔ Encourage detailed messages. "Please leave a message of up to three minutes, and we will get back to you by day's end." If you encourage a lengthy message, the caller is more likely to convey complete information, reducing the need for telephone tag after the call.

✔ If at all possible, include the option of pressing zero to speak with a real, live person.

✔ If you can't fully respond to the caller's request within the specified time period, call with a polite explanation and tell when you will have a response.

✔ Voice mailboxes have limited storage capacity. Delete messages regularly to ensure that new messages can be stored.

✔ Regularly call your own voice mail to see that it's working and that the message is current.

The minute that your voice mail starts to sound like that of a big, faceless corporation, move quickly to put your small business personality back into it. Customers choose small businesses in large part for their personal touch. Don't let voice mail or other systems encroach on that small-business advantage.

Many businesses boast that their signage is their most effective means of attracting first-time visitors. But before banking on your sign to reel people in, realize that when people respond only to your signage, they're making spur-of-the-moment, drop-in visits — perhaps at a time when they're short of both time and money. Instead, work to achieve *destination visits* by making impressions and cultivating interest well in advance of prospects noticing your sign and walking through your door.

Leading people to your business

Don't expect people to find your business on their own. Instead, lead them to your door. If your business relies on a heavy volume of consumer visits, convey directions in ads, mailings, and other advance communications. You can even invest in directional road signs or billboards if appropriate. At the very least, be sure that when visitors arrive at your business — whether you're located in a corporate high rise or a home office — they are welcomed with a sign that presents your business name along with instructions on how to reach your front door.

Parking

If people have to drive to your business, is it clear where they should park? If a parking fee is involved, do you have a validation program that customers know of in advance? Is the parking area clean, well marked, and capable of making a good impression? Have you saved the nearest spots for customers, rather than for your own car or for those of your employees? (How many times have you driven up to a parking space only to see the spot nearest to the door marked "Reserved for Manager"? And what do those three simple words tell you about your standing as a customer?)

Nearing your front door

As a prospect approaches your entrance, does your business look open and inviting? Here's a list of questions to consider:

✔ Is your signage visible and professional?

✔ Do signs and window displays clearly indicate what your business does?

✔ Is the entrance easy to find?

 ✔ Is your entryway signage welcoming — or is it papered with negatives such as "No UPS," "No Smoking," "Deliveries Use Back Door," or "No Outside Food or Beverages"? You need to add only a few words to state your rules in a positive way. "Let us hold your umbrella and packages while you shop" sure beats "No backpacks."

✔ If your business success relies on foot traffic, do your windows have show-stopping capacity? Stand back and look hard. If necessary, improve your displays by adjusting lighting to cut glare, or by replacing small objects with big, bold items that are magnets for attention. Use mirrors to slow people down and also to help them adjust their dispositions (remember, people automatically put on a friendly face when they look in the mirror), both of which are likely to benefit your business.

The moment of arrival

Walk step by step through the process of approaching and entering your business. Forget for a minute that this is *your* business. Imagine how it feels to a stranger. Does it convey the right attitude and make the right set of impressions? If you're striving for the feel of a private, invitation-only club, then you want first-timers to literally feel the exclusivity. To broaden your appeal, see that you eliminate all barriers while increasing the sense of warmth and welcome. Consider the following:

✔ Is your entry area impeccably clean?

✔ Is it decorated to make a strong statement about the nature of your business, its customers, and its products?

✔ Do your surroundings present and promote *your* business, or do they inadvertently promote other businesses whose logos happen to appear on calendars, posters, coffee cups, and other items that sneak their way into your environment? Rather than making your lobby a display for others, turn it into a showcase of your own products, your clients, or your staff. If you want customers to be proud to associate with your business, proudly spotlight your offerings.

✔ Is there a clear "landing area" — a place where a visitor can pause upon entry and receive a good first impression?

✔ Does your business offer an obvious greeting — either by a person or a welcoming display?

✔ If you have a customer waiting area, do people head straight for it or do they pause and look for an invitation before entering? In some businesses, a thermos of fresh coffee, a stack of logo ID cups, and a welcoming sign are all it takes to break the ice. Other times, you may need to remodel or at least redecorate to break down obstacles and enhance the sense of welcome.

✔ If customers consistently stop in a certain area or study a particular display, consider that area as prime marketing real estate and think of ways that you can enhance it to deliver the strongest possible statement on behalf of your business.

What it's like to be a customer in your business

Take some time to role-play, following the path that customers take through your business:

✔ **Stop where they stop.** Stand in an inconspicuous spot and watch what people do when they enter your business.

- How long do they wait until someone greets them?

- Do they look around for a clue regarding what to do next?

- If you're a retailer, do they see a bottleneck at the cash register as their first impression? If so, how often do they make a U-turn and leave before they get all the way into your shop?

✔ **Shop like they shop.** Study what it's like to purchase your product. Note the impressions you make as customers encounter your business at different phases. Where do points of concern or resistance arise? How can you alleviate obstacles that hinder the decision to buy or the ability to enjoy dealing with your business?

- If you have a service business, and customers want to know how your charges add up, be ready with answers. Create a brochure or handout describing your services and fee structure.

- If they want to touch the merchandise, build appropriate displays.

- If they need to try before they buy, offer samples, fitting rooms, before-and-after photos, or other ways to experience your product.

- If they want to browse, display products at eye level and give them room to stop and shop, realizing that narrow aisles and tight spaces drive people — especially women — right out the door.

✔ **Wait where they wait and for as long.** Test your customer service from a customer's viewpoint. Look at how they react to the way they are treated by your business.

- Have you provided chairs in areas where they end up waiting?

- In areas where customers pause, have you placed displays that move them toward buying decisions?

- If spouses, children, or friends accompany customers, have you created entertainment areas and appropriate diversions?

- If their visits consistently last longer than an hour, do you provide some form of refreshment?

- Watch for nonverbal complaints about a lack of attentiveness. Do customers glance at their watches or fidget while waiting for employees to handle phone calls, deal with other customers, or complete deskwork? Be aware that customers use waiting time as the single most important factor in gauging your customer service, so plan accordingly.

In designing your business environment, balance your operations and internal needs against the wants and needs of your most important asset: your customers.

Online encounters

To cyberspace customers, your Web site *is* your business. The big difference, though, is that you can't be there to personally welcome them or to right wrongs should something go awry. Instead, your Web site needs to do it all. As you build your online presence, be vigilant about adhering to your company's image while creating a site that works flawlessly and efficiently — just as you would expect your physical environment to work.

Chapter 16 is full of information to help you achieve your marketing objectives online. Here are some quick things to keep in mind as you develop an online presence that supports your business image:

✔ **Your Web site will rarely make a first impression for your business.** With more than four billion Web pages and some 50 million Web sites out there, the chances of a customer randomly wandering onto your site are remote. Plan to lead people to your site through your ads and marketing materials, through online links to your site, and through efforts that maximize your site's performance in search engines.

✔ **Your Web site *can* make a *final* impression for your business.** If it crashes, is slow to load, or is too confusing to navigate, visitors won't return.

✔ **Be aware that people arriving at your site may not know where they are.** They may be coming from search engines, referrals, or links, and they may not know that they've arrived in your Web space. Or they may arrive at an internal page of your site, so be sure that every page features your name or logo along with a link to your home page.

✔ **Remember that online customers are like any other customers.** They are not of another world; they are not isolated to online encounters. They are the same people who see your magazine ads, walk by your display windows, find you in the Yellow Pages, and meet you at dinner parties. If you want your Web site to work for your business, make it *part* of your business. Integrate its look, content, and offerings with the rest of your marketing program, right down to the style of type you use, the kinds of messages you present, and the way you display your business name and logo. For more information, turn to the advice on establishing and maintaining a consistent image in Chapter 7.

Managing a few trillion e-mail impressions

Sometime in the late 1990s (sounds like ancient history, doesn't it?), the number of e-mail messages eclipsed the volume of traditional letters sent by businesses. Yet while traditional correspondence is routinely formatted, proofread, printed, and filed, e-mail messages are sent spontaneously, often with no standard policy and rarely with a company record for future referral.

Such an informal approach to e-mail is fine as long as your staff member is simply sending a thank-you note or a quick update to a customer. But what if the message includes a fee estimate? Or a notice that client-requested changes will result in an additional thousand dollars of expense? And what if the staff member is no longer with your company when the customer questions the bill?

For the sake of your business, set a few e-mail guidelines:

- ✔ **Unify all company e-mails by use of a common signature.** A *signature* or *sig* consists of a few lines of text that show up at the end of every e-mail message. Usually it includes the name of the person sending the message, a tag line that tells what your business does, your Web site address, your street address, and your phone number. You can create a signature in almost any e-mail program. Go to the help function for instructions.

- ✔ **Set a tone and style for e-mail messages.** In well-managed businesses, traditional letters go out on letterhead, are printed in a consistent type-face, and use a consistent style and clear, professional language. Consider e-mail a dressed-down version of your formal correspondence. It can be more relaxed and more spontaneous, and it can (and should) be more to the point — but it can't be impolite or unprofessional.

- ✔ **Respond to e-mail within 24 hours.** People expect a different level of response to e-mail than to other forms of correspondence. An e-mail that isn't answered promptly falls into the category of phone calls that are placed on endless hold or customers who wait in three-minute lines. The customer service impact is devastating. Answer e-mails quickly, even if it's a one-line note offering a complete answer within a week.

- ✔ **Establish a system to print and file e-mails** that contain any form of pricing or delivery promise.

Before you hit the Send button

Measure your e-mail policies against these standards:

- ✔ **Keep messages short** and use paragraph breaks to avoid the visual dread of a long block of type.

- ✔ **Add punctuation, but use it sparingly.** E-mail messages seem to come in two types: the kind that includes no punctuation or the kind that sprinkles punctuation like salt. Sentences that begin with capital letters and end with periods are good. Strings of five exclamation marks are not. When in doubt, revert to what you learned in English 101.

✔ **Keep "emoticons" out of business correspondence.** Also called "smilies," they don't all convey happiness. You'll encounter emoticons conveying a smile :-), a frown :-(, or even a grin :-D. They're crudely capable of showing what you mean, but in most cases they are as appropriate in the business environment as a swimsuit.

✔ **Limit abbreviations to those in common use.** E-mail is peppered with terms such as LOL (laughing out loud), BTW (by the way), and IMHO (in my humble opinion). Stick to widely understood abbreviations like ASAP, FYI, or OK, and leave ones like TNSTAAFL (there's no such thing as a free lunch) on the cutting room floor.

✔ **Stick to the basics as you format e-mail.** Avoid using stationery, colored background, or unusual type styles.

✔ **Use uppercase and lowercase.** Typing in all uppercase — using all capital letters — means one thing in cyberspace: You're screaming.

The ten commandments of e-mail

E-mailers have established some do's and don'ts. The following list of ten has circled cyberspace numerous times:

✔ Thou shalt include a clear and specific subject line.

✔ Thou shalt edit any quoted text down to the minimum thou needest.

✔ Thou shalt read thine own message thrice before thou sendest it.

✔ Thou shalt ponder how thy recipient might react to thy message.

✔ Thou shalt check thy spelling and thy grammar and not rely on spellcheck alone.

✔ Thou shalt not curse, flame, spam, or USE ALL CAPS.

✔ Thou shalt not forward any chain letter.

✔ Thou shalt not use e-mail for any illegal or unethical purpose.

✔ Thou shalt not rely on the privacy of e-mail, especially from work.

✔ And the Golden Rule of e-mail: Thou shalt not send unto others that which thou findest hateful to receive.

Two terms in these commandments may need an explanation: To *flame* is to "fight fire with fire" by sending hostile replies to those who annoy others online. More often than not a flame inspires a flame, starting a flame war that benefits no one. And *spam* is unsolicited commercial junk mail sent via e-mail. (See Chapter 13.)

As you adopt the commandments, add one more. Follow the standard advice about what to do with a message written in anger: Save it overnight and reread it in the cool light of dawn.

Creating an Impression Inventory

The only way you can be sure that you're making a consistent impression in your marketplace is to take inventory and study every communication you have with prospects, customers, and others who deal with your business.

You can take an impression inventory using a simple form. Across the top of a sheet of paper label five columns with the words listed in bold and described here:

- ✔ **Impression points:** In this column, list every item that carries your name or logo into the marketplace. Use the "Impression Points" list following this section to trigger your thoughts. No item is too small to include. If your ad is a work of art, but your proposal cover is ratty, the negative impact of one will cancel out the positive impact of the other. Every impression counts.

- ✔ **Target market:** Define the purpose of each communication. Is it to develop a new prospect or to communicate with an existing customer — or maybe a little bit of both? If your business has a number of customer types or product lines, you may want to get even more specific. For instance, one ad for an insurance agency may target property insurance prospects, and another may target life insurance prospects. By defining the different purposes, the agency will be able to gauge how much it is investing in the development of each product line.

- ✔ **Who's in charge** of each impression point? Many impressions that affect a company's image are made by those who don't think of themselves as marketers. Nine times out of ten, no one is thinking about marketing when a cost estimate is presented, a bill is sent, or a purchase order is issued. The key is to think about the marketing impact way in advance so that you create materials and usage systems that advance a positive image for your company.

- ✔ **Costs involved:** What does each communication cost in terms of development, media, printing, or other expenses? Once you know the answer, you can add up what you're spending on business development, customer retention, and marketing of each product line. You may be surprised to find that you're over-supporting some functions and under-supporting others, and you can adjust accordingly.

- ✔ **Evaluation:** Jump to the next section, "Rating Your Marketing Communications," for tips on how to evaluate your communications.

With the headers in place, your next step is to list down the left side all the "impression points" that apply to your business. To speed the process, you can add to or subtract from the following list:

Impression Points

Advertising and Sales Materials

Newspaper ads	Direct mailers
Magazine ads	Sales literature
Television ads	Brochures
Radio ads	Newsletters
Phone book ads	Printed materials (menus, rate cards, instruction sheets, and so on)
Other directory ads	
Community publication ads	Videos, DVDs, or CDs
Web site or search engine ads	Speaker support materials (overheads, PowerPoint slides, and so on)
Transit ads and outdoor boards	Presentation materials (proposal covers and so on)
Other ads	

Signage

Building signage	Event signs
Entry door sign	Posters
Department signs	Office displays
Trade show signs	

Correspondence

Letters	Purchase orders
Memos	Invoices/statements
E-mail	Business cards
Faxes	Envelopes
Estimates	Package labels

Publicity

News release stationery	Press kit folders

Logo Items

T-shirts	Specialty items (pens, coffee cups, paperweights, gift items, and so on)
Baseball caps	
	Shopping bags

When your inventory is complete, answer the following questions:

- ✔ Are you allocating your efforts well? Are you spending enough on efforts to keep your current customers happy, or are your efforts too heavily weighted toward getting new people through the door — or vice versa?

- ✔ Do your communications fit your image and objectives? Answer this question for every item, whether it's an ad or a logo-emblazoned coffee cup. Be sure that each contributes to the image you're trying to etch in your marketplace, rather than to some decision made long ago based on the powerful presentation by a sales representative.

- ✔ Is your image consistent, professional, and well suited to the audiences that matter most to your business?

Use your inventory as you fine-tune your communications. Then file it in a safe place. If you ever decide to change your name, logo, or overall look, this list will remind you of all the items that you need to update.

Rating Your Marketing Communications

Pull samples of stationery, ads, signs, brochures, coffee cups, T-shirts, and any other items that carry your company name or logo. Line them all up and put them through this test:

- ✔ Does your business name and logo look the same every time you make an impression?

- ✔ Do you consistently use the same colors?

- ✔ Do you consistently use the same type style?

- ✔ Do your marketing materials present a consistent image in terms of look, quality, and message?

Study your samples and isolate those that don't fit with the others, perhaps because they use outdated or inaccurate versions of your name or logo. Or maybe the colors are wrong or the tone is inconsistent. Possibly the message is witty or silly when the rest of your communications are fact-filled and serious. Or the caliber may be unprofessional compared to the rest of your materials.

Cull the inappropriate items and then look at what's left.

✔ Does the consistent portion of your marketing materials accurately reflect your business?

✔ Do your marketing materials adequately appeal to your target market?

- If you know that your customers value top quality, do your marketing materials convey a top-quality company? Do your ads convey quality? Do you apply your logo only to prestigious advertising items? If you're a retailer, are your shopping bags the finest you can afford? If you're a service company, do you present your proposals in a manner that reinforces the caliber of your firm while affirming your customer's taste level?

- If your customers value economy above all else, do your materials look too upscale? If so, they may inadvertently telegraph the wrong message.

- If your customers choose you primarily for convenience, do your materials put forth that assurance? Or, if you believe that your highest virtue is your reliability, do you convey that attribute through a flawless commitment to a reliably consistent projection of your identity?

In forming opinions about your company, your market relies on the impressions it gets from your communications.

Use your impression inventory as the basis for rating the image you project to your market. As you get ready to adjust and improve the quality of your communications, turn to Chapter 7 for everything you need to know about managing your image, setting a creative strategy to guide your communications, and writing an image style guide to cast your image rules in cement.

Chapter 7

Establishing Your Position and Brand

"*W*e're just a small business," you may be thinking. "We're not Nabisco or Nike, with a bazillion-dollar ad budget and a global market. We're just 12 people trying to build a half million dollars in sales. We hardly need a brand."

Guess what? You do need a brand.

A brand isn't some mysterious, expensive treasure available only to the rich and famous. And it isn't just for mega-marketers, though most certainly they all have one.

Branding simply (well, maybe not all *that* simply) involves developing and consistently communicating a set of positive characteristics that consumers can identify with and relate to your name. If those characteristics happen to fill a meaningful and available position in their minds — a need they've been wanting and trying to fill — then you just scored a marketing touchdown, and that half-million-dollar sales goal will be way easier to reach.

This chapter is about paving the road for marketing success by building a brand, focusing on a market position, and aligning all your communications under a creative strategy that leads to a single image customers trust and rely on. That's how small businesses become large, and *that's* what marketing is all about.

Brands Live in the Minds of Customers

When people hear your name, they conjure up a set of impressions that influence how they think and buy. Those thoughts define your brand.

Your brand resides in your customer's mind as a result of all the impressions made by encounters with your name, your logo, your marketing messages, and everything else that people see and hear about your business.

Something as basic as your business address contributes to how your brand is perceived. For that matter, every time someone walks into your business and looks around, visits your Web site, meets an employee, or glances at your ad, that person forms an impression that leads to a mind-set about your business.

If a person knows your business's name, you have a brand in that person's mind. It may not be the brand you want, and it may not be as well known as you wish it were, but you *have* a brand.

You can have a powerful brand without having a power brand

Levi's is a power brand. It's more powerful than Wrangler, Lee, or Guess. All are brands. All convey an identity and a promise. But one is known internationally and by all age and demographic groups, whereas the others have a more narrow influence and, therefore, less marketing power. The power of your brand comes from the degree to which it is known.

Your small business probably will never have a globally recognized "power brand" simply because you don't have (and for that matter don't need) the marketing horsepower that would fuel that level of awareness.

But you *can* be the most powerful brand in your target market. All it takes is

- Knowing the brand image that you want to project
- Having commitment and discipline to project your brand well
- Spending what's necessary to get your message to your target market
- Managing your marketing so that it makes a consistent impression that etches your desired brand image into the mind of your target prospect

Consistency builds brands

When your marketing communications create a single impression for your business, they build a strong brand. Stay consistent in your marketing by

✔ Projecting a consistent look

✔ Projecting a consistent tone in your communications

✔ Projecting a consistent level of quality, demonstrated by consistent communications, consistent products, and consistent services

If you notice a word used *consistently* (hint, hint) in the preceding instructions, write it down and remember it: Be consistent.

Stick with your brand. Don't try to change your brand image unless you're certain that it's no longer appropriate for the market. (And if that's the case, you better be prepared to change your business — because your brand is the public representation of your business.)

Imagine how tired the people at Campbell's Soup must be of their label, but imagine what would happen to their sales if they abandoned it simply because a fickle marketing manager said, "Let's try something new."

Consistency builds brands. And brands build business.

Branding makes selling easier

If you need a motivating fact to boot you into branding action, here it is. Branding makes selling easier, and here's why. People want to buy from companies they know and like — companies they trust will be there well into the future. A good brand puts forth that promise.

With a well-managed brand, your company hardly needs to introduce itself. Within your target market, people will already know your business, its personality, and the promise you make to customers — all based on what they've seen and heard through your marketing communications.

Without a well-managed brand, you'll spend up to half of every consumer contact trying to introduce your business and make your case, while some well-known Brand X down the street can spend that time making the sale.

An essential online ingredient

Without a brand, you have to build the case for your business before every sale. Doing that is tough work in person and even tougher work online, where you can't be there to make introductions, inspire confidence, counter resistance, or break down barriers.

People are buying everything online — from contact lenses to cars — without the benefit of demonstrations or test-drives. Why? Because customers arrive at e-businesses with confidence in the brands they are buying. If they don't see a brand they know, the odds of the online purchase occurring plummet. But if they see a brand they know and like, then they'll check the price and terms, make their selection, and purchase the product.

Branding facilitates sales and spurs business success all the way from Main Street to the cyberhighway.

Six steps to brand management

Good brand management follows certain steps.

1. **Define why you're in business.**

   What does your business do? How do you do it better than anyone else?

   Refer to Chapter 5, which can help you put into writing the reason that your business exists and the positive change you aim to achieve.

2. **Consider what you want people to think when they hear your name.**

   What do you want current and prospective employees to think about your business? What do you want prospects, customers, suppliers, associates, competitors, and friends to think?

   You can't be different things to each of these different groups and still have a well-managed brand. The brand image held by each of these groups has to synch into one identity — one *brand* — that people will trust and believe.

   For example, if you want employees to think that you pay the very best salaries in your competitive arena, you can't also expect customers to think that you provide the most bare-boned, low costs in the market. Likewise, you can't have an internal company mind-set that says "economy at any price" and expect consumers to believe that no one cares more about product quality and customer service than you do.

   Figure out what you want people to think when they hear your name. Then ask yourself whether that brand image is believable to each of the various groups with whom you communicate. If it isn't, decide how you need to alter your business to make achieving your brand image possible.

3. **Think about the words you want people to use when defining your business.**

   Ask your employees, associates, and customers this question: When people hear our name, what images do you think come into their minds?

   If everyone is saying the same thing — and if those words are the words you *want* associated with your name — you have a well-managed brand. If gaps occur, you have your brand-management work cut out for you.

   List words that you want people to link to your business and be certain that you live up to that desired image. Then lead people to the right conclusions by presenting those characteristics — that brand image — consistently and repeatedly in your marketing communications.

4. **Pinpoint the advantages you want people to associate with your business.**

   Figuring out these benefits helps you land on the advantages you want to communicate in your marketing communications. It also leads to your definition of the position you want to own in the consumer's mind (there's way more on this topic in the upcoming section, "Filling a Meaningful Market Position").

5. **Define your brand.**

   Look at your business through a customer's or prospect's eyes as you define your brand. What do people say — and think — about your business? Why do they choose your business and prefer to buy from you again and again? How would they define your brand?

   Boil your findings down to one concept — one brand definition — that you honestly believe you can own in the minds of those who deal with your business. Following are examples of how four widely known brands are generally perceived by the public:

   - Volvo: The safest car

   - CNN: The all-news channel

   - Google: The top Internet search engine

   - Starbucks: The most inviting coffeehouse experience

6. **Build your brand through every impression that you make.**

   Flip back to the Impression Points table in Chapter 6. Every item on that list is either a brand builder or a brand detractor, depending on how well it projects your brand with clarity and consistency.

A well-managed brand creates a strong emotional connection, and a strong emotional connection fosters loyal customer behavior. Protect and project your brand through every representation of your business in the marketplace.

Filling a Meaningful Market Position

Positioning involves figuring out what meaningful and available niche in the market your business is designed to fill, filling it, and performing so well that your customers have no reason to allow anyone else into your market position.

The tricky thing about positioning is that it's not something *you* do to your business; it's something the market does for you. Customers position your company in their own minds. Your job is to lead them to their positioning conclusions through your branding and marketing communications efforts.

How positioning happens

When people learn about your business, subconsciously they slot you into a business hierarchy composed of the following:

- **Me-too businesses:** If the mind slot — or position — that you want for your business is already taken, you'll have to convince consumers to switch allegiances on your behalf, and that's a tough job. The best advice to a "me-too" business is to find a way to become a "similar-but-different" business. Instead of simply opening your town's umpteenth pizza shop, open the only one in a trendy new neighborhood, or the only one that offers New York–style pizza by the slice, or the only one that uses recipes from Southern Italy in a trattoria setting. Your distinction better be a pretty compelling one, though, because you're going to have to convince people that 1) your difference is worth hearing about and 2) your difference is worth changing for.

- **Similar-but-different businesses:** These are businesses that market a meaningful difference in an already crowded field. If your town has three accounting firms, but you open the first one that caters specifically to small businesses, then you have a meaningful point of distinction. And if you communicate that distinction well, you're apt to win an available position in the minds of entrepreneurs and small business owners. Depending on the nature of your business, your positioning distinction may be based on pricing, inventory, target market, service structure, or company personality. The most important thing is that the difference matter to your target market.

- **Brand-new offerings:** If you can be the first to fill a market's needs, then you have the easiest positioning task of all. But you must jump into the market skillfully and forcefully enough to win your way into the consumer's mind before anyone else can get there.

First-in-a-market businesses and first-of-a-kind products have to market fast and fastidiously because, in the end, being first isn't as important as being first into the consumer's mind.

Determining your positioning strategy

The easiest way to figure out what position you hold is to determine what hole would be left in the market if your company closed tomorrow. In other words, what does your business offer that your customers would have a hard or impossible time finding elsewhere? Other questions that will lead to your positioning statement include the following:

✔ How is your offering unique or at least difficult to copy?

✔ Is your unique offering something that consumers really want?

✔ Is your offering compatible with economic and market trends?

✔ With which businesses do you compete and how are you different — and better?

✔ Is your claim believable?

Don't aim for a position that requires the market to make a leap of faith on your behalf. If a restaurant is known for the best burgers in town, it can't suddenly decide to try to jump into the position of "the finest steakhouse in the state." Leapfrog doesn't work well when the game is positioning.

Determine what has built your success to date. Develop your position around that distinct attribute. Here are a few examples of positioning statements:

✔ Skyliner is a residential development offering families the finest view in Pleasantville.

✔ Treetops is an alpine inn hosting the most pampered ski vacationers in the East.

✔ *Small Business Marketing For Dummies* is a friendly guide packed with low-cost, high-impact advice especially for do-it-yourself small business marketers.

See how it works? A positioning statement is easy to construct. Just apply the formula you see in Figure 7-1.

Figure 7-1:
This formula
helps you
build a
positioning
statement.

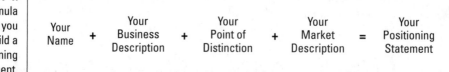

Your Name + Your Business Description + Your Point of Distinction + Your Market Description = Your Positioning Statement

Your desired position must be

✔ Available

✔ Consistent with the character and offerings of your business

✔ Believable and desirable to the target market

As you write your statement, avoid these traps:

✔ **Don't try to duplicate a position in an already crowded category**.

✔ **Don't base your distinction on a pricing or quality difference that a competitor can take from you.** For instance, you're only egging your competitors on if you position yourself as "the lowest priced" or "the most creative." With effort, a competitor can beat you on either front.

✔ **Don't hang your hat on a factor you can't control.** For example, too many resorts have ended up red-faced after positioning themselves as "the region's only five-star resort," only to lose a star or have a competitor gain one.

Conveying Your Position and Brand through Tag Lines

Your *tag line* is the phrase that helps consumers link your name to your business brand and position. A tag line (also called a *slogan*) provides consumers with a quick, memorable phrase that gives an indication of your business brand and position in just a few words.

The New York Times is famous for its tag line, "All the news that's fit to print." BMW ads say, "The ultimate driving machine." Altoids became famous with, "Curiously strong peppermints." www.adslogans.co.uk/hof/ has tag lines compiled by the Advertising Slogan Hall of Fame.

Tag lines translate a company's positioning statement into a marketing phrase meant to serve as a customer magnet. Following is how the *For Dummies* brand might be summarized in a positioning statement, and how the brand is presented in its trademarked tag line.

Positioning statement: For Dummies business and general reference books are lighthearted but not lightweight survival guides that demystify confusing or intimidating topics and give readers everything they need to know without making it seem like a big deal.

Tag line: A Reference for the Rest of Us!

Good tag lines have the following attributes:

- ✔ They're memorable.
- ✔ They convey your brand image.
- ✔ They present key customer benefits.
- ✔ They differentiate your business from competitors.
- ✔ They evoke a positive feeling.
- ✔ They're unique. For example, they won't work when linked to a competitor's name.
- ✔ They fit your branding strategy.
- ✔ They don't trigger sarcastic retorts.
- ✔ They don't sound like a corporate committee wrote them.

If you adopt a tag line, make it an official element in your marketing communications and use it with your logo on all printed materials. Here are some tips on using your tag line:

- ✔ Treat your tag line as part of your logo. Specify the type style and the relationship between the size of your tag line and the size of your logo, so that the slogan doesn't overpower your symbol.
- ✔ Include your tag line along with your logo in all printed presentations except in e-mail, where your tag line will appear as the sole representative of your brand and position unless your program allows inclusion of your logo. (The help function in your e-mail program will explain how to create an e-mail signature.)

Advancing Your Brand through a Creative Strategy

Your *creative strategy* is the plan that directs the development of all your marketing materials. It defines

- ✔ Your target market
- ✔ The believable and meaningful benefit you offer to your market
- ✔ How you present your personality in your communications

Writing your creative strategy

You can write your creative strategy in three sentences that define the purpose, approach, and personality that will guide the creation of your marketing communications, following this formula:

1. "The purpose of our marketing communications is to convince [insert a brief description of your target market] that our product is the most [describe the primary benefit you provide to customers]."

2. "We will prove our claim by [insert a description of why your distinct benefit is believable and how you will prove it in your marketing]."

3. "The mood and tone of our communications will be [insert a description of the personality that all your communications will convey]."

Following are sample strategies for two fictitious businesses:

- ✔ **Glass Houses, a window washing service:** The purpose of our marketing communications is to convince affluent homeowners in our hometown that our service is the easiest and most immediately gratifying way to beautify their homes. We will prove our claim by guaranteeing same-week and streak-free service, by promising four-month callback reminders, and by offering special three-times-a-year contract rates so that homeowners will never have to think about window cleaning after their first call to us. The mood and tone of our communications will be straightforward and clean — just like our service.

- ✔ **Bookworms, an independent bookshop:** The purpose of our marketing communications is to convince residents and visitors that our bookstore is the most friendly, welcoming, and informative place to browse and discover great reading material. We will prove our claim by extending invitations to enjoy free staff recommendations, refreshments, and reading areas in our store and by including reading choices and staff reviews in all our ads. The mood and tone of our communications will be friendly and intelligent, conveying the kind of casual confidence and enthusiasm that members in a book club express to one another.

Using your creative strategy

Every time you create an ad, a direct mailer, a voice-mail recording, or even a business letter or an employee uniform or dress code, be 100-percent certain that your communication is consistent with the creative strategy that you've established to guide your business personality. Here are some ways to do so:

- ✔ **Use your creative strategy to guide every representation of your business — and your brand.** Start by looking around your business to see that your physical space projects the tone you want for your business. If your creative strategy stipulates a discreet tone for your business, you won't want prospects to encounter a rowdy atmosphere with music blaring when they walk into or call your business. Carry that same discipline into every marketing communication.

- ✔ **Create each new marketing communication with your creative strategy in mind.** Whether you're developing a building sign, a Web site, or a splashy ad for an expensive magazine, insist that the final product adheres to your creative strategy.

- ✔ **Fine-tune your creative strategy annually.** Each year as you update your marketing plan (see Chapter 22), review your creative strategy. You may decide to reach out to a different target market, or you may decide to present a different marketing message based on your assessment of market opportunities. But hold tight to your definition of the mood and tone of your communications. (Flip back to the section "Consistency builds brands" for a reminder on why your look and tone need to be reliable indicators of your brand image.)

Writing Your Image Style Guide

Well-branded organizations have firm rules about how their logos may be presented, what type styles and colors may be used in marketing materials, how certain words are used, and when and how tag lines, copyrights, and trademark indicators apply — called *style guidelines*. They protect the consistency of your business image in the marketplace. Before a print shop, a specialty-advertising producer, a staff designer, an outside marketing firm, or any other supplier creates marketing materials on your behalf, share your style guidelines to steer the outcome of their efforts.

Controlling your logo presentation

Your logo is the face of your business on marketing materials. Ensure that it is presented cleanly and without unnecessary alteration by asking and answering the following questions in your style guidelines:

- ✔ When your logo appears in black ink, what color backgrounds may be used?

- ✔ When your logo appears in white ink (called a *reverse*), what color backgrounds may be used?

- ✔ When your logo appears in color, what ink color or colors may be used? The person who designed your logo should specify ink colors from the Pantone Matching System used by nearly all printers.

- ✔ What is the smallest size that can be used for your logo?

Indicate in your guidelines that your logo must be reproduced from original artwork or a professionally produced reproduction, and never from a photocopy or previously printed piece, because the quality will be inferior.

Deciding on your type style

A quick way to build consistency is to limit the type styles you use in ads, brochures, signs, and all other communications. Choose one font (also called a *typeface*) for headlines and one for ad copy. If your company prints technical materials (instruction guides, warranties, operating or assembly instructions, or other copy-intensive pieces), you might designate a third, easy-to-read font for small print and long-text applications.

Serif type is type with short, decorative flourishes at the start or finish of the letters, while *sans serif* (literally "without serif") type features letters with no adornments. The serifs help guide the eye from letter to letter and are particularly useful for long paragraphs or pages of information.

This is an example of serif type.

This is an example of sans serif type.

The font you choose for your marketing materials should reflect the personality of your company. If you want to convey an old-fashioned or traditional tone, you probably need a serif type. But if you want your materials to appear informal or very clean and straightforward, sans serif type is an appropriate choice.

In addition to specifying fonts, you may want to define usage preferences.

- ✔ Research has proven that people read copy that uses both uppercase and lowercase letters with greater ease than they read copy printed in all capital letters. For legibility, avoid using all capital letters unless the headline or copy block is extremely short and easy for the eyes to track.

- ✔ Especially if your target market has aging vision, try to keep text or body copy at no smaller than 10 points in size.

  - This is 8-point type.

  - This is 10-point type.

  - This is 12-point type.

  - This is 14-point type.

- ✔ Avoid reversed type (light type on black or dark backgrounds, as shown in Figure 7-2) if you expect people to read your words easily. If, for design purposes, you decide to reverse type, keep the type size large.

- ✔ Limit the number of fonts that you combine in any single marketing piece, unless you're trying through your design to create a cluttered look.

Figure 7-2:
Reversed
type.

This is an example of reversed type.

See Chapter 11 for more on selecting and using type.

Copy guidelines

Copy refers to the words, text, or content of your marketing materials. As you establish style guidelines, define how you want your copy prepared.

- ✔ If certain words in your marketing materials require copyright (©), trademark (™), or registered trademark (®) symbols, then list these words in your style guidelines.

- ✔ Indicate in your guidelines if you want your marketing materials to carry a copyright notice in very small (usually 6-point) type at the bottom of your material. For example: © 2005 John Doe. (Go to www.copyright.gov for more information.)

✔ If you plan to send printed materials over national borders, ask your attorney if you need to include a line reading "Printed in U.S.A." If so, include the instructions in your guidelines.

✔ Decide which words you prefer to have capitalized. For example, perhaps your style preference is to say your business is located in "Southern California" and not "southern California." Or maybe you want your business to be "The Candy Factory" and not "the Candy Factory."

✔ Determine whether you want to ban certain words. For example, a real estate developer may prohibit the word *lots* in favor of the word *homesites*. A public relations firm may rule out the term *PR* and insist the words be spelled out to read *public relations*.

Chapter 8

Getting Strategic before Getting Creative

- -

- -

Creative. The very word turns confident people queasy and rational people giddy. It prompts otherwise buttoned-down small business owners to say such outrageous things as "Let's dress up like chickens" or "Let's show our products as animated characters dancing the can-can" or such well-intended but pointless things as "Let's cut through the clutter" or "We have to think outside the box."

Far, far less often are you apt to hear the creative conversation turn strategic, with statements like "Let's talk in terms that matter to our target prospects" or "Let's define what we're trying to accomplish."

By focusing on your communication objective *before* dreaming up your creative concept — by getting strategic and *then* getting creative — you'll steer past the mistakes that shoot too many ad budgets into the great abyss where wasted dollars languish. This chapter shows you how.

Good Communications Start with Good Objectives

Copywriters and designers are talented and creative, but they're rarely telepathic. They can't create marketing materials that meet specific objectives if their instructions don't include what they're trying to accomplish.

So who is supposed to define the objective, set the strategy, and aim the creative process? Well, get ready, because that task falls to the person responsible for marketing, which is probably, well, *you*.

In blunt terms, the creation of good marketing materials begins with you.

Putting an end to shot-in-the-dark marketing instructions

You can hit your marketing target almost every time if you take careful aim. Read the following examples of creative instructions and note the differences:

> Example 1: "We need to build sales. Let's run some ads."

> Example 2: "We need to run ads to convince teenagers that by shopping after school on weekdays they will enjoy our best prices in a club atmosphere because we feature live music, two-for-one café specials, and weekday-only student discounts."

Example 1 forces those creating the ad to guess what you want. It will likely lead to a process that involves round after round of revisions as the creative team tries to read your mind about your target market, promotional offer, creative concept, ad copy, and media schedule.

Example 2 tells the ad creators precisely which consumers you're targeting, what you want to say, the offer you want to make, and the action you're hoping to achieve. It allows development of an appropriate concept and media plan — probably on the first try.

As the chief marketer for your business, it's your job to give those who produce your ads the information they need to do the job right the first time.

Dodging the creative landmines

There's an old saying among marketers that half of all ad dollars are wasted, but no one knows which half. You can move the dividing line between what works and what doesn't by planning in advance to avoid three wasteful errors:

> ✔ **Mistake #1:** Producing marketing materials without first defining objectives, leading to the production of materials that address neither the target prospect nor the marketing objective

✔ **Mistake #2:** Creating marketing materials that are too "hard-sell," asking for the order without first reeling in the attention and interest of the prospect.

✔ **Mistake #3:** Creating self-centered marketing messages that focus more on what a business wants to say about itself than about the benefits that matter to a prospect.

Deciding on a Goal for Every Single Marketing Communication

Before you undertake any marketing effort — from a quick sales call to an elaborate advertisement — define whom you're trying to influence, what you're trying to get the market to do, and what message you want to promote to accomplish your aim.

Here is a template you can use when setting communication goals. Just insert the appropriate text for your business in the parentheses.

This (ad/brochure/sales call/speech/trade booth display, or so on) *will convince* (describe the target market for this communication) *that* (describe the action that you hope to achieve) *will* (describe the benefit they will realize) *because* (state the facts that prove your claim).

Writing a Creative Brief

Your communication goal defines *what* you're trying to accomplish. Next, complete a "creative brief" to explain *how* you'll get the job done.

Each time you create an ad, write a speech, make a sales presentation, plan a brochure, or compose an important business letter, start by running through the questions on the creative brief to focus your thinking. For all major projects — or for any project that you plan to assign to a staff member, free-lance professional, vendor, or advertising agency — take time to put your answers in writing. Then pass them along so they can serve as a valuable naviga-tional aid.

Figure 8-1 provides a format to follow. Answer Questions 1 through 7 (you can find more advice on each step later in this chapter), and your briefing instructions will be complete.

1. Who is the target prospect?

The target audience: Who are the people most apt to respond to this marketing effort? Describe them in terms of geographic location, demographic facts, and tendency to purchase a product like yours.

2. What do they currently know or think about us and our product or service?

Current Perceptions: Are you trying to reinforce current thoughts about your product/service, or are you trying to change minds? What wrong impressions, if any, do you want to correct?

3. What do we want them to know or think — and do?

Desired Outcome: Write a one-sentence description of the major idea you want prospects to receive from this marketing effort, and the action you want them to take. Remember: a single marketing communication can only accomplish so much.

4. Why should they believe us?

Supporting Facts: Don't create a laundry list of features you offer, but a statement of the unique benefits customers can count on.

5. What information does this marketing effort need to convey?

Mandatory Instructions: What information must you include? If you know you need to include legal or copyright lines, logo or tag line, Web address, contact information specific photos, and so on, state your requirements here.

6. How will we evaluate this marketing effort?

Success Measurements: State what you expect this effort to accomplish so that it can be designed to accomplish your objectives.

Figure 8-1:
Guide to
writing a
creative
brief.

7. Project guidelines, Timeline, Budget.

Specifications: If you want it done right the first time, provide all the facts and figures before the creative planning begins. Don't withhold information, especially about your budget. If you have limited funds, say so.

Targeting your market

Start with everything you know about your prospects (see Chapter 2 for more information) and then boil your knowledge into a one-sentence definition that encapsulates the geographic location, the lifestyle facts, and the purchasing motivators of your target prospects.

Here is the target market statement for a real estate developer:

> The prospect is a resident of Montana, aged 40+, married with children living at home, with a professional career, upper-level income, and an affinity for travel, outdoor recreation, status brands, and high levels of service.

Dealing with prospect perceptions

If you want your marketing efforts to change market perceptions, you need to start with knowledge about what your prospects currently know and think about your business or product. Use your own instincts and those of your staff and colleagues to answer the following questions:

✔ Have prospects heard of your business?

✔ Do they know what products or services you offer?

✔ Do they know where you're located or how to reach you?

✔ Do they see you as a major player? If they were asked to name three suppliers of your product or service, would you be among the answers?

✔ How do they rate your service, quality, pricing, accessibility, range of products, and reputation?

✔ Do you have a clear brand and market position or a mistaken identity in their minds?

Be candid with your answers. Only by acknowledging your shortcomings can you begin to address them through your marketing efforts.

A new destination resort might write the following prospect opinion assessment:

> The majority of our prospects are not aware of our existence, but among those familiar with our name, we are known to provide an experience competitive with the best resort offerings in our state. We need to reinforce the opinions of our acquaintances while extending awareness to our prospects and especially to those opinion leaders whose recommendations are most valued by our affluent and socially connected target market.

Stating your desired outcome

Some advertisers use the tired phrase "more bang for the buck" as they work ineffectively to pack a dozen thoughts into a sales letter, a 30-second radio commercial, a postcard mailer, or a miniscule print ad.

Don't be greedy. Present one clear idea, and chances are good that you'll *communicate* one clear idea. But if you try to present two or three messages, you're likely to communicate nothing at all.

Four out of five consumers read only the headline in a print ad; they absorb no more than seven words off a billboard; and they take one idea away from a broadcast ad — providing that they don't tune out or skip over the ad altogether.

What single idea do you want prospects to take away from this particular marketing effort, whether it's a sales call, a display window, an ad, or any other form of communication? As you answer, follow this process:

1. **Step out of your own shoes and stand in those of your prospect.**

2. **Think about what your target prospect wants or needs to know.**

3. **Develop a single sentence describing what you want people to think and what motivating idea you want them to take away from this communication.**

Here is the desired outcome for a computer retailer targeting senior citizens:

> We want senior citizens to know that they're invited to attend our Computer 101 open houses every Wednesday afternoon this month where they can watch computer and Internet demonstrations, receive hands-on training, and learn about our special first-time computer owner packages that include in-home installation and Internet hook-up.

Watch what you ask for. Be sure that you can handle the outcome you say you desire.

If you aren't geared up to answer the phone, handle the foot traffic, or fulfill the buying demand that your ad generates, then you have failed strategically even though you succeeded — wildly — on the advertising front.

Consider this example: A one-man painting company decided to rev up business by placing a series of very clever small-space ads in the local newspaper. The ads touted impeccable service, outstanding quality, affordable estimates, and prompt response. The ads won attention, action, and advertising awards. The problem is, the painter couldn't keep up with the phone calls, the estimates, or the orders. Prospects — who had been inspired by the great ads — ended up signing contracts with the painter's competitors instead.

The moral of the story is to expect a miracle from good advertising and to be prepared to get what you ask for.

Conveying benefits versus features

To be believable, your marketing materials need to make and support a claim. *The easy way* is to list your features (the oldest moving company in the east, under new management, the only manufacturer featuring the X2000 widget, 10-year winner of our industry's top award, yada yada yada . . .). *The effective way* is to turn those features into benefits that you promise to your customers. The difference between features and benefits is that features are facts, and benefits are personal outcomes.

Table 8-1 shows you exactly what this crucial difference means.

Table 8-1	Features versus Benefits		
Product	*Feature*	*Benefit*	*Emotional Outcome*
Diet soda	One calorie	Lose weight	Look and feel great
Flower arrangements	Daily exotic imports	Send unique floral presentations	Satisfaction that your gift stands out and draws attention
Automobile	Best crash rating	Reduce risk of harm in accidents	Security that your family is safe
Miniature microwave	1.5 cubic feet in size	Save dorm room space	Make room for the floor's only big-screen TV

Every time you describe a *feature* of your product or service, you're talking to yourself. Every time you describe the *benefit* that your product or service delivers, you're talking to your prospect, because consumers don't buy the feature — they buy what the feature does for them. Here are some examples:

 ✔ Consumers don't buy V-8 engines. They buy speed.

 ✔ They don't buy shock-absorbing shoes. They buy walking comfort.

 ✔ They don't buy the lightest laptop computer. They buy the freedom to work wherever they want.

Follow these steps to translate features into benefits:

1. **State your product or business feature.**

2. **Add the phrase "which means."**

3. **Complete the sentence and you are forced to state the benefit.**

    The Feature + "Which Means" = The Benefit

Here's an example using the diet soda mentioned in Table 8-1: Diet soda has one calorie (that's the feature) *which means* you can lose weight and look and feel great (that's the benefit).

Naming your "have-to-haves"

Ad designers call it "death by a thousand cuts" when marketers respond to every creative presentation with, "Yes, but we have to include. . . ."

If you know that you need to feature a certain look or specific information or artwork, say so up front — not after you see the first creative presentation. And keep the list of have-to's as short as possible. Here are some guidelines:

✔ **Have-to #1:** Every communication has to advance your brand image (refer to Chapter 7 for information about defining your image). Provide a copy of your image style guide whenever you assign a staff person or outside professional to help with the development of marketing material.

✔ **Have-to #2:** Be sparing with all other have-to's. Every time you start to say, "we have to include . . ." stop and check yourself with this self-test:

• Is this element necessary to protect our brand?

• Is it necessary to protect our legal standing?

• Is it necessary to prompt the marketing action we want to achieve?

• Is it necessary to motivate the prospect?

Let necessity — not history — guide your answers.

Deciding how you'll measure success

Small businesses are critical of their marketing efforts — after the fact.

After an ad has run its course, you'll hear such criticism as, "That ad didn't work, it didn't make the phone ring, and it sure didn't create foot traffic." Yet if you ask to see the ad under question, you'll find that it includes no reason to call, no special offer, a phone number that requires a magnifying glass, and no address whatsoever.

If you want consumers to take action, set your expectation *before* the concept is created and define your measurement standard in your creative brief.

Specifying your specifications

Know the specifications of your job before you start producing it — and especially before you assign the production task to others.

- ✔ **Set your budget and be frank about how much you can spend.** Small business owners often worry that if they divulge their budgets, the print shop or agency or media outlet will spend it all — whether they need to or not. But the strategy usually backfires. If suppliers *don't* know the budget, they *will* spend it all — and then some — simply because no one gave them a not-to-exceed figure to work with. The solution is to hire suppliers you trust, share your budget with them (along with instructions that the budget cannot be exceeded without your prior approval), and then count on them to be partners in providing a cost-effective solution. (See Chapter 9 for information on how to control costs when working with advertising agencies and freelance talent.)

- ✔ **Know and share deadlines and material requirements.** If you have already committed to a media buy, attach a media rate card to your creative brief so that your designer can see the specifications directly from the publication and not through your translation.

- ✔ **Define the parameters of nonmedia communication projects.** For example, if you're asking for speechwriting assistance, know the length of time allocated for your presentation. If you're requesting materials for a sales presentation, know the number of people expected to attend and therefore the number of handouts you'll want to take with you.

What the creative team doesn't know can cost you dearly in enthusiasm and cost overruns if you have to retrofit creative solutions to fit production realities. Communicate in advance to keep everyone happy.

Chapter 9

Hiring Help for Your Marketing Program

· ·

· ·

*Y*ou're a small business marketer. Most likely you're not a trained marketing strategist, media buyer, award-winning designer, or stop-'em-in-their-tracks copywriter.

You're also human. You have 24 hours in every day, and perhaps you've suddenly realized that even by giving up sleep you can't come up with enough time to run your company, develop your products and services, build your customer base, maintain your business relationships, *and* produce and place your own ads.

Or maybe you have the time but lack the professional touch or creative talent to create great ads, brochures, Web sites, or promotions on your own.

Or, best of all, maybe you've arrived at the point where your business has simply grown so large that you can no longer implement its marketing programs on your own.

Perhaps all you need is occasional help from a designer, copywriter, Web site designer, or media buyer. Or maybe it's time to graduate to "client" status by hiring an advertising agency to help polish and project your image. Either way, you need to know where to find marketing professionals, how to manage the screening and selection process, and how to participate in a relationship that works to your immediate and lasting advantage. That's what the following pages are about.

Can You Afford to Hire Professional Help?

When advertising agencies first came into being, they sold their services in return for the 15-percent commission that newspapers, magazines, and radio stations offered when agencies provided the media with ready-to-use ad materials. As an example, if an agency provided professional material when placing a $1,000 ad for a company, the media let the agency keep $150 — or 15 percent — as the agency commission. The agency then used the $150 to cover the cost of its effort on behalf of the client.

Today, businesses communicate their marketing messages through television ads and in many other forms that involve production costs that far outweigh 15 percent of media costs, and agencies can no longer perform under the 15-percent formula.

Still, 15 percent of your marketing budget is a good place to start as you try to decide whether your budget is big enough to cover the cost of outside professional assistance. Table 9-1 shows examples for companies with sales of $100,000 to $2 million. The middle column shows the marketing budget if the businesses allocated 5–10 percent of sales revenue for marketing. The third column shows how much the companies would spend if they allocated 15 percent of the marketing budget to the purchase of professional services.

Table 9-1	Should You Bring in Marketing Pros?	
Sales	*Marketing Allocation (5%–10% of Sales)*	*Professional Services Allocation (15% of Marketing Allocation)*
$100,000	$5,000–$10,000	$750–$1,500
$200,000	$10,000–$20,000	$1,500–$3,000
$500,000	$25,000–$50,000	$3,750–$7,500
$1,000,000	$50,000–$100,000	$7,500–$15,000
$1,500,000	$75,000–$150,000	$11,250–$22,500
$2,000,000	$100,000–$200,000	$15,000–$30,000

As you hire pros, be aware that fees range upwards from $50 an hour, depending on whether you are hiring freelance writing and design services or whether you need marketing consultation and advice. Here are a few practical guidelines for hiring outside professionals:

✔ Companies with sales revenue under $500,000 should probably limit their purchase of outside talent to on-call copywriting and design services.

✔ Companies with sales of over a million dollars may be wise to invest in an annual consultation by a marketing professional.

✔ As the marketing budget nears $100,000 to $200,000, consider retaining an advertising agency — one large enough to offer the quality services you need but small enough to consider your business important — to help leverage your marketing budget through strong creative messages and targeted media purchases.

Knowing When It's Time to Get Help

When it comes to marketing, getting help is an indication of success. It means that you've decided to strengthen the image and message you project in the marketplace. It also means that you're willing to invest some of your hard-won profits into your business-building effort.

As with most business investments, you can't afford to dive in too soon, nor can you wait too long. Here's when to bring in the pros:

✔ **When you're creating a long-life marketing piece.** If you're creating a logo, ad campaign, major brochure, or some other piece that will represent your business for months or years to come, invest in professional assistance if you're not certain that your own talents are up to the task.

✔ **When doing it yourself takes you or your staff away from more profitable activities.** Focus on doing what you do best and contract with marketing professionals to do what they do best. You'll profit doubly by building your business while investing in professionally produced marketing materials.

✔ **When your annual budget for marketing communications reaches $50,000.** Add up what you've budgeted for brochures, advertising, direct mail, and other outreach efforts. If the total exceeds $50,000, consider hiring freelance creative professionals to help you build a strong message and a coordinated look for your company.

✔ **When the budget for a single marketing effort exceeds $10,000.** If you're putting significant dollars behind a direct-mail program, brochure, ad campaign, or marketing effort, don't risk your investment trying to do it yourself unless you're certain of your capabilities.

Where to Turn for Help

As your business grows, your marketing needs may exceed the time or the talent that you have to devote to producing your marketing materials. As you lift the weight off your own shoulders, here are some ways to get help:

- ✔ You can tap in-house, staff talent.
- ✔ You can turn to print shops or media ad departments for free or almost-free production services.
- ✔ You can hire freelancers, who are independent contractors available by the hour for short-term projects.
- ✔ You can hire an advertising or public relations agency to handle your work as a project or as part of an ongoing assignment.

Tapping in-house talent

Many entrepreneurs take the first step away from doing it all themselves by assigning the coordination of marketing functions to an employee or associate.

When assigning the task to those already on or added to your payroll, weigh the following considerations.

Assigning the marketing task to a staff member

As you add the role of marketing management to the responsibilities of an existing staff member or associate, here's what you need to do:

- ✔ Write a job description and list qualifications for the ideal person to handle your marketing. Before assigning the task to a staff member, be sure that person meets the criteria.
- ✔ If the staff member doesn't possess the expertise to perform the assignment well, consider what kind of training (and training costs) will be necessary.
- ✔ The staff person who will take on the marketing duties probably doesn't have idle time in which to perform the new marketing assignment. Consider which current responsibilities you will shift, and to whom.
- ✔ Define what resources this person will require in order to do the job. You may need to invest in design or production-tracking software, subscriptions to professional publications, professional education, and support staff.

Hiring a marketing manager

By hiring a person to handle your marketing program, you may be able to delay the decision to hire an agency — because you'll have a person on staff who can handle the coordination and marketing management role. But as you budget for the position, realize that no one person can do it all — design, copywriting, Internet marketing, public relations, and media planning and buying. Plan accordingly by budgeting for freelance talent in addition to the line item that you budget for your new marketing manager.

Forming an in-house agency

Some companies calculate the commissions that their media buys will generate and decide to form an in-house agency so that they can keep the money under their own roofs.

An *in-house agency* (also called a *house agency*) is a company department set up to function as an ad agency that serves only one client — the company of which it is a part.

Forming an in-house agency involves the following steps:

- ✔ Establish a marketing department that has the expertise to plan, produce, and place ads.

- ✔ Establish your agency with media organizations to confirm that you qualify for the discount offered to recognized agencies. Check with publications and stations that serve your market to learn the criteria they use to recognize an agency and to see that you meet the requirements.

- ✔ Plan to pay media bills promptly in order to qualify for the commission.

Businesses flirt with the idea of forming an in-house agency because they want to qualify for media commissions. But in order to earn commissions, you have to spend money — a lot of money — on media. Even if you're spending $150,000 on media buys, the commissions are hardly enough to fund the bare-bone costs involved in staffing your own ad agency. Do the math: Fifteen percent of $150,000 is $22,500, not enough to pay the salary and benefits of an assistant, let alone someone with proven expertise to write, design, and produce ads that can enhance your image in the marketplace.

Using free or almost-free resources

This section is short. You get what you pay for, and if you don't need much, then free is a wonderful price. If you're only adding a tag line to a pre-produced industry broadcast ad or are dropping your logo and address into a manufacturer's newspaper ad, then you hardly need to invest in high-priced assistance. Hand your instructions over to a media production department, ask for a proof, and keep your billfold in your pocket because you probably won't have to pay a thing.

Likewise, if you're reprinting an existing brochure with only minor type changes, or if you're creating a simple brochure or small-space ad using an established design template, then a designer at your print shop or newspaper is apt to be an ideal and economical resource.

But . . . if you want a big creative idea, a unique concept, a striking design, or memorable creative quality, then budget accordingly and hire professionals who can spend the time and effort necessary to create a piece capable of enhancing and advancing your unique brand image.

Hiring marketing professionals

Small business owners hear the term "advertising agency" and instinctively grab hold of their billfolds — with good reason. The myth is a reality when it comes to the feeling that advertising agencies — and freelance professionals too, for that matter — are expensive. They charge hourly fees that start in the mid-$50s and climb to $150 or more in a hurry.

A print ad produced by professionals may cost anywhere from $500 to five figures, depending on whether you're looking at a simple black-and-white ad for the local daily or a splashy full-color ad designed for a slick monthly magazine. Staggering as the numbers are, don't let them scare you off. Not yet. First, do the following:

- ✔ Take an objective look at your advertising compared to that of your competitors. Ask yourself whether your business would profit in terms of image, impact, and market responsiveness if you invested more in ad creation and production.

- ✔ Estimate the potential profit you might realize if your ads were even 5–10 percent more effective in inspiring market action.

If you decide that the impact of professionally produced marketing materials justifies the expense involved (and usually it does), you can turn to a range of professionals who can help you out. They include advertising and public relations agencies, graphic design studios, self-employed freelance graphic artists and copywriters, and media planners and buyers.

✔ **Ad agencies, public relations firms, and design studios** are set up to handle entire jobs, from strategic and concept development through design and copywriting, production management, and overseeing printing, ad placement, and direct mailings. They have systems in place to handle multifaceted tasks and they have teams of professionals they can assign to your job. They also serve as brokers — screening, selecting, and managing photographers, printers, and marketing specialists on your behalf. Most assign a liaison, usually called an account executive, to serve as your primary contact and advocate. As a result, you have a team of people helping you, but you deal with only one person, who will hold all the others accountable on your behalf.

✔ **Freelancers** are specialists in particular fields such as strategic planning, copywriting, design, illustration, and media planning. Freelancers work on an hourly basis and gladly accept project work, whereas agencies often prefer longer-term client commitments. While most freelancers work independently, often they are part of a creative network that can serve as a virtual team for your project. Minimally you can count on one freelancer to recommend creative professionals for other aspects of your project.

In deciding what kind of expertise to hire, follow these tips:

✔ Hire professionals whose talents and fees fit your situation. If you want a photo of a new employee to send with a news release to the local paper, you hardly need to hire a photographer who charges $1,000 a day to take the mug shot. And you don't need a public relations consultant whose fee is $100 an hour to write a two-paragraph news release.

✔ If you have a staff member who is able to coordinate the various steps of your production and ad placement process, you can hire freelancers rather than an agency. But if you need management as well as creative expertise, turn to an agency that is set up to offer full service and to assume the coordination role.

Some general guidelines can help you select the best resources. For example, a designer is your answer if you need a logo, stationery, or a design solution for a brochure or ad. A copywriter can help if you need text for brochures or ads. A media planner or buyer helps with media placement of pre-produced ads. Public relations agencies are skilled at special event planning, promotions, publicity generation, and crisis management. A full-service ad agency is the best approach if you're undertaking several of these activities as part of your overall marketing program, or if you want an ongoing partner in developing your marketing image, message, and materials.

Choosing and Working with an Advertising Agency

Before you can select a marketing partner, here's what you need to know:

- **Your needs:** What kind of service are you seeking? Are you looking for help with a single important project — perhaps the creation of an advertising campaign, a major brochure, an annual report, or a big promotion? Or are you seeking an agency to help build your image on a long-term basis? Know what kind of partnership you're after before contacting agencies. Some agencies welcome project work, while others prefer to work with clients on a long-term basis.

- **Your priorities:** Some businesses want an agency with a reputation for delivering award-winning creative concepts. Others seek agencies with demonstrated experience in a particular industry or market segment. Some value economical solutions above all else. Others want an agency with a name-dropping client roster, proven government or industry relations, or even strong social or business connections. Before beginning your search, decide which aspects of an agency's offerings are most important to you and evaluate capabilities accordingly.

- **Your budget:** Define how much you plan to spend over the coming year on ad production, media placements, marketing materials, and promotional efforts. Then share the financial facts with your top-choice agencies. Small businesses hesitate to reveal budgets that they think might sound meager, plus they're afraid to "let the wolf in the hen house" by telling an agency how much money is budgeted. Advice: Establish a trusting partnership by being open from the get-go. If your budget doesn't fit an agency's client profile, it's best to know before you spend time trying to establish a mismatched relationship.

Defining your selection criteria

Before beginning the agency selection process, answer these questions:

- **What are you trying to accomplish?**

  Put your objectives in writing. Are you trying to establish and build a brand? Do you want to introduce a product? Do you need to reverse a sales decline or jumpstart stagnant sales? Is your objective to launch a long-term effort to build market share?

✔ **What do you value in an agency?**

Are you looking for an agency that specializes in a certain kind of media —
such as broadcast, print, online advertising, or direct mail? Do you want
an agency that specializes in the production of brochures and printed
material? Is it important to you that the agency can develop and implement cooperative advertising programs?

Are you seeking an agency that is known for its award-winning creative
work? Realize that clients pay for breakthrough creative advertising in two
ways. First, it takes time and therefore money to develop and produce
highly creative and attention-getting advertising. Second, it takes brave
clients to approve highly creative concepts. Clients of award-winning
agencies talk about the sweaty palms they experienced in approving both
the concepts and the budgets for ads that went on to win not just awards
but market share. Be sure that you're willing to invest on both fronts if
"creative" is your highest advertising value.

✔ **What do you bring to the table?**

To get and keep the attention of a good agency, you need at least one
and preferably two or all three of the following attributes:

- **A good budget:** You need a budget big enough to do the job and to
  allow the agency a decent profit.

- **A product or service around which an agency can create high-
  visibility ads:** Face it. Agencies want to produce work that will be
  noticed by other clients. Certain kinds of products allow for more
  attention-getting advertising than others do. Agencies throw in
  nonbillable time and even forgo some profits to produce ads upon
  which they can build not only your reputation but their own as
  well. Such ads are the type that air on major stations or that run in
  high-circulation consumer magazines versus low-readership trade
  or business magazines.

- **A client mind-set that allows for creative excellence:** Agencies
  lose enthusiasm quickly when clients deal out "death by a thousand cuts." If you want your agency to stay enthused and effective,
  provide clear advertising objectives, maintain a streamlined and
  efficient concept approval process, and allow the agency the creative freedom to do great work on your behalf.

Creating your agency short list

Make a short list of the firms that you believe fit your needs and provide a
good match for the attributes you seek in a marketing firm. In creating your
list, follow these steps:

1. **Decide how many agencies you want to interview.**

   If your project is fairly simple or your budget is pretty tight, start with a list of only one. You have a better chance of getting the agency's attention by telling the agency that it's your top choice and by eliminating the need to "compete" for a budget in which there is likely very little profit. If your budget is larger, you have more clout, so start with a list of no more than four agencies.

2. **Get the names of agencies that match your needs.**

   Ask for agency recommendations from trusted business colleagues. Or contact owners or marketing managers at companies that resemble yours in size and that have particularly strong advertising to ask who produces their work. Advertising managers at your local newspaper or radio or television stations are another good resource, as are the sales representatives of major print shops in your area. They know which agencies consistently submit professional work on time.

3. **Finalize your short list.**

   Answer the following questions before putting a prospective agency on your list:

   • Do they handle and care about accounts our size?

   • Do we have confidence in their expertise and experience?

   • Will their creative style fit our brand and company culture?

   • Do they have the talent we need? Sometimes small businesses hire very small agencies with the belief that smaller firms have lower overhead and therefore lower costs. But if your agency has to subcontract to get your job done, you may end up paying marked-up costs for services that it buys on your behalf.

Requesting proposals

Contact the CEO of each agency on your short list to convey the following:

✔ Invite the CEO's agency to present its capabilities and to discuss its interest in working with your firm.

✔ Describe your marketing objectives, your target market, and whether you're seeking help on a finite project or an ongoing relationship.

✔ Ask that any or all of the following information be submitted in advance of the interview: samples of agency work, biographical sketches of key staff, a client list, a list of clients gained and lost in the past two years, relevant case studies of agency work, a description of expertise in your industry or market area, and billing procedures including hourly rates and commission or markup policies.

✔ Detail your timeline. Ask the CEO to confirm within a certain number of days whether the agency will participate in your agency search. State the day by which you'd like the agency's capabilities summary submitted to your office (allow agencies a few weeks to prepare this response). Give the dates on which you will be scheduling interviews, along with the day that you will make your decision and begin work with your new agency.

✔ Provide the name of the person to contact initially and throughout the agency search process.

Here's what *not* to do when requesting a proposal:

✔ Don't get overly prescriptive as you describe your needs. Tell *what* you want to accomplish through the agency relationship but not *how* you want to accomplish it. Leave room for the agency to bring its point of view and expertise to the task.

✔ Don't ask the agency to submit speculative work (in other words, free sample solutions). It isn't fair, and it isn't a good indication of an agency's abilities. Agencies work *with* clients, not *for* them. If you want to "sample" the firm's style, propose a small-project budget and be ready to play your role as the client — working with the agency on a solution to your marketing need.

✔ Don't withhold information. If an agency asks for the names of others being considered for your account, share your list. If they ask what you've done in the past that has and hasn't worked, provide a brief summary.

Keep track of how you feel about the way each agency interacts with your company, even during the preinterview period. Your impressions will be useful as you weigh the issues of chemistry and compatibility.

Agency presentations and interviews

The agency presentation and interview is the final step in the agency selection process. Follow these tips:

✔ Name your agency review committee, being sure to include the person who will be working most closely with the agency once it is selected. The agencies deserve to know who will be making the decision, and the process will go more smoothly if you confirm the selection participants in the beginning and then stick with your decision.

✔ Choose one member of your review committee to field queries from all agencies. Doing so helps ensure that all agencies get the same information and also helps you compare agency styles as interpreted by one of your team members.

✔ Schedule up to two hours for each agency presentation, with roughly half the time allocated to an informal question-and-answer period.

✔ Consolidate interviews so that no more than a week elapses between the first interview and the final analysis and decision.

✔ Tour each agency before the presentation unless the presentations are held at the agencies. Doing so gives you a sense of how each agency works and a feel for the atmosphere in which they create.

✔ Keep the interviews as relaxed as possible. The goal isn't to put anyone on the spot or to watch rehearsed performances, but to learn how the agency interacts — among itself and with your team.

✔ Complete a worksheet following each presentation. This can be as simple as a list of attributes that are important to your business and a space to rank each agency on a 1–10 scale. For example, if "broadcast media planning" is important to your business, list that category and rank each agency from 1–10 on how well it convinced you of its expertise in this area. Then compare your impressions of each firm's capability to determine which one seems to best address your needs.

Putting the client-agency agreement in writing

Most agencies prepare a contract that defines the role the agency is to assume for the client, the compensation arrangement, ownership of work produced under the contract, and how the relationship may be terminated. If your new agency doesn't offer you such a contract or memo of agreement, ask for one and be certain that you both sign and keep a copy on file.

Good questions to ask agencies

When interviewing agencies, consider any of the following questions to help determine the agency's mission, style, culture, and values:

✔ How would you characterize the strengths of your creative department?

✔ Do your copywriters and designers have direct contact with clients?

✔ How will your chief executive officer be involved or maintain contact with our account?

✔ How do you define "good advertising"?

✔ If you had to name an attribute that sets your agency apart from all others, what aspect would you spotlight?

✔ Would you mind if we talked with a few of your current clients about their impressions of and experiences with your agency? Could you provide us with several names?

There is no single standard contract, but all contracts should define certain issues and agreements, including but not limited to the following points:

- ✔ **The products or services that the agency is to work on.**

- ✔ **The responsibilities that the agency is to assume for the client:** The contract might list specific services to be provided, or it might cover the issue with a broad brush by stating that the agency is to provide "services customarily rendered by an advertising agency." This section of the contract also defines agreements that protect the interests of the client, including, but not limited to, stipulations that the agency may not act as an advertising agency for any products that compete directly with the products of the client; the agency must maintain confidentiality on behalf of the client; and the agency must be responsible for obtaining rights to photographs, artwork, copyrights, and other proprietary materials that it uses on the client's behalf.

- ✔ **The client's obligations to the agency:** This part of the contract includes a definition of the client's role, including the client's agreement to provide information as needed to allow the agency to do its job, agreement to pay for work in progress if a job is canceled by the client prior to completion, and agreement that the client will be responsible for determining accuracy and ownership of materials that it provides to the agency for use in client advertising. If the contract covers a time span (versus a project), the client often agrees not to hire another agency to work on the products or services covered by this contract without prior notice.

- ✔ **Agency compensation:** No one likes to talk about money, but if you dot all the i's in the contract, your client-agency relationship will be easier forever after. The contract should define whether you will pay the agency a fee, a percentage of your budget, or a combination of the two. It should define how the agency will be reimbursed for purchases it makes on your behalf, including whether those charges will be billed with or without markups or commissions (see the following section for an explanation of how commissions and markups work). It also describes the time frame within which your payments are due to the agency, how you can qualify for prompt payment discounts offered by media or suppliers, and how the agency will be paid for work that exceeds the scope of the general agreement and budget.

- ✔ **Project accountability:** Many contracts stipulate that the agency must submit and gain written approval of a timeline and cost estimate for each project undertaken on the client's behalf. The agency agrees to adhere to approved cost estimates and timelines unless otherwise authorized by the client. The client agrees to pay for cost overruns incurred as a result of client-requested changes to agency work that has been previously approved by the client.

✔ **Ownership of materials:** Just because you pay for advertising materials produced for your company by your agency doesn't mean that you necessarily own them. Be sure that your contract covers this issue. Ideally, it says that any material presented to your company by the agency becomes the property of your company upon payment for the services rendered. Be aware, though, that even if you own the agency's work on your behalf, you don't necessarily own unlimited rights to the artistic materials included in that work. Photos, illustrations, original artwork, and even voice and acting talent are usually purchased with limited usage rights. When the agency is buying outside art or talent on your behalf, you need to ask whether the purchase covers limited usage rights, unlimited usage rights, or outright ownership.

✔ **The term of the relationship:** The contract might remain in existence until it is "canceled by either party," or it might cover a finite period.

✔ **How the contract can be terminated:** This is the "prenuptial" part of the contract. It tells how the agency will be paid during the termination period, how contracts that can't be canceled will be handled, and how client materials will be returned from the agency.

Most agencies prepare and submit the contract to you so that all you need to do is review it carefully (preferably with your attorney), sign it, and keep it on file for future reference. As you sift through all the legalese, keep repeating the mantra "An ounce of prevention. . . ."

Understanding how agency fees are calculated

Most agencies are compensated by a combination of fees for time expended and commissions or markups on purchases made on your behalf. While a growing number of agencies and freelancers are moving toward a straight fee-based method of compensation, and while others are willing to negotiate the amount by which they mark up expenses, the following explanations describe what are still the most common calculations on agency invoices.

Commissions: When an agency buys a $1,000 newspaper ad for a client, if the newspaper allows the agency a 15 percent commission, then the agency bills the client $1,000, pays the newspaper $850, and keeps the $150 commission as part of its compensation.

Newspaper ad charge billed to client	$1,000
Less 15% commission to recognized agency	-$150
Agency payment to media	$850

Markups: When the agency makes a purchase from a supplier who doesn't offer a commission, the agency generally marks up the expense instead. To make the math work, though, the agency marks the charge up not by 15 percent, as you'd guess, but by 17.65 percent in order to arrive at the same level of compensation. Following is an example for an $850 printing job.

Printing charge to agency	$850
Plus 17.65% agency markup	+$150
Printing charge to client	$1,000

When reviewing contracts or approving estimates, ask agencies and freelancers to define their markup structures so that you're clear on the percentages being charged and in a position to negotiate if the numbers seem too high.

Working with your agency

The best advice for building a great client-agency relationship is to give clear instructions and then trust your agency — share your marketing plan, your budget, and your hopes. In everyday terms, building a great relationship means that you do the following:

- ✔ Provide your agency with all the information it needs to do the job right the first time around.

- ✔ Boil down your input. Don't make your agency read encyclopedia-length documents to figure out your marketing plan, advertising strategy, or positioning statement.

- ✔ Be frank about your budget. Don't act like a high roller (money is *always* an object). At the same time, don't withhold funds for fear the agency will spend it all unnecessarily.

- ✔ Spend your time questioning project estimates rather than arguing after-the-fact over the bills.

- ✔ Hold up your end of the bargain by providing information and approvals when you said you would.

- ✔ Set a time for regular status calls or meetings.

- ✔ Pay on time.

- ✔ Pay for your changes. If you change your mind when you see the final proof of your marketing materials, expect to take responsibility for the last-minute additional expenses and extra hours involved.

- ✔ Be open to ideas.

✔ Be constructive with your criticism.

✔ Set up a decision-making process and then stick to it. Eliminate the words "let's just run it by so-and-so" from your vocabulary. Ads never get better as they go through a committee process.

✔ Stay involved. A direct correlation exists between great agency work and great interest at the top levels of the client organization. That doesn't mean that you should be cocreating ads. It does mean that you should care about the objective, the strategy, and the creative rationale.

✔ Review the relationship once a year with both sides present.

✔ Be the agency's best client. How? Just follow the preceding advice and send over an occasional gift or note of thanks.

Hiring Help for Web Site Design

Hiring a Web design firm involves many of the same steps involved in hiring an agency, plus a few additional ones, described in this section.

More than anything else, start by knowing what you want to achieve. With detailed specifications in hand, Web designers can do a better job of creating their bids, plus you'll be able to make apples-to-apples comparisons, since all design companies will be responding to the identical request.

Creating a request for proposal

Your request for a Web site design proposal should include the following:

✔ **Brief background information on your company.** Notice the word *brief*. The design firms aren't trying to learn how to manage your company; they just want to learn your business purpose and online marketing objective so that they can create a successful Web site.

✔ **A description of the kinds of people you expect to visit your site.** Again, reduce it to a sentence, or a sentence for each visitor group.

✔ **Your site storyboard.** This can be a simple outline of how you think your site should work. Here's an example for a florist's site:

SAMPLE SITE MAP

Home

Flower Arrangements

Catalog

> Prices
>
> How to Order
>
> Wedding Center
>> Wedding Ideas
>>
>> Prices
>>
>> Sample Packages
>>
>> Ordering Guide
>
> Contact Us
>> Phone, E-mail, Fax, Street Address
>
> Map

- ✔ **How you plan to drive traffic to the site:** If you plan to use your Web site as a way to bring new people into your business, then you'll probably want to be listed and ranked with search engines, and the designers need to know this in advance. They also need to know the key terms that you want the search engines to find.

- ✔ **The addresses of sites that are similar in look and complexity to the one that you would like to create.**

- ✔ **Copies of current marketing materials that represent your image guidelines.**

- ✔ **The level of site testing you expect from the design firm, and what you plan to do on your own:** One way or another you'll want to be sure that your site comes up quickly even for users with slow modems, that it works with various browsers, and that each link works and goes where it's supposed to go.

- ✔ **The ways you plan to evaluate your site:** This will help the designers know what kinds of site traffic analyses and reports you will need, which will affect the overall site design. (See Chapter 16 for information on ways that you can analyze your site effectiveness.)

 The top reasons that Web site design costs run over budget are 1) unclear purpose and 2) content that wasn't ready when it was needed. Shave unnecessary cost overruns by being prepared, not changing your mind frequently, and having your content ready to hand off when it is needed.

Seeking responses from design companies

If you're building a relatively simple and inexpensive site, interview a few firms, choose the one that instills the most confidence, and ask that company for a cost estimate and design proposal.

On the other hand, if your site is complex, you might ask for bids from two or three capable firms.

1. **Draw up a list of good Web site design firms.**

   Ask business associates for the names of reputable Web site design companies. Also, look at the sites of local businesses. As you find ones you like, call and ask who created them.

2. **Narrow the list to those firms you want to consider.**

   As you narrow your design firm choices, call each one and ask for a list of sites they have designed. As you view the sites, if you can't figure them out or don't like the look, take the company's name off your list. Focus on the companies that build sites you like and that you think your customers will understand.

3. **Ask for proposals from only a few design companies.**

   Reach outside your local area if necessary to find the right talent, but do so realizing that communication over a distance may be harder and more time-consuming, and therefore more costly.

Evaluating proposals

As you evaluate proposals, consider the following:

- ✔ Did the company respond to your request? Did it meet your requested proposal delivery date? Did it address the specific topics you outlined?

- ✔ Do you understand what the company says it will provide? If not, ask for clarification. Assume nothing.

- ✔ Call references. Ask whether the firm was easy to work with, if it stuck to the budget, if it produced quality work, and what happened when problems arose.

- ✔ Compare work samples.

- ✔ Clarify who will actually be doing the work and decide whether you have confidence in the talents and working style of that person.

Signing a contract

Most Web design firms will have a contract for you to sign, but if they don't, make sure you have one created. The contract should cover the following:

✔ **An estimated cost of the site design:** This should include a breakdown of design time and outside costs involved.

✔ **What the estimate covers:** Has the firm based its estimate on the total number of hours it thinks will be involved? Has it provided a breakdown of estimated costs involved with the delivery of such elements as graphics, navigation, testing, and other site-creation tasks so that you can go down the list and be sure that all necessary tasks are covered? Are time and costs for travel, if any, included? Is a round of changes included, or will changes lead to additional costs?

Include a clause stating that the cost estimate cannot be exceeded without your prior written authorization. As you work with the designers to construct your site, you may make decisions that alter the scope and therefore the cost of the project. This clause assures that you understand how your requests will impact the price of creating your site — *before* you see the surprise on an invoice.

✔ **The payment due date:** Many Web design companies require a partial payment at the onset of the project. This payment schedule is standard, but make sure that you aren't required to pay the balance until the site is live, tested, and fully functioning. Put into writing the fact that final payment is based on your sign-off and acceptance of the site.

✔ **What happens if the site doesn't work:** Stipulate in the contract whether the design firm has to absorb the cost of alterations required to fix dead links and site crashes within a specified period.

✔ **Penalties for nonperformance:** State that you will pay less if the firm doesn't meet the deadlines or the expectations.

✔ **Performance milestones:** Include a timeline that sets dates for major steps in the process, including your deadline for providing content (and in what format).

✔ **Ownership:** Make sure that the contract stipulates your ownership of the site and all its components. Many small businesses overlook this point only to find out later that they don't own the site and that they have to start all over if they choose to revise the site using a different designer.

Handing off the content

Content includes the storyboard, text for each page, pictures, and any other graphics to be included in your site. Because you're the expert on your business, most likely you will build the content or at least oversee its development and provide it in a ready-to-go form to the design firm. You'll make the process go smoother if you follow these suggestions:

✔ Create and provide the content in an electronic format that meets the agreed-upon specifications, so that you eliminate unnecessary costs and errors.

✔ The closer you can get your content to finished form, the less time (and therefore money) the designer will spend building your site.

✔ Be concise and clear with your instructions regarding how you want the content to appear.

✔ Don't send your content in dribs and dabs.

✔ Review your content carefully before you hand it off. Complete all your editing *before* the designers begin working on the site — not after, when changes cost time and money.

Part III
Creating and Placing Ads

The 5th Wave   By Rich Tennant

"Okay, so maybe the Internet wasn't the best place to advertise a product that helped computer illiterate people."

In this part . . .

When it comes to advertising, the money can really fly. Part III puts you in the pilot's seat, arming you with advertising terminology, ad creation guidelines, and media selection advice that will help you steer your advertising investment to a successful takeoff.

Consider the next three chapters to be your guide to navigating the world of advertising, complete with everything you need to know to create and place ads that work in print, broadcast, and outdoor media.

Chapter 10

Mastering Advertising Basics and Media Planning

In This Chapter

▶ Using advertising to move the market to action

▶ Choosing the best media for your business

▶ Creating ad schedules

Advertising is the stand-in mouthpiece for your business in the marketplace. It goes where you can't — carrying your message into the homes, offices, televisions, computers, mailboxes, and car radios of your prospects and customers. When it is successful — when it is creative, entertaining, understandable, and compelling — advertising goes even farther. *Great* advertising goes right into the minds and hearts of customers, which is where brands live and thrive.

Contrary to popular belief, though, great advertising rarely makes the sale for your business. Advertising paves the way, but the sale happens later, after your prospect is motivated by your ad to call or visit your business, request more information, or buy your product.

This chapter offers the information you need to set reasonable expectations for your advertising and to make wise media selections and placements. The field of advertising is baffling and complex, but the following pages should make it feel a whole lot less foreign.

Moving the Market through Advertising

Ask any small-business person what advertising is and you'll probably hear the word *expensive* somewhere in the answer. That's because advertising is the means by which businesses, organizations, and individuals buy their way into prospects' minds.

By definition, advertising is how businesses inform and persuade potential and current customers through messages purchased in various media such as newspapers, magazines, television and radio stations, outdoor boards, and Web sites.

Image versus product advertising

Marketers talk about brand advertising, product advertising, promotional advertising, call-to-action advertising, and other terms capable of setting your head spinning. Basically, ads fall into two categories: ads that promote a company's image and ads that aim to prompt a consumer action, as described in the following two definitions:

> If an ad's sole purpose is to build awareness and interest, it is considered an *image ad.* Image ads are also called *brand ads* or *institutional ads.*

> If an ad's sole purpose is to present an offer and prompt a corresponding action, it is considered a *product ad.* Product ads are also called *promotional ads, response ads,* or *call-to-action ads.*

Image-plus-product advertising — the have-it-all approach

Brand advertising is an indulgence that many small businesses, who need every ad to deliver a measurable prospect action, can't afford. Yet call-to-action advertising works best if the prospect already has a favorable impression of the company — achieved through brand advertising.

It's a classic catch-22, but one with a good solution.

Instead of choosing between brand ads and product ads, choose total-approach ads that build brand awareness, present your offer, *and* prompt consumer action. To create ads that do double and triple duty, follow these steps:

1. **Establish a creative strategy to reign over the creation of all ads, brochures, and communications in your marketing program.**

   See Chapter 7 for step-by-step advice on how to define a creative strategy and uniform look for your communications — and how to build a strong brand image as a result.

2. **Establish a creative brief to guide the development of each new ad or other communication effort.**

See Chapter 8 for a sample format you can follow before launching the preparation of any new ad.

3. **Hand both your creative strategy and your creative brief to those who will produce your ad.**

Insist on materials that fit your image *and* meet your advertising objectives. That way your ads will build your brand while promoting your product, which is like having your cake and eating it, too.

Talking to the right people

The great advertising executive Fairfax Cone once said, "Advertising is what you do when you can't go see somebody."

You wouldn't spend your business days calling on people who aren't able or likely to buy your products, and you shouldn't spend your money advertising to unlikely prospects either. Before committing dollars to advertising, know your prospect and do everything you can to talk to only that kind of person.

Your prospective customer is

- ✔ Someone who matches the profile of your best existing customers. (See Chapter 2 for information on profiling your customers.)
- ✔ Someone who wants or needs the kinds of products or services you offer.
- ✔ Someone who can easily access your business, whether by a personal visit or by phone, mail, or Internet contact.
- ✔ Someone able to purchase from you, by reason of financial ability or ability to meet any qualifications required to buy or own your product.

The Internet allows you to serve people all over the globe. But before you consider the world your market, turn to Chapter 16 to assess whether you offer the kind of product people will reach through cyberspace to buy.

Creating Ads That Work

Good ads grab attention and lead consumers exactly where they want to go:

- ✔ Good ads present *what* the prospect wants to buy.
- ✔ Good ads present offers that are sensitive to *how* and *when* the prospect wants to buy.
- ✔ Good ads affirm *why* the prospect wants to buy.

Good ads persuade, convince, and nudge prospects into action, all without any apparent effort. They meld the verbiage with the visual and the message with the messenger so the consumer receives a single, inspiring idea.

Creative teams will tell you that making an ad look so simple takes a lot of time and talent — and they're right. If you're spending more than $10,000 to place an ad or more than $100,000 on annual media buys, consider bringing in pros to help you out.

Bringing in the pros

Chapter 9 offers advice about hiring freelancers or an advertising agency to rev up your creative horsepower. For ad production, here are the resources you'll most often rely upon:

- **A copywriter** writes the headline and motivating copy or, in the case of broadcast ads, the ad script. This person needs to be a good communicator who is capable of writing simply, clearly, and directly to your target prospects, using a single-minded approach to grab and hold the prospect's attention and to achieve the ad objective.

- **A designer** arranges your ad so that it is visually appealing, using a layout that draws the viewer's eye to the correct starting point before guiding it with effortless movement through the ad elements.

- **A producer** is necessary if you're creating a radio or television ad, a video, or a multimedia show. The difference in quality and impact between do-it-yourself and professional productions is big and undeniable. Your TV station or cable company can produce your ad, but realize that in return for low production costs, you'll need to bring your own creativity to the task to avoid ending up with an ad that looks and sounds like all the other station-produced creations.

Starting the creative process

Ease into the creative process with these ideas:

- Review your positioning statement (see Chapter 7) and your *Unique Selling Proposition,* or *USP.* Your USP defines your competitive advantage. It describes the distinct benefit that consumers receive only by buying from your business. It is why your business is capable of drawing attention, distinguishing itself from your competition, and winning prospect buying decisions and customer loyalty.

- List good things you've heard customers say about your product.

- ✔ Recall words that you use during sales presentations.

- ✔ Dig around for every product fact and figure you can get your hands on. Buried in the details may be the item that unleashes a winning concept.

- ✔ Define the kinds of people who *won't* want your product. (Defining non-buyers is a good way to uncover things about those who *will* buy.)

- ✔ Think of why a prospect will want to take action. Imagine a likely prospect and consider that person's perceptions, desires, and needs.

- ✔ What do you want people to do after seeing this ad? Do you want them to feel differently, to tell a friend, to pick up the phone, to ask for more information, to purchase the product?

Landing on the big idea

The *big idea* is to advertising what the brake, gas pedal, and steering wheel are to driving. (See why they call it *big?*) Here's what the big idea does:

- ✔ It stops the prospect.

- ✔ It fuels interest.

- ✔ It directs prospects toward the desired action.

"Think Small" is an historic example of a big idea. Volkswagen used it to stun a market into attention at a time when big-finned, lane-hogging gas-guzzlers ruled the highways. "Think Small" — two words accompanied by a picture of a squat, round car miniaturized on a full page — stopped consumers, changed attitudes, and made *the Bug* chic.

Big ideas are

- ✔ Attention-getting

- ✔ Memorable

- ✔ Compelling

- ✔ Persuasive

- ✔ Capable of conveying the benefit you promise

- ✔ Appealing to your target market

An idea qualifies as a big idea only if it meets *all* the preceding qualifications. Many advertisers quit when they hit on an attention-getting and memorable idea. Think of this: A slammed door is attention-getting and memorable, but it's far from compelling, persuasive, beneficial, or appealing.

Brainstorming

Brainstorming is an anything-goes group process for generating ideas through free association and imaginative thinking with no grandstanding, no idea ownership, no evaluation, and definitely no criticism.

The point of brainstorming is to put the mind on automatic pilot and see where it leads. You can improve your brainstorming session by

- Flipping through magazines and newspapers for inspiration. Pick up copies of *Advertising Age* and *AdWeek* (available at newsstands and in most libraries) for a look at the latest in ad trends. Also include fashion magazines, which are a showcase for image advertising.

- Looking at competitors' ads.

- Looking at your own past ads.

- Thinking of how you can turn the most unusual attributes of your product or service into unique benefits.

- Doodling. Ultimately an ad is a combination of words and visuals. See where your pencil leads your mind.

- Widening your perspective by inviting a customer or a front-line staff person to participate in the brainstorming session.

If you're turning your ad creation over to a staff member or to outside professionals, you may or may not decide to participate in the brainstorm session. If you do attend, remember that there is no boss in a brainstorm. In a brainstorm session, every idea is a good idea. Bite your tongue each time you want to say, "yes, but . . ." or "we tried that once and . . ." or "get real, that idea is just plain dumb."

At the end of the brainstorm, gather up and evaluate the ideas:

- Which ideas support the ad strategy?

- Which ones present the consumer benefit?

- Which can be implemented with strength and within the budget?

Any idea that wins on all counts is a candidate for implementation.

Golden rules

Chapters 11–13 focus specifically on creating and placing print, broadcast, and direct mail ads. The following rules apply to *all* ads — regardless of the medium, the message, the mood, or the creative direction:

- Know your objective and stay on strategy.
- Be honest.
- Be specific.
- Be original.
- Be clear and concise.
- Don't overpromise or exaggerate.
- Don't be self-centered or, worse, arrogant.
- Don't hard-sell.
- Don't insult, discriminate, or offend.
- Don't turn the task of ad creation over to a committee.

   Committees round the edges off strong ideas. They eliminate any nuance that any member finds questionable and crowd ads with details that matter more to the marketers than to the market. An old cartoon popular in ad agencies is captioned, "A camel is a horse designed by committee."

Capturing Prospects with a Media Plan

It's a harsh reality that many prospects disappear on the route between your advertising and your cash register (for proof, see Chapter 17). But with a strong media plan, you can increase the number of prospects you bring into your sphere of influence — and almost as an automatic result you'll increase your number of new customers as well.

Make media decisions based on answers to these four questions:

- **What do you want your ad to accomplish?**

   If you want to develop general awareness and interest, use media that reach a broad and general market. On the far end of the spectrum, if you want to talk one-to-one with those who have expressed interest in your product, you'll want to bypass mass media in favor of direct mail or other one-to-one communications (see Chapter 13).

- **Who and where are the people you want to reach?**

   When it comes to advertising, trying to be all-inclusive is a bankrupting proposition. The more precisely you can define your prospect (see Chapter 2), the more precisely you can choose your media vehicles.

If you know that your prospects are teenagers, you can ask publications or stations to describe what percentage of their circulation or audience reaches that age group. If your prospects have a particular interest — maybe they snowboard, own pets, or drive SUVs — ask for a demonstration of how the medium under consideration reaches that target group, and which sections or programs capture the highest percentage of people with that affinity.

✔ **What are you trying to say, and when do you need to say it?**

If you need to show your product in action, use television or perhaps print ads that allow for clear reproduction of a series of photos. If you have a tremendous amount of explaining to do, you'll probably rule out radio or television, where you're timed by the second. If you have a very immediate message, such as a one-week special event, steer away from monthly magazines that are in circulation long after your offer is history.

✔ **How much money is in your media budget?**

Set your budget before planning your media buy. Doing so forces you to be realistic with your media choices. By following this advice, you also save an enormous amount of time because you don't have to listen to media sales pitches for approaches that are outside your budget range.

The media menu

Mass media reach many people simultaneously. Advertisers divide mass media into four traditional categories and one new category:

✔ **Print media:** Includes newspapers, magazines, and directories

✔ **Broadcast media:** Includes television and radio

✔ **Outdoor media:** Includes billboards, transit signs, murals, and signage

✔ **Specialty media:** Includes items imprinted with an advertiser's name and message

✔ **New media:** Includes Internet advertising, Webcasts, Web pages, and interactive media

The opposite of mass media is *one-to-one communications,* such as personal presentations, telemarketing contacts, direct mailings, and other means of contacting your prospects individually.

Mass media pros and cons

Each form of mass media has advantages and drawbacks. For a quick overview, see Table 10-1 later in this chapter.

Newspapers

Newspapers, particularly metropolitan and suburban area ones, are the number-one choice for small businesses trying to reach local markets.

Here are the advantages of newspaper advertising:

- **Broad coverage:** Newspapers can reach a lot of readers within a geographically concentrated area.

- **Engaged readers:** Newspaper readers expect and look for ads. They are willing to spend time absorbing substantial amounts of ad information on product features, pricing, promotions, and buying information.

- **Targeted sections:** Advertisers can place ads in the sports, travel, food, home, or other section that best matches prospect profiles.

- **Geographic zones:** Many newspapers allow advertisers to place ads only in copies that reach specific geographic areas within the overall newspaper circulation area.

- **Predictable timing:** Newspapers are usually read promptly upon receipt, allowing for timely delivery of ad messages.

- **Minimal advance planning:** Ads run within days of your decision.

- **Flexibility:** Most newspapers sell ad space as small as one column wide by one inch deep, or any multiple of that size up to a full page or even a *double truck,* an ad that spreads over two facing pages.

- **Low production and placement costs:** Black-and-white ads can be produced relatively quickly and inexpensively, and newspaper placement costs are among the lowest of all mass media, although multiple placements are necessary to achieve adequate levels of consumer impact.

Here are the drawbacks to newspaper advertising:

- **Limited ability to target prospects:** Advertisers pay to reach the full (or zone) circulation even if only a minor portion of readers fit the advertiser's prospect profile.

- **Minimal youth audience:** Newspaper readership is heaviest among the 35+ age group and weakest among younger age groups.

- **Short life span:** Newspapers are usually read quickly and discarded.

- **Two-dimensional presentations:** Newspapers cannot provide the attention-grabbing sound and action of broadcast ads.

- **Print quality limitations:** Unless you produce and pay to place full-color ads, plan to limit your art selections to high-contrast black-and-white photos and line illustrations.

✔ **A jam-packed environment:** Although many newspapers are stringent about maintaining a positive balance of news over ads, still the pages are filled with headlines, stories, photos, and ads. All these elements contribute to visual "clutter" and compete for the reader's attention. Generally the largest and best-designed ads win.

Magazines

Most magazines fit into two categories:

✔ **General interest magazines:** Consumer magazines or *glossies* (so called because of their shiny, high-grade paper and premium-quality printing) dominate most newsstands. Their readers share specific interests, such as travel, cooking, sports, fitness, fashion, celebrity lifestyles, home decorating, world affairs, and on and on.

✔ **Trade magazines:** These publications are also called *business to business* (B2B) and *vertical* magazines (because they reach vertical versus broad or horizontal markets). They're read primarily by people in targeted industries and services.

Here are some advantages of advertising in magazines:

✔ **Targeted readership:** You can reach people with defined interests.

✔ **Engaged readers:** Magazine readers generally dedicate time to read the contents carefully.

✔ **Credibility:** Readers tend to associate the credibility of the advertiser with the credibility of the publication.

✔ **Targeted editions:** Many magazines allow an advertiser to place ads in issues that reach only a select portion of the magazine's full distribution.

Inquire about regional zones that reach only northwest, southwest, or central states, for example. Some magazines even allow the purchase of select metropolitan areas, whereas others bind editions for particular professional subscriber groups.

✔ **Classified or directory ad sections:** For advertisers who can't afford to buy or create magazine display ads, many magazines offer classified ad and directory ad sections at a dramatically lower placement rate.

✔ **Merchandising materials:** Ask about complementary easel-back display cards featuring your ad, provided by many magazines as added-value enhancements to advertisers.

Many small businesses place an ad in a major magazine only a few times, and then they leverage their investment by displaying the merchandising materials long after the magazine is out of date.

✔ **High-quality printing:** Magazines can deliver superb color and photo reproduction of your ad, plus they offer a range of creative opportunities such as fold-out pages, fragrance chips, and sound devices — most of which cost a small fortune in return for the hope of making a big impact. But even without the razzmatazz, well-designed magazine ads can stop readers with near-perfect presentations of show-stopping photos, along with lengthy copy (if appropriate) and reply cards to prompt responses.

✔ **Long life span:** People read magazines at a relaxed pace during leisure hours. Then they often keep issues or pass them along to others.

Magazine advertising does have its drawbacks:

✔ **High production and placement costs:** A full-page, full-color consumer magazine ad can run into tens of thousands of dollars. Although you can cut costs by placing only in a regional edition, you still need to invest in quality design, photography, and production to create an ad capable of competing in the upscale magazine environment. For advertisers with limited resources, large-circulation consumer magazines are rarely a cost-effective way to reach prospects, although they are a powerful way to establish awareness and build credibility.

✔ **Unpredictable response schedule:** Count on magazines for long-term awareness and interest rather than for immediate response. Magazines land in mailboxes and on newsstands over a several-week period and may not be opened or read for weeks after that.

✔ **Long lead times:** Magazine ad placement commitments are usually required months before the magazine actually reaches the consumer.

Directories

The most visible directory is the Yellow Pages. There's an old saying that "Small businesses *are* the Yellow Pages," because small businesses place the majority of all ads in the phone directory. Directories offer these advantages:

✔ **Action-oriented readers:** Directories reach people when they're ready to buy or at least ready to get information leading to a buying decision.

✔ **Credibility:** If a business is listed in a directory, readers assume that the company is established in the marketplace.

✔ **Low production costs:** A simple ad lasts a full year.

Here are the drawbacks of directory advertising:

✔ **An overwhelming number of categories:** Deciding where to list an ad can be a difficult and expensive proposition.

✔ **Competing directories:** New phone books seem to pop up constantly, and even the stalwart directories are breaking into subdirectories that compound advertiser costs and decisions.

✔ **Long lead time:** Directories require ad commitments far in advance of publication, and ad materials remain in the marketplace for at least a year with no ability to pull out or make alterations.

✔ **Competing ads are grouped together:** Directories make it easy for prospects to comparison shop, forcing advertisers to compete via ad size, use of color, and strength of marketing claim.

Outdoor and transit advertising

Outdoor advertising is a love-it-or-hate-it reality that includes roadside billboards, bench signage, transit vehicle ads, and other means of putting ad messages into the great outdoors.

Advantages of outdoor advertising include the following:

✔ **Unavoidable and repetitious:** Passersby can't change channels when they see your sign. You have a captive audience that tends to travel the same route daily, allowing you to drill your message in via repetition or frequency.

✔ **Geographically pinpointed:** You know in advance exactly where your sign will sit, so you can make your message directional (for instance, "Take Next Exit").

Here are the drawbacks of outdoor advertising:

✔ **A moving market:** Unless the sign is at a stoplight or railroad crossing, people will read it at 35 miles per hour or more. Keep messages to seven words that can be grasped in a couple seconds. With transit signs, you have more time, but also a greater need to either entertain or inform.

✔ **A diverse market:** Many viewers may not be potential customers.

✔ **Presentation difficult to control:** Your ad is susceptible to vandalism, weather, and dirt, and the environment may not suit your brand image.

✔ **Expense of high-traffic locations:** Ads posted in locations where masses of people will see them cost more than ads placed on side roads and back alleys.

✔ **Long lead time:** Boards need to be reserved early, and most companies require multi-month commitments, making outdoor advertising a poor choice for short-term, time-sensitive announcements.

Radio

Radio advertising offers these advantages:

✔ **Rate flexibility:** You can bargain, barter, and ask for bonus spots. An unsold radio ad slot represents foregone revenue that can't be recaptured — like an unoccupied hotel room — so radio sales reps are usually willing to wheel and deal.

✔ **Targeted audience:** Auditing services provide demographic research to help you determine whether a station reaches those who fit the age, gender, and lifestyle of your prospect. You can target your buys based on listener profile, geographic reach, time of day, and program format.

✔ **Last-minute decisions:** As long as ad time is available (which isn't always the case during Christmas and political campaign periods), you can schedule your ad up to hours in advance, and you can update your ad almost to the last minute before it airs.

✔ **Immediate:** Many listeners are in their cars when they hear radio ads, which is why live remote broadcasts work to build traffic for advertisers. Radio also delivers immediate messages in support of other media advertising. For instance, your ad can say, "Check out our ad in Sunday's paper," or "Check today's mail for our half-off coupon."

✔ **Ad length choices** range from sponsorships ("This weather report is brought to you by . . .") to 15-second, 30-second, and 60-second ads.

✔ **Intrusive and involving:** Especially if ads are creative and well produced, they can draw listeners in, create mental images, and advance direct offers. Most good ads include a clear call to action.

Radio advertising does have its drawbacks:

✔ **Now you hear it, now you don't:** The listener can't rewind to hear your phone number again. If the listener was tuned out when your ad played, you can't reach him or her until you pay to re-air the ad.

✔ **A distracted audience:** Listeners have access to many commercial stations, plus they can opt to tune into public radio, satellite radio, Internet radio, CDs, or personal digital music players.

✔ **Repetition is necessary and costly:** Most advertisers pay to air their ads many times weekly on a number of different stations in an effort to reach target prospects at least three times each. They also invest in the production of several ads to avoid boring the market with a single ad played over and over again.

✔ **Station switching:** The listener can change stations if your ad isn't adequately compelling during its first few seconds.

Television

Sometime in the late 1950s the television replaced the fireplace as the center of the household, and homebodies have been transfixed by it ever since. It is the most intrusive, costly, and powerful advertising medium of all and as an advertising medium it requires careful thought and commitment.

Consider these advantages of television advertising:

- ✓ **Abundant airtime:** Between cable and broadcast TV, hundreds of ad slots are available hourly, even in the smallest media markets.

- ✓ **Targeted audiences:** You can schedule ads to reach viewers in certain geographic areas, during certain day parts or programs, or on networks that appeal to specific interests, such as MTV or ESPN.

- ✓ **Image-enhancing:** TV is considered the advertising major league. A well-produced ad transmits a prestige that goes beyond the message. Print advertisers use the phrase "as seen on TV" for a reason. Television ads build credibility and excitement for advertisers.

- ✓ **Emotion-evoking:** Television brings together sight, sound, special effects, color, and well-cast actors to create a sensual impact on viewers.

Drawbacks of television advertising include the following:

- ✓ **Professional ad creation required:** This is show-and-tell at its best. You need to create an ad that illustrates your message while using the fewest possible words and only one or two selling points — while still managing to mention your name a few times and keeping the overall ad clear, entertaining, and memorable. Television advertising usually calls for an investment in professional assistance.

- ✓ **Fragmented audiences:** People have endless viewing choices. In addition to TV stations, they can turn their attention to rented movies, computer games, or the Internet, to name a few alternatives.

- ✓ **Commercials galore:** Heavy advertising makes TV a cluttered environment.

- ✓ **Low-cost ads stand out, unfortunately:** Low-budget ads can look amateurish or sloppy when aired next to high-cost commercials.

- ✓ **Complex buying time arrangements:** Buying airtime is complicated and usually merits investment in a media planner or expert buyer.

Table 10-1	Mass Media Comparisons		
Media Vehicle	*Cost Realities*	*Advertising Considerations*	*What This Medium Does Best*
Newspapers reach a broad market within a specific geographic area.	Inexpensive cost per thousand readers. Inexpensive ad production.	Deadlines allow for quick ad placement decisions.	Good for announcing sales and offers to adults within a geographic area on a frequent basis.

Media Vehicle	Cost Realities	Advertising Considerations	What This Medium Does Best
Magazines reach target markets that share specific characteristics and interests.	Advertisers pay for access to highly targeted audience. Advertisers must invest in quality ad design and production.	Ad commitments are due months before publication date. Magazines remain in circulation for long periods of time.	Good for developing awareness, credibility, and interest in complex or high-investment products.
Directories reach prospects at the time of their purchasing decision.	Costs are based on number of categories and ad size chosen by advertiser. Production costs are minimal.	Ad commitments are due months before publication date. Ads are in the market for a year with no chance for revision.	Good at establishing credibility, providing reason to choose one business over others, and reaching prospects when they're ready to take action.
Outdoor Advertising reaches an audience within a geographic area on a repeated basis.	Placement costs are based on traffic counts. Requires investment in sign design/production.	Prime locations are reserved well in advance. Ad commitments usually span a multi-month period.	Good at building name awareness and product interest through a single-sentence message.
Radio reaches a defined local audience — if they're tuned in — with a verbal message.	Airtime is inexpensive and negotiable, but costs more during peak listening times.	Repetition of ad is important. Last-minute decisions and short-term schedules are possible.	Good for building immediate interest and prompt responses to newsy or urgent messages.
Television reaches a defined audience — if they're tuned in — with visuals and sound.	Reaching large audiences is expensive. Good TV ads often involve significant production budgets.	Repetition of ads is important. Local ads compete for attention with top-quality national ads.	Good at engaging viewer emotions and empathy while explaining or demonstrating products and building credibility.

The Making of a Media Schedule

The same advertising budget can be spent a number of different ways, depending on how you decide to balance three scheduling considerations: *reach*, *frequency*, and *timing*.

Balancing reach and frequency

Reach is the number of individuals or homes exposed to your ad. In print media, reach is measured by circulation counts. In broadcast media, reach is measured by gross rating points (see Chapter 12 for information on broadcast ad terminology).

Frequency is the number of times that an average person is exposed to your message.

Your schedule needs to achieve enough reach (that is, your message needs to get into the heads of enough readers or viewers) to generate a sufficient number of prospects to meet your sales objective. It also needs to achieve enough frequency to adequately impress your message into those minds — and that rarely happens with a single ad exposure.

If you have to choose between reach and frequency — and nearly every small business works with a budget that forces that choice — opt to limit your reach to carefully selected target markets and then spend as much as you can on achieving frequency within that area.

The case for frequency

Ad recall studies prove that people remember ads in direct proportion to the number of times they are seen. Here are some facts about frequency:

- One-shot ads don't work — unless you opt to spend a few million dollars to air an ad on the Super Bowl. Even then, part of the audience will be away from the tube, replenishing the guacamole dish or grabbing beer from the refrigerator.

- You need to place an ad as many as nine times to reach a prospect even once. That means you need to place it as many as 27 times in order to make contact three times — the number of exposures it takes before most ad messages sink in. If your ad runs in a publication with a devoted readership, or on a program that viewers tune into with regular conviction, the placement requirement goes down, but especially in the case of radio ads, the 27-time schedule generally holds true.

Why? Because each time your ad airs, a predictably large percentage of prospects aren't present. Either they're tuned out or distracted, or maybe your creative approach or offer failed to grab their attention.

- Frequency increases an individual's responsiveness to your ad message.

- Frequency increases the number of people who notice your ad.

✔ Frequency increases advertiser recognition.

✔ Frequency increases overall responses to an ad.

Reach creates awareness, but frequency changes minds.

The case for using only a few media vehicles

Frequency and concentrated ad campaigns go hand-in-hand. A *concentrated campaign* gains exposure using a limited number of media outlets.

Instead of running an ad one time in each of six magazines that reach your target market, a concentrated campaign schedules your ad three times each in two of the publications. Or, instead of running a light radio schedule and a light newspaper schedule, a concentrated campaign bets the full budget on a strong schedule that builds frequency through one medium or the other.

A concentrated ad campaign offers several benefits:

✔ It allows you to take advantage of media volume discounts.

✔ It can give you dominance in a single medium, which achieves a perception of strength and clout in the prospect's mind.

✔ It allows you to limit ad production costs.

✔ It ensures a higher level of frequency.

Timing your placements

No small business has enough money to sustain media exposure 52 weeks a year, 24/7. Instead, use one of the scheduling concepts shown in Figure 10-1.

Reversing the forgetting curve

Here's some information to remember — if you can!

In the late 1880s, German researcher Hermann Ebbinghaus quantified the rate at which people forget. You may not need formal statistics to confirm that most people forget 90 percent of what they learn in class within 30 days.

Get this: Most of the forgetting takes place in the first hour after contact with new information, and by the time two days have passed, only 30 percent of the information is retained.

This *forgetting curve* is why ad repetition is so important to marketers. Through schedule frequency, prospects encounter your message and just when they are about to forget it, they encounter the information again . . . and again.

	Jan	Feb	Mar	Apr	May	June	July	Aug	Sept	Oct	Nov	Dec
Continual												
Flighting												
Front Loading												
Heavy-Up												
Pulsing												

Figure 10-1: Showing how ad schedules can vary.

✔ **Flighting:** Ads run or air for a period of time and then go dormant before reappearing with another but lesser *flight* of ads. To succeed in flighting, start with a heavy enough schedule to make a strong market impression. That way, your business will benefit from the residual awareness until you come back in with a light schedule to rekindle awareness, go dormant, and then reappear with a heavy schedule.

✔ **Front-loading:** Saturate the market with a heavy schedule of ads and then pull back to a more economical schedule that aims to maintain the awareness you bought during the early days. Front-loading is often used to announce openings, promote new products, and jumpstart idle sales.

✔ **Heavy-up scheduling:** Heavy-up schedules are similar to front-loaded schedules, except that they rely on saturation advertising schedules (also called *blitzes*) to be repeated several times a year.

✔ **Pulsing:** With this on-and-off schedule, you're in the media, then you're dormant, then you're in, then you're dormant, with no variations.

Evaluating Your Advertising Efforts

Armchair quarterbacking is a popular after-the-ad-runs activity. But your advertising will be more effective if you set objectives and plan your evaluation methods early on — back when the plays are being called — not after the fumble has already occurred.

Generating ad responses

The easiest way to monitor ad effectiveness is to produce ads that generate responses and then track how well they do, following these suggestions:

- Give the prospect a reason to respond. Offer a brochure, a free estimate, or some other reason to contact your business.

- For ads that will be evaluated based on phone activity, create an ad that presents a reason to call, along with an easy-to-read, toll-free number.

- If you plan to evaluate based on increased foot traffic or cash register activity, present a compelling and time-sensitive offer and be prepared to track which media worked to originate customer activity.

Keying responses

A *key* is a code used to facilitate an advertiser's ability to track the ads that produce an inquiry or order. Here's how to key your ads:

- **Add a unique extension to your phone number,** keyed to indicate response to a certain medium or ad concept. Train those who answer the phone to record the extension number as they process the inquiry.

- **Add a key to coupons that you include in print ads and direct mailers.** For direct mailers, the key might indicate the mailing list from which the inquiry was generated. For print ads, the code could match up with the publication name and issue date. For example, BG0214 might be the key for an ad that runs on Valentine's Day in *The Boston Globe.*

- **Feature different post office box numbers on ads running in various publications or on various stations.** Alert those who open your mail to attach all envelopes to inquiries so that you can monitor not only the number of responses per medium, but also the effectiveness of each medium in delivering prospects that convert to customers.

Here are ways to use ad keys to evaluate advertising effectiveness:

- **Test headline or ad concepts** by placing several ads that present an identical offer. Track responses to measure which ads perform best.

- **Compare the cost effectiveness of various media buys** by measuring the number of responses against the cost of the placement.

Chapter 11

Creating Print Ads

● ●

In This Chapter

▶ Creating, producing, and placing newspaper and magazine ads

▶ Writing good headlines and ad copy

▶ Using signage and outdoor advertising

▶ Making phone book and directory ad decisions

● ●

For many small businesses, advertising means one thing: the Yellow Pages. Others wade further into the world of print media by placing newspaper and magazine ads. And especially in smaller towns — where billboard rentals are available at less than bank-breaking rates — small business marketers turn to the great outdoors to display their headlines and logos.

If print advertising is the route you take into your prospect's mind, this chapter offers advice for negotiating, buying, creating, placing, and evaluating the ads that carry your message to your market. Advice for broadcast ads follows in Chapter 12. For Web advertising, Chapter 16 has information on banner and text ads, along with all kinds of other information about putting the Internet to work for your business.

If advertising isn't your business megaphone — if you're among the many small businesses that turn to publicity, promotions, direct mail, and other one-to-one vehicles to market your business — turn straight to Part IV, which is packed with information on how to spread your marketing message without advertising.

But if you're a print advertiser, let the following pages serve as your guide.

Writing and Designing Your Ads

In the best print ads, the headline, copy, and graphics work together to capture attention, inspire the target market, promote the benefits of the product, prompt the desired consumer action, *and* advance the brand.

The *headline* is the print ad's major introductory statement. It is the large-type sentence or question that aims to stop readers in their tracks, target the right prospects, and pull them inside the ad to read, as commentator Paul Harvey would say, "the rest of the story."

Copy is the term for the words that fill the body of an ad. Good copy talks directly to the prospect. Its point is to connect with and persuade the reader. Instead of following the standard rules of grammar, copy usually is written to sound like people talk. It is conversational yet crisp, poetic yet to the point, and, above all, convincing.

Packing power into headlines

REMEMBER

Four out of every five people who see your ad will read only the headline. Here's where the rest of the readers go:

- One reader will see your headline and move on because he doesn't have time to study the details at the moment.

- A second one will see the headline and rule herself out as a prospective customer because she doesn't want or need what you're offering, or can't buy what you're offering at this time.

- The third reader may find your headline all that's needed to reinforce an existing (hopefully positive) opinion.

- The fourth (should you be so lucky) will find the headline powerful enough to trigger the desired consumer action.

- The fifth one is stopped by your headline and inspired to dive into the ad copy in a genuine desire to learn more. Oh lucky day!

Attributes of a good headline

Your headline has to pack marketing power. It is your only chance to communicate with 80 percent of your prospects and it's your hook for baiting the other 20 percent into your marketing message. If your headline doesn't grab and inspire, your body copy doesn't stand a chance. Here's what your headline needs to do:

- Flag the attention of your prospect by saying, in essence, "Stop! This message concerns you."

- Appeal to your target prospect individually and immediately.

- Promote an answer or solution to a problem.

- Convey a meaningful benefit.

- Advance your brand image.

As if the preceding weren't already a heavy load, the headline has to accomplish those things in words that people can read and grasp in five seconds.

Luckily, headlines come with a lot of creative elbowroom:

- ✔ They can be short or long, as long as they're irresistibly compelling.
- ✔ They can sit anywhere on the page — at the top, in the middle, or along the bottom.
- ✔ They can present a single word, a stand-alone phrase, a complete sentence, or a question.

Headline how-to's

Whether you do it yourself or call on the talents of a professional copywriter or advertising agency, follow these headline tips:

- ✔ **Lead with your most powerful point.** Too many ads use a clever come-on for a headline and then divulge the benefit somewhere toward the end of the copy — where few will see it. Flip the sequence. Punch up your headline and use your copy to back up your claim.

- ✔ **Turn features into benefits.** If you say that your product works at double the speed of competing products, you've stated a feature. If you say that the consumer can save the equivalent of two days of vacation, you've stated a benefit. If you add that the extra vacation days are a free bonus with every purchase, you've fuel-injected the message.
- ✔ **Use both uppercase and lowercase letters.** Large-type headlines set in all capital letters are harder to read and, as a result, easier to overlook.
- ✔ **Don't end your headline with a period.** The last thing you want is to encourage the reader to stop at the end of the headline.
- ✔ **Be believable.** There's an old line about advertising: *If it sounds too good to be true, it probably is.* Beyond that, media ad departments screen ads and reject ones that advance deceptive messages.

Amping up your headline language

As you develop headlines, consider the following advice:

- ✔ **Positive statements carry power.** Consider the difference between *save time* and *work less;* or between *feel great* and *reduce pain.* Or, using a familiar political campaign example, think of the difference between *investing tax dollars* and *spending tax dollars.* In each case, the first statement presents a desired outcome; the other conjures up a nagging problem.

✔ **Use strong, compelling language.** Once you've landed on a headline, go through and see if you can push more impact into the words. If your headline says *stomach*, ask yourself whether *guts* would be more forceful.

✔ **Find words that help readers form mental images.** Instead of saying *reduce fear*, paint a picture by saying something like *eliminate white knuckles."*

✔ **Avoid technical terms** and always use words that most people will understand.

✔ **Use the word *you*.** It's the most magnetic word in advertising. Every time you get ready to write *we*, turn the spotlight to the consumer by using *you*.

✔ **Tell *how*.** People are attracted to the feeling of interaction conveyed by the word *how*. Write a headline that includes *how to . . .* or *how you . . .* to up your chances that the prospect will continue on to the first line of the ad copy.

✔ **Use power words.** Whenever you can, grab your readers' attention with the long-proven power of words such as *free, new, save, better, now,* and other words that communicate that your offer is special and worth reading about.

Writing convincing copy

The first sentence of your ad copy only has to do one thing: Make the reader want to continue to the second sentence. The second sentence needs to lure the prospect on to the third sentence. And so good ad copy goes, carrying consumers through your ad, building credibility and trust, and convincing readers of the merit of your message, until, finally, it makes an irresistible offer and tells exactly how to respond.

As you lead prospects through your ad, work to accomplish the following points:

✔ **Tell your basic story.** Provide a description of your offering, your unique selling proposition, the benefits that a buyer can count on, and information that backs your claim.

✔ **Provide an action inducement.** Offer a proposition or invitation.

✔ **Sweeten your offer.** Add a guarantee, special financing terms, trade-in opportunities, a promotional price or package, special options, a free or limited-time trial, or other offers to increase consumer responsiveness.

✔ **Add a deadline.** Consider a limited-time offer, a promotion that involves only the first 100 respondents, or the statement *while supplies last.*

✔ **Explain what to do next.** Don't assume that prospects know your address, which exit to take, what area code and number to dial, your Web address, or other details about how to reach you. Explain what, why, when, and how to respond.

As you review your copy, imagine that you're face to face with your prospect and the person is saying, "Well, let me think about it; right now I'm just shopping." Then add statements of value, action inducements, or other ideas to overcome prospect hesitation.

If your ad includes prices, see "Presenting prices" in Chapter 3 for advice on how to convey costs while inspiring readers.

Making design decisions

Advertisers, ad agencies, and the media have spent enormous amounts of time and money to determine what does and doesn't work in the design of print advertisements. There is no pat formula — life in the marketing world isn't quite that easy — but when readers are asked which ads they remember positively, the following design traits emerge.

A picture is worth a thousand words

Whenever you can, include an attention-getting visual element in your ads, following these tips:

✔ **Use art.** Ads with stopping power nearly always have a photograph, an illustration (a drawing, cartoon, or other art), or both. Sometimes the art presents the product. Sometimes it shows the product in use. Sometimes it is relative to the product through *borrowed interest.*

For example, a restaurant ad might feature art of the entryway (the product), a photo of diners at a set table (the product in use), or an illustration of a sprig of rosemary or bundle of herbs (borrowed interest).

✔ **Let your visual *show* what your headline and copy are *telling.*** You don't have to be literal. An ad for housekeeping services could feature a mop, broom, and vacuum cleaner. The ad may be more effective, however, if it communicates the benefit of more free time by showing a person in a bubble bath, feet propped up on the rim, open magazine in hand, in an immaculately clean setting.

Keep it simple

Streamline your design to help readers focus on the important points of your ad. Here are two ways to keep your ad design uncluttered:

- ✔ **Frame your ad with wide-open space.** Isolate your ad from those around it while providing the visual relief toward which the reader's eye will naturally gravitate.

- ✔ **Make your ad easy to follow.** As a prospect's eyes sweep from the upper-left corner to the bottom-right corner, will he be able to grasp your message and see your name and logo before exiting to the next page? If your ad lacks an obvious focal point or if two design elements compete for dominance, the reader is apt to pass over the ad altogether.

Knowing your type

You can choose styles of type right from your computer screen, but choosing the *right* type is an art that makes a tremendous difference in how your ad looks and, even more important, how easy your message is to read. Chapter 7 includes a section on choosing and sticking with a type style for your marketing materials. As you work on ad designs, you may find it helpful to know some of the following terminology.

A *typeface* is a particular design for a set of letters and characters.

- ✔ Garamond is a typeface.
- ✔ Helvetica is a typeface.
- ✔ Times New Roman is a typeface.

A *type family* is the full range of weights and styles available in a typeface. For example, you can stay within the Helvetica type family and select bold, italics, and light versions in a great number of sizes. Helvetica, **Helvetica Bold**, and *Helvetica Italic* are all part of the Helvetica type family.

A *font* is the term used for a full set of characters (letters, numbers, and symbols) in a particular typeface and size.

- ✔ This is a 12-point Garamond font.
- ✔ **This is a 10-point Garamond bold font.**
- ✔ This is an 8-point Garamond italic font.

The general rule is to choose one typeface for your headlines and one for body copy. Limit the number of typefaces and sizes that you use in an ad, unless you're intentionally trying to achieve a jam-packed or cluttered look (as might be the aim of a carnival promoter or a retailer announcing a giant warehouse clearance event).

- ✔ **Headlines** need to be attention grabbing, so designers usually choose typefaces that are capable of standing out while also communicating clearly. Choose *sans serif* typefaces, which have no decorative lines at the ends of the straight strokes in the characters. Probably the most popular sans serif typeface is clean-cut Helvetica.

- ✔ **Body copy** needs to be easy to read, so designers often opt for *serif* typefaces such as Garamond, Century, or Times New Roman because they're designed with flourishes (serifs) that serve as connectors to lead the eye easily from one letter to the next.

Designing every ad to advance your brand

Small businesses have small budgets to start with. Don't reduce the impact of your investment by changing the look of your ads from season to season or, worse, from week to week. Here are some ways to advance your brand:

- ✓ **Find an ad look and stick with it.** Settle on a recognizable format that readers can link to your name and brand. Not only will a consistent ad design gain you marketplace awareness and impact, it also will save time and money by eliminating the need to redesign every new ad.

- ✓ **Prominently present your name.** Huge advertisers can get away with postage-stamp-sized presentations of their logos because their products and ad looks are so familiar. Small business budgets don't allow for that level of awareness, so make your name apparent in every ad.

- ✓ **When in doubt, leave it out.** This adage is good advice for do-it-yourself ad designers (and all other designers, too). As you consider tossing in an additional type font, different type size, ornamental border, or any other design element, remind yourself that good design is usually the result of subtraction — not addition.

Translating ad production terminology

Even if you pay the pros to produce your ads, it still helps to know the language of print ad design and production:

- ✓ **Ad proof:** This is the checking copy of your ad and the last thing you'll see before the presses run. When you review ad proofs, look closely at type set in all capital letters, which is where many typos slip through. Read your phone number twice and doublecheck your address. See that mandatory information (copyright lines, trademarks, photo credits, and so on) is in place. Then hand the proof to the best proofreader in your organization for a second review before you initial your approval.

- ✓ **Display advertising:** Print ads that combine a headline, copy, art elements, and the advertiser's logo in a unique design are called *display* ads. All-word ads are called *classified* or *directory* ads.

- ✓ **Four-color:** This is the term for the process used to achieve full-color printing, because (flash back to second-grade art class) all colors can be created from the primary colors of blue, red, and yellow (or, in print terms, cyan, magenta, and yellow). The most elaborate photo can be separated into these three colors and then reproduced by laying one ink color over the next until the image is rebuilt to match the original. Black (the fourth "color") is used for type and other details.

- ✓ **Spot color:** This is color used to highlight an otherwise black and white ad.

Making sense of print media rate cards

Every publication has a rate card that defines pricing, deadlines, and mechanical and copy requirements. Here are some definitions of key terms:

- ✔ **Bulk or volume rate:** A reduced rate offered to businesses that commit to place a certain amount of advertising over a contract period. Increased volume results in decreased rates.

- ✔ **Closing date or deadline:** The date by which ad material must be to the publication if your ad is to appear in a certain issue.

- ✔ **Cash discount:** A discount allowed by media to advertisers who pay promptly. Watch your bill and reduce the cost of your media charges by up to 2 percent by settling your bills quickly.

- ✔ **Column inch:** A column inch is 1 column wide by 1 inch high. Most newspapers measure ad space in column inches, though they used to measure by the *agate line,* which equals $\frac{1}{14}$ of an inch. Once in a while you'll still see ad rates quoted in agate lines. Just multiply by 14 to arrive at the price per column inch.

- ✔ **Cost per thousand (CPM):** This is the cost of using a particular medium to reach a thousand households or individuals. (You'd think that the abbreviation would be CPT, but the accepted term uses M, the Roman designation for thousand.) CPM allows you to compare the relative cost of various media options.

  The CPM formula: Media rate ÷ circulation or audience × 1,000 = CPM

  If a full-page newspaper ad costs $2,200, and the circulation is 18,000, the CPM $122.22. ($2,200 ÷ 18,000 × $1,000 = $122.22)

- ✔ **Combination rate:** This is a discounted rate offered to advertisers who buy space in two or more publications owned by the same publisher or by affiliates in a syndication or publishing group.

- ✔ **Earned rate:** The rate that you pay after all discounts are applied.

- ✔ **Flat rate:** The cost of advertising with no discounts.

- ✔ **Frequency discount:** A reduced rate offered by media to advertisers who run an ad a number of times within a given time period.

- ✔ **Local or retail rate:** A reduced newspaper ad rate offered to local or retail businesses. If you are placing ads in an out-of-town paper but selling your product through or in connection with a local business, see whether the local business can place your ad or if you can receive the local rate by mentioning the local business in your ad.

- ✔ **Make-good:** This is a no-charge repeat of your ad, which you can request if your ad ran with a publisher error or omission.

✔ **Open rate:** The highest price you'll pay for placing a particular ad one time with no discounts. Also called the *one-time rate* and the *basic rate*.

✔ **Pick-up rate:** Many newspapers offer a greatly discounted price when advertisers rerun an ad with no changes within a five- or seven-day period.

✔ **Short rate:** The amount you'll owe to the publisher if you don't earn the rate for which you contracted. If you sign a contract to run a certain amount of advertising but over the contract period you run less advertising than anticipated, you will owe the publisher the difference between the rate for which you contracted and the rate you actually earned.

Placing Newspaper Ads

There are more opinions about what works in newspaper advertising than there are newspapers, and that adds up to a lot of differing ideas. Some advisers tell you to avoid the Sunday edition and the day that the grocery store ads appear because they're crammed with ads and yours will get lost in the chaos. Others counter with the fact that those big and busy issues are crammed with ads because they're the best-read papers of the week. Some people tell you to place clever, small-space ads with high frequency, and others advocate dominating the paper with big-format ads even if you can afford to run them only on a few carefully chosen dates.

Most of the advice you hear is absolutely right — but only some of the time. So how do you proceed?

✔ **Know your target prospect** so that you can make an educated guess about which days and sections of the paper that person is likely to read.

✔ **Know your ad strategy** (see Chapter 8) so that you can time your placements to accomplish your advertising objective.

✔ **Know how newspaper advertising works** so that you can prepare a schedule that takes advantage of media discounts.

Scheduling your placements

Myths are rampant about which day gets the most readership, but the fact is this: From Monday through Friday, the number of people who open their papers varies only 3 percent, with Tuesday's paper outpulling the others because in most markets it carries the food ads. If you want your ad to generate results, heed these tips:

✔ **Place your ad on the day that makes sense for your market and message.** Here are some examples:

- If your target prospect is an avid price shopper, don't miss the issues full of grocery ads.

- If your target is a sports fanatic, advertise in Monday's sports section where your prospect will be reading the weekend recaps.

- If you're promoting weekend dining or entertainment, advertise in the Thursday and Friday papers and in entertainment sections — unless you're trying to influence prospects in out-of-town markets, in which case you'd better run your ad Tuesday and Wednesday to allow time to make weekend travel plans.

- If your ad features an immediate call to action (*Call now for a free estimate*), don't choose the weekend papers if you're not open to handle the responses.

✔ **Advertising in the Sunday paper usually costs more — and delivers more.** The number of single-copy sales is 10–40 percent higher on Sundays than on weekdays. What's more, readers spend up to three times as long with the Sunday paper as they do with weekday papers, and Sunday's paper tends to have a longer shelf life. Even if your newspaper charges a premium for Sunday ad placements, calculate the cost per thousand and you're likely to find that the cost of reaching readers is cheaper on Sunday than on any other day.

Small-budget ad-sizing tips

Even though more readers note full-page ads than half-page ads, and more note half-page ads than quarter-page ads, there's good news for small-budget, small-size advertisers.

Partial-page ads pull fewer readers — but the reader numbers don't drop as fast as the cost of the space does. For example, while a full-page ad pulls about 40 percent more readers than a quarter-page ad, the quarter-page ad costs roughly a quarter of the price. As you work out a small-budget ad plan with your advertising salesperson, here's some general advice to follow:

✔ **If you have to choose, opt for frequency over size.** Plan the largest ad that you can afford to run multiple times and don't worry if the most you can afford is only a partial page.

✔ **Match your ad size to the size of your message.** If you're opening a major new location, go for the biggest ad you can afford. But if you're promoting a $5.99 product, a big splashy ad is likely to be overkill.

✔ **Aim to dominate the page.** Even partial-page ads can have a page-dominating effect. Span the width of the page with a ⅙-page horizontal ad. Or run a half-page vertical ad, which echoes the shape of a full-page ad and dominates the page as a result. Long, skinny one-column ads that run all the way down the page also draw attention, especially if they're placed along the outer-edge of the paper.

✔ **If you're not the biggest, be the most consistent.** Ask your newspaper representative about a Top-of-Mind Awareness (TOMA) program that offers outrageous discounts in return for the commitment to run your ad — however tiny — several times a week, 52 weeks a year.

Requesting your ad placement

Right-hand page, as far forward as possible is repeated like a mantra by print advertisers. But there's no solid proof that an ad on the right page of an open publication does any better than one on the left page, and the same can be said for other hallowed rules about ad placement. In fact, research shows that newspaper ads placed above the fold pull no more readers than those placed below the fold, and ads next to editorial content pull the same as those next to other ads. It depends on the ad — not on the placement.

Have you created an ad that will draw attention regardless of where it appears in the paper?

Once you know you have a strong ad, *then* decide whether you will reach your prospects if your ad runs anywhere in the paper (called a *run of paper* or *ROP* placement) or whether you need to request — and possibly pay extra for — a *preferred position.* The following advice will help you make your placement decisions:

✔ Make an "if possible" request with your ROP ad placement. Most papers do their best to honor reasonable placement requests with ROP orders — at no extra charge, but on a space-available basis. Ask for placement in the front section, sports section, business section, or any other preference. But be willing to settle for what you paid for — which is placement anywhere in the paper. Most readers flip through nearly all the paper on a daily basis, and that's why most advertisers are confident rolling the dice with ROP ads.

✔ Ask about special rates for display ads placed in the real estate section and the classified section, as well as in special interest supplements that target your specific market.

✔ If your ad has a coupon, tell your ad representative in advance so it can be placed on an outer edge of the page for easy clipping and also so it won't be positioned against another coupon on the flip side of the page.

✔ Leverage your budget. Work with your newspaper to arrive at a contract rate based on the nature of your business and your advertising volume. Ask about a contract addendum assuring that a certain percentage of your ROP placements will be in a preferred placement.

Taking advantage of the classified section

The classified section is the bargain basement of the newspaper. It's where you'll find great ad prices and readers who are intent on taking action.

Classified ads come in two types:

✔ **Small-print classified ads:** These ads are typeset by the newspaper and arranged into interest categories.

✔ **Classified display ads:** These ads feature headlines, illustrations, special type styles, and advertiser logos. They're available in sizes smaller than those accepted in the rest of the paper, and they stand out on the otherwise all-type pages.

Classified ads follow the same guidelines as all other print ads:

✔ Use a short headline to draw readers in. Small-print classified ads are all set in the same typeface. The only way to gain attention is with a headline set in boldface capital letters.

✔ Write your ad to talk directly and personally to a single target prospect.

✔ Avoid abbreviations unless you're certain that most people will understand them.

✔ Place your ad in a number of classified categories if it appeals to more than one interest area.

✔ Tell how to contact you and give the reader a reason to call — to request an estimate, learn the price, view the product, schedule an appointment, or take some other action.

Placing Magazine Ads

When a full-page, color ad in *Time* magazine costs hundreds of thousands of dollars, you may wonder why small businesses should even bother considering magazine advertising. The reason is that thousands of small circulation (and vastly more affordable) magazines exist — plus, many of the best-known magazines print regional or even city editions in which you can place an ad for a fraction of the full-edition price.

Most small businesses limit their magazine ads to publications that serve particular business or interest groups, or — especially in the case of those in the travel industry — to city or regional travel magazines.

Selecting magazines

Review the magazines that serve your industry or your target market. A good reference is the *Standard Rate and Data Service (SRDS)* advertising source-book, which is available on the reference shelves of many public libraries. The catalog features data provided by business and consumer magazines as well as by broadcasters, direct marketing houses, and other media resources. You can research a specific magazine or look up an interest area to find the various magazines serving readers in that category.

Say that your business sells software to small banks, and you want to run ads in magazines read by small institution bankers. Go to the *SRDS Business Publications Advertising Source Directory,* turn to the Banking section, and you'll find 20 pages of magazines ranging from the *ABA Banking Journal* to *U.S. Banker.* Each entry lists the magazine's editorial profile, editorial personnel, ad representatives, page dimensions, deadlines, and rates including commissions, discounts, and color charges.

Scheduling placements

As you schedule magazine ads, consider the following:

- **Frequency matters.** Be sure that your budget is big enough to place your ad in the same magazine at least three times over a three- to six-month period. Or, if you want to advertise during a single month, choose three magazines with similar readership profiles and run your ad in each one, building frequency for your message through what is called *crossover readership* between publications.

- **Magazines have long lead and response times.** For example, if you're trying to inspire spring vacation business, your magazine ads will have to run well in advance of the March and April vacation months in order to allow prospects time to read your ad, request information, and make plans. Unlike newspaper and broadcast ads, response to magazine ads builds slowly and continues for months and even years into the future.

- **Full-page ads dominate, but partial-page ads compete well.** Partial-page ads frequently share the page with other ads and end up toward the back of the magazine, but they also share the page with editorial content, which means that readers often spend more time on the page.

✔ **Concept and design will make or break your ad.** If you're advertising in a high-quality and costly magazine, definitely, *definitely* invest in professional copywriting, design, and production to create an ad that represents you well in the highly competitive ad environment.

✔ **Success stories are built on frequent placements of small, well-designed, black-and-white ads.** If you can't afford the production and placement of a full-color ad, but you want to reach a magazine's readership, run a small black-and-white or classified ad in the magazine. Use the space to invite readers to *request our color catalog, visit our Web site,* or some other invitation that allows you to use the small ad space to lead readers to a larger, full-color presentation of your business.

✔ **Work with magazine ad reps.** Explain your business, your desire to reach the magazine's circulation, and your budget realities. If you have an ad that is produced and ready to go, ask to be contacted when *remnant space* (last-minute, unsold ad space) is available — usually at a fraction of the regular cost. Also inquire about regional editions or any other means of placing your ad at a reduced rate.

✔ **Take advantage of merchandising aids available to advertisers.** The magazine may have a *bingo card* that invites readers to circle numbers for additional information from advertisers. All you have to do is offer a brochure or other free item. You'll receive labels for all respondents — a great way to gather inquiries and build your database (see Chapter 13).

Ask for *tear sheets* mounted on boards reading *As Seen In XYZ Magazine* for display in your business.

✔ **Reprint color ads for use as direct mailers.** Amortize the cost and leverage the credibility of being a major magazine advertiser by turning the ad into a direct mailer (see Chapter 13).

Using Billboards and Out-of-Home Advertising

Out-of-home ads include billboards, transit displays, waiting bench signs, wall murals, building or facility signs, vehicle signs, movie theatre billboard-style ads, and even flyover signs. Look around your market area. See where your prospect is apt to be waiting, standing, or sitting, and you'll probably find an advertising opportunity, usually accompanied by the name of the company to contact for advertising information.

The most frequently used form of out-of-home advertising involves billboards. Nearly every town (except those in billboard-free Alaska, Hawaii, Maine, and Vermont) has one or two companies that own most of the boards. Contact them to find out about available locations, costs, and contracts. Or, when you see a billboard in a desirable location, look along the bottom of the sign for the owner's name and then call for availability and cost information.

In scheduling billboard ads, a few key terms apply:

- ✔ **Circulation** is measured by the number of people who have a reasonable opportunity to see your billboard or sign message.

- ✔ **A full showing** or *#100 showing* describes the number of boards necessary to reach 100 percent of the mobile population in a market at least once during a 30-day period. A half showing (or #50 showing) reaches 50 percent of the mobile population. Anything less than a #25 showing is not considered adequate frequency for an advertising campaign, although the placement of one or two boards may be useful as directional signage.

In placing and creating billboards, two truths prevail:

- ✔ **Location is everything.** When you make an outdoor ad buy, you will receive a map or list of locations. Drive by the sites to be sure that they are in areas that reach your prospects and enhance your image. (While you're at it, check how well the sign is lit for nighttime visibility.)

- ✔ **Ads must pass the at-a-glance test.** Most viewers look at a billboard for five seconds, read seven words, and take away two ideas — your name and the reason to buy your product. Use large, legible type with adequate spacing between letters, words, and lines, strong color contrasts, and graphics that can be seen and understood in a flash.

Yellow Pages and Directory Ads

If consumers are apt to start a search for a business like yours with a phone call, you need to be in the Yellow Pages — in print and online. Even if customers reach your business through personal referrals, you'll still want a listing (though not necessarily an ad) to help them find your address or phone number.

Research conducted for the Yellow Pages Publishers Association finds that:

- ✔ Nearly half of those looking up a business in the Yellow Pages are trying to contact a specific establishment.

- ✔ Six out of ten consumers turned to the Yellow Pages to solve a need with no particular business preference.

Creating and placing directory ads

To get your money's worth out of your directory ads, do some advance planning. Use the following as a checklist:

✔ **Choose the right classifications.** Each category you add costs more money, so limit your entries to the sections your prospects are most apt to check. New businesses should place only in one most promising category and test results for a year before increasing exposure.

✔ **Choose the right size.** In the Yellow Pages, biggest isn't always best. Begin by studying how many businesses appear in your Yellow Pages category. If your crowd isn't very big, you hardly need a large ad to stand out in it. Also consider the nature of your competitive arena. In some business categories, the most established and respected firms run the smallest and most subdued ads. Think about your own experiences: If you're looking for a plumber, you might look for large ads as an indication that the plumber is established and large enough to meet your immediate plumbing needs. But if you're looking for a good corporate attorney or business advisor, you might shy away from the largest ads, assuming that smaller, discreet ads better represent respected professionals who don't need to clamor for business.

✔ **Choose whether to add color.** Study the section where your ad will run. See whether color is necessary to compete on the pages. If you opt for color, read the rate card carefully because color charges vary from one directory to another but always mount up quickly.

✔ **Choose the right directories.** Before investing in independent and upstart directories, ask for proof regarding how they will be distributed. Then do your own research. If you know owners of businesses with ads in the directory, call to ask how well the book worked. Or get old copies of the directory and compare ads in your category. If your competitors were in the book a few years ago and are either out of it this year or in with reduced-size ads, read your findings as proof that the ads pulled less-than-impressive results. Small-budget and service-based businesses should start with one directory and expand based on results.

✔ **Write the right ad.** Regardless of size or color, what your ad says determines its success. Research shows that directory readers are looking for 1) a solution and 2) a business they can trust. Your ad will appear alongside ads for your competitors — so present the unique, beneficial attributes that set you apart and make you the best choice.

Consumers consider the following kinds of information valuable:

• Offers of brochures, catalogs, demonstrations, estimates, and so on

• Listings of products or brands (including logos)

• Special qualities and services

- Professional endorsements or affiliations

- Length of time in business

- Business open hours

- Map or directions to the business

- Parking instructions

- Phone, fax, and toll-free numbers, and Web site address

- Street address

- Credit card options

- Bonding, licenses, and related information

✔ **How should your ad look?** Keep it clean and simple. Yellow Pages are a cluttered ad environment. Use a strong border to set your ad apart. Prominently display your phone number and address so they stand out. And whether you use your own designer or let the directory create your ad, insist that the ad match your unique brand image.

When placing a Yellow Pages display ad, include a line in your alphabetical listing that reads *See our ad on page XX.* Or, if you decide not to place a display ad, consider an *in-column ad* that expands your alphabetical listing into a bordered presentation for your business. Finally, don't use ads in other media to direct prospects to see you in the Yellow Pages. If you do, you'll be sending them not only to your ad, but to ads for all your competitors as well.

Using the online Yellow Pages

Local market customers increasingly search online listings instead of printed directories. Some of the big-name sites include `local.google.com`, `superpages.com`, `smartpages.com`, `switchboard.com`, and `yellowpages.com`. Go to `www.telephonebook.com` for a list of online Yellow and White Pages sites and then visit various ones to see that your business is included with an accurate, complete listing.

Chapter 12

Broadcasting Ads on Radio and TV

- -

In This Chapter

▶ Figuring out how much airtime to buy

▶ Understanding broadcast media terminology

▶ Adhering to broadcast ad guidelines

▶ Producing radio and television ads

▶ Advertising with infomercials

- -

*W*ith television sets in more than 98 percent of U.S. homes and radios in the dashboards of 95 percent of all cars, it's unquestionable that your customers are tuned in to the broadcast world. If you want your advertising to meet them there, this chapter helps you prepare your strategy and master the terms and guidelines that apply to broadcast advertising, whether on radio or television.

Venturing into the broadcast advertising arena is a lot like taking a first-time trip to a foreign territory. The language is new (*avails, dayparts, GRPs, TRPs, flights, reach* — yikes!) and the rules are different from other, more familiar environments.

As you plan your foray into the world of broadcast ad production, scheduling, and placement, count on the following pages to help you translate the lingo and guide your decisions.

Buying Airtime

If you're placing ads on just a few stations in your own hometown market, you can probably handle the task on your own. But if your marketing needs involve multiple market areas, or if you're spending more than $10,000 on a media buy, use a media buyer to wheel, deal, apply clout, and bring the kind of muscle that comes from experience in the field. (See Chapter 9 for help choosing and hiring media buying professionals.) You'll pay an hourly fee or a percentage of your overall buy, but you'll save time and confusion and almost certainly you'll obtain a better schedule and price. If you're using an advertising agency to create your ad, media planning and buying usually come as part of the service.

If you're going to do it yourself, begin by requesting a rate kit for each station you believe will reach your target market. The rate kit contains the following:

- ✔ Audited research including statistical profiles of the age, gender, and consumer buying patterns of the station's audience
- ✔ Descriptions of network affiliations
- ✔ Summaries of advertising success stories
- ✔ Sample advertising packages
- ✔ Rate cards

Use the rate card as a cost guideline. In broadcast, prices vary depending on availability, time of day, time of year, and the commitment you're willing to make to the station. Stations throw in added-value enhancements and bonus schedules to win your business. Ask and you just might receive.

Station and ad buying terminology

Get acquainted with the following terms before talking with media representatives:

- ✔ **Area of dominant influence:** Also known as *A.D.I.* The area that a station's broadcast signal covers.

- ✔ **Availability:** Also called *avail.* A broadcast advertising time slot that is open for reservation. Except during holiday and political seasons, most stations have plenty of avails even at the last minute.

- ✔ **Call letters:** A station's identification, for example (borrowing from the old TV sitcom), WKRP in Cincinnati.

- ✔ **Dayparts:** Segments of the broadcast day.

  Radio time is generally segmented into the *morning drive time* (6 to 10 a.m.), *midday* (10 a.m. to 3 p.m.), *afternoon drive time* (3 to 7 p.m.), *evening* (7 p.m. to midnight), and *late night* (midnight to 6 a.m.). The drive times draw the most radio listeners and the highest ad rates.

  TV time is priced highest during *prime time,* which runs from 8 to 11 p.m. The next most expensive ad buys are in the hours adjacent to prime time, called *early fringe* (5 to 8 p.m.) and *late fringe* (after 11 p.m.).

✔ **Flight:** A schedule of broadcast ads concentrated within a short time period, usually followed by a *hiatus,* or period of inactivity. Ad flights create a level of awareness that generates a *carryover effect,* causing prospects to think that they "just heard" your ad even when it has been off-air for several weeks.

✔ **Increments:** Stations sell ad time in lengths — called *increments* — of 10 seconds (written as *:10s* and called *tens*), 15 seconds (:15s), 30 seconds (:30s), and 60 seconds (:60s).

When buying radio time, :60s are usually only slightly more expensive and sometimes no different in price than :30s. If you opt for the longer ad, though, be sure you can create an interesting, entertaining ad capable of holding listener attention for a full minute. The rule in radio is to use only as much time as you need to say what needs to be said. If your offer is easy to explain, a :30 might be all you need. Shorter ads (:10s and :15s) are used as reinforcements, rotating into a schedule of :30s or :60s to build frequency through short reminder messages.

The majority of all television ads are :30s.

✔ **Network affiliate:** A station that is affiliated with a national broadcast network (such as ABC, NBC, CBS, and FOX), usually resulting in higher news credibility and larger audiences. A station not affiliated with a network is called an *independent station.*

✔ **Sponsorship:** Underwriting a program in return for on-air announcements (called *billboards*) that tell the sponsor's name and tag line or brief message.

On commercial stations, advertisers can sponsor reports such as the helicopter traffic update or the daily weathercast. Or they can sponsor a public service message: *This safe driving reminder is brought to you by the doctors and nurses of St. Vincent's Hospital.*

On public broadcast stations, sponsorships are the major vehicle available to advertisers. Many financial planners, medical and legal professionals, and other service providers use program sponsorships to gain awareness without looking promotional. When you hear *This program is brought to you with the generous support of . . .,* you're listening to a sponsorship announcement.

✔ **Spot:** The term *spot* has several meanings in broadcast advertising:

- It refers to the time slot in which an ad runs. *We're going to run 30 spots a week.*

- It refers to the ad itself. *We're going to produce three spots to rotate over a month-long schedule.*

- It refers to television time purchased on specific stations rather than on an entire network. *We can't afford a million-dollar Super Bowl network buy, so we're going to spend $500 to make a spot buy on our local channel.*

✔ **TAP or Total Audience Plan:** A radio package that includes a specified number of ads spread throughout each of the dayparts, allowing the station to decide on the schedule as long as it plays the agreed-upon number of your ads in each time period. Ads that run as part of TAPs are called *rotators*. TAP programs are usually the most affordable packages offered by stations. Still, negotiate the deal. Ask about weighting the schedule toward the dayparts when your prospects are most apt to be listening, or see whether the station will throw in additional spots to enhance the schedule. It's okay to beg — just don't get greedy!

Achieving broadcast reach, frequency, and rating points

Reach is the number of people who hear your ad or, in the case of television, the number of households that are tuned in when your ad airs. *Frequency* is the number of times that an average prospect is exposed to your ad. The accepted rule is that a broadcast ad needs to reach a prospect 3 to 5 times before it triggers action, which usually requires a schedule of 27 to 30 ad broadcasts. Chapter 10 has more information about how reach and frequency work together in advertising schedules to put your message in front of enough prospects enough times to make a marketing difference.

Increase advertising impact by opting for frequency over reach. Instead of airing ads on ten stations (wide reach), choose two of the stations and talk to the same people repeatedly (high frequency).

It takes reach to achieve awareness, but it takes frequency to change minds.

How much is enough?

The age-old question among broadcast advertisers is how much and how often ads need to air. This is where rating points come to the rescue. A *rating point* measures the percentage of the potential audience that is reached by a broadcast ad. If an ad airs during a time that is calculated to reach 10 percent of the potential audience, then it earns ten rating points.

The ratings are based on actual market performance, measured through surveys conducted by firms such as Arbitron and A. C. Neilsen. The findings have an admitted margin of error, but they remain the best way to compare broadcast audiences within a market area. Stations subscribe to the findings and share the numbers with advertisers as part of their sales efforts.

Decoding the rating points

In scheduling ads, you'll hear reference to two kinds of rating points.

Gross rating points (GRPs) are the total number of rating points delivered by an ad schedule, usually over a one-week period. If you air 30 ads in a week, each reaching an average of 5 percent of the total potential audience, your schedule will achieve 150 GRPs.

Target rating points (TRPs) are measured exactly like GRPs, except they count only the audience that matches your target audience. If your target market consists only of men age 35+, then your TRPs are measured as a percent of the men 35+ who hear or see your ad.

GRPs measure your *total* reach; TRPs measure your *effective* reach.

Most media planners agree on the following scheduling advice:

- ✔ **150 GRPs/month is the rock-bottom minimum.** If your budget can't cover a schedule with 150 GRPs over a month-long period, the effort likely won't be worth the investment.

- ✔ **To build awareness, schedule at least 150 GRPs for three months in a row.** You can divide your schedule into 50 GRPs every week or 75 GRPs every other week, but commit to a multi-month schedule if you expect broadcast advertising to result in awareness for your business.

- ✔ **Buy up to 500 GRPs/month if you're trying to blitz the market.** For grand openings and major promotions, you need the kind of major impact that only high-frequency broadcast buys can deliver. A month-long *heavy-up* schedule involves as many as 500 GRPs.

You can make a broadcast buy without ever mentioning rating points, but don't. Stations will gladly present you with people-language proposals — for example, "30 spots at an average of $25 each." But what are you really getting for your money? Follow up with a request: "Would you calculate how many gross rating points that schedule delivers? Also, what percentage of the audience fits our target profile of men age 35+?"

Bartering for airtime

Barter is the exchange of merchandise or services rather than monetary payment for advertising time. A restaurant might trade for ad time by catering a station's holiday party, or a hotel might swap lodging packages for use in on-air drawings. Here are a couple ways to barter for airtime:

- ✔ You can trade a product or service that the station wants or needs — either for its own use or for use in on-air promotions.

✔ You can trade your product to a third-party business that then trades a like value of time or product to the station. (For example, you trade $1,000 of plumbing services to a contractor who then trades $1,000 of contracting services to a station's remodeling project, and the station gives the contractor $1,000 of airtime which you get as your end of the deal.)

Unless you're making a direct trade with the station, bartering takes time and expertise. For assistance, look online or in the Yellow Pages for *Barter Services* or inquire with your media planner about making barter contacts.

If you decide to barter for your ad buys, here are the advantages:

✔ You can buy airtime without spending actual money.

✔ You can leverage your budget. You may be able to trade for airtime at one and a half to two times your product value (for example, $1,500 of airtime for $1,000 of product). Even a straight trade ($1,000 of airtime for $1,000 of product) saves money over a cash buy because your product price includes profit.

When bartering, proceed with exactly the same care you would exercise if you were making cash purchases of media time:

✔ See that the schedule delivers adequate reach and frequency.

✔ Verify that the station reaches your target audience.

✔ Be sure that the timing matches your marketing plan.

✔ Include an expiration date on the product certificates you provide as part of your agreement. You don't want to end up paying for this year's advertising out of ad budgets in years to come.

✔ Be careful that on-air promotions involving your products are consistent with your business image and contribute to the strength of your brand.

Broadcast Ad Guidelines

Whether you're producing a television ad or a radio ad, some general broadcast advertising guidelines apply.

Establishing your own broadcast identity

Over time, you want listeners or viewers to recognize your business before they even hear your name. Consider the following identity-building techniques:

✔ **Sound:** Have the same announcer serve as the voice in all your ads.

✔ **Style:** Establish a broadcast ad style — for example, an ongoing dialogue between the same two people, or ads that always advance a certain kind of message.

✔ **Music:** If you use music or sound effects, use the same notable background in all your ads.

✔ **Jingles:** Jingles are musical slogans that play in broadcast ads. Some people love them, some hate them, and sooner or later almost everyone tires of them. Before investing in a jingle, first be sure you will air enough broadcast ads to achieve an association between the jingle and your name. Second, the jingle must be appropriate to your brand image. Any station or studio can direct you to jingle producers.

Writing your ad

Don't write your own ad. Instead, write your ad strategy and objective and then bring in professional help to develop your concept and write your script. Follow these tips:

✔ **Be strategic.** Start by setting your ad strategy (see Chapter 8).

✔ **Know your objective.** Write a creative brief (again, see Chapter 8) summarizing whom you want the ad to talk to, what you want it to accomplish, and what market action you want it to inspire.

✔ **Develop your ad concept.** Your concept should be capable of grabbing and holding audience attention without stealing the spotlight or distracting attention away from your ad message (see Chapter 8). This is where professional writers really earn their fees.

✔ **Grab audience attention.** You have three seconds before your audience is gone — out to the refrigerator or over to another station.

✔ **Tell a story.** In a 30-second ad, you have about 20 seconds to inform, educate, entice, and entertain — and even less if you cede time to a jingle or other sound effects. The other seconds get divided between an attention-getting opening and your ad identification and call to action. Be sure to do the following in your ad:

- Feature your name (or product name) at least three times.

- Feature your call to action at least once, preferably twice.

- If you include an address, provide an easy locator (for example, *Just across from the train station*).

Turning your script over to the producers

When it's time to begin production, radio or TV stations usually offer to help you out. When you use station talent, follow these steps:

✔ **Review work samples.** As you watch or listen to each ad, ask yourself whether your impression of the advertiser is enhanced by the ad, or does the ad create a negative image about the company's commitment to quality? If you like what you see and hear, inquire about pricing, which at station-based studios is likely to be free or close to it.

✔ **Make your selection.** Produce your ad at one studio and provide all other stations with duplicate copies, called *dubs*. Don't allow each station to air its own version of your ad. Frequency works only when people hear the same ad repeatedly.

✔ **Obtain a budget.** Request detailed allocations for studio time, tape and materials, music fees, talent, editing time, other costs, and ad duplication. Particularly, review the costs and usage restrictions for music, sound effects, and talent, following these tips:

    • **Music and sound effects:** Studios have access to libraries of rights-free or nominally priced music and sound effects. As you make selections, confirm costs and usage rights. Some rights are outright (you can air the ad wherever and whenever you want at no additional fee), whereas others cover only the designated exposure and are renewable (meaning you pay again) for further use. Prerecorded music available through music libraries is referred to as *needle-drop* and usually comes with a reasonable fee.

    • **Talent:** Your ad will involve an announcer and likely actors as well. For locally aired ads, you'll probably use talent provided by the studio. If you use members of a union, such as the Screen Actors Guild, be prepared for higher rates, paperwork, *and* more experienced talent. When using nonstation talent or recording outside the studio, obtain talent releases. Figure 12-1 presents a simple format, although you should check with your production company and your attorney to be sure that you're using an appropriate form.

✔ **Meet with the talent.** Before rolling tape or cameras, ask the talent to perform a dry run of the ad. Take time to correct the pronunciations of your name and products if necessary and alter sentences that contain tongue twisters. Trim time-gobbling extra words and do a final read to be sure the ad sounds right and fits within the allocated seconds.

If you don't like what you see or hear, speak up. Announcers can adjust their voices to sound younger, older, happier, sadder — or as if they're talking to children instead of adults, or to a single person rather than a whole group. A good ad agency or production facility director can handle the talent direction for you, representing your thoughts while adding professional expertise.

TALENT & MODEL RELEASE FORM

Project: _____

Business: _____

For valuable consideration I do hereby authorize (name of company) _____
or those acting on its authority to:

■ Record my participation and appearance on video tape, audio tape, film,
photograph, or any other medium

■ Use my name, likeness, voice, and biographical material in connection with those
recordings

■ Exhibit or distribute such recording in whole or in part without restrictions or
limitations for any educational or promotional purpose deemed appropriate by
(name of company) _____

I have read this agreement before signing below, and understand its contents.

Name (Print) _____

Address _____

City, State, Zip _____

SSN (for paid talent only) _____

Phone number _____

Signature _____ Date _____

Signature of parent or guardian if talent is under 18 years of age

_____ Date _____

Witness signature _____ Date _____

Figure 12-1:
Sample
talent
release
form.

Wanna be a star?

Think long and hard about serving as your own ad talent. Even if you're your firm's best advocate, you aren't necessarily its best spokesperson. Do you have the best voice and appearance to serve as your own on-air talent? Can you commit the time? Can your advertising build a story around you, thereby making your appearance part of your message and not just a substitute for paid talent? Do you *want* to be the spokesperson? If you're considering selling your business in the future, will your presence in your advertising help or hinder that effort?

✔ **Attend the editing session.** Editing is where dollars burn quickly. Make and approve decisions on the spot to avoid the need for a repeat session.

Review your ad outside of the studio with its perfect sound system and lack of interruptions. Sit in your car, preferably in traffic, or in your living room while kids race through after school. Turn your ad on while others are around to see whether they stop to tune in. Turn it on halfway through to see if it still presents a coherent message. Then review it a dozen more times to see whether it can hold your interest without driving you to distraction.

Producing Radio Ads

In 30 or 60 seconds, a good radio ad grabs attention, involves a listener, sounds believable, creates a mental picture, spins a story, calls for action, and manages to keep the product on center stage and the customer in the spotlight — all without sounding pushy, screamy, obnoxious, or boring.

Done perfectly, a radio ad is a one-on-one conversation with a single target prospect, written and produced so well that the prospect hears the introduction and says, in essence, "Ssshhh, be quiet, you guys, I need to hear this. It's talking to me."

Writing to be heard

Great writers tell you to *write out loud* when you create radio ads. Here's how:

✔ **Use straightforward language** that is written exactly how people talk.

✔ **Write to the pace people talk,** not to the pace at which they read.

✔ **Include pauses.** People need time to think, and the announcer needs time to breathe.

✓ **Cut extra verbiage.** You wouldn't say *indeed, thus, moreover,* or *therefore* if you were explaining something exciting to a friend, so don't do it in your radio script, either.

✓ **Rewrite elaborately constructed sentences.** Don't expect listeners to track through phrases linked together with *who, which,* and *whereas.* Instead of *The new fashions, which just came off the Paris runways where they made international news, are due to arrive in Chicago tomorrow at noon* try *The newest Paris runway fashions arrive in Chicago tomorrow at noon. You're invited to a premiere of the world's leading looks.*

✓ **Tell listeners what to do next.** Prepare them to take down your phone number *(Have a pencil handy?),* or at least repeat your number for them. Most important, help them remember your name so they can find you in the phone book or online. (Warning: Don't waste radio time telling people to *look us up in the Yellow Pages,* especially if your competitors overshadow your presence there.)

Radio do's and don'ts

Use the following checklist of ideas to employ and landmines to avoid:

✓ Do stick with a single theme in each ad.

✓ Do make a simple offer that calls for immediate action.

✓ Do generate leads by making no-risk offers for free estimates, free brochures, or free information.

✓ Do limit a 30-second ad to 60 or 70 words *unless* it includes an intentionally rapid-fire conversation.

✓ Do use radio as a complement to other advertising: *Look for our coupon in Friday's paper.*

✓ Do say your name three times.

✓ Do match your ad to the format of the stations you air it on. If you advertise on a country western station, you'll hardly want an ad with new-age music in the background.

✓ Don't expect the ad to make the sale; use it to make the contact.

✓ Don't advertise products with a bunch of disclaimers.

✓ Don't fast-talk the prospect.

✓ Don't use incomprehensible jingles.

✓ Don't use weak attempts at humor.

✓ Don't talk to yourself. *We've been in business 25 years. . . . We're excited over our new inventory. . . . We're open until 10 p.m.* Instead, turn every statement into a consumer benefit (*Shop 'til 10 nightly!*) if you want to hold listener attention — and you do!

Producing TV Ads

People spend more time with the television than with any other advertising medium. *I saw it on TV* has become a mark of having made it into the advertising major leagues. To get there, though, be prepared to make a financial commitment. Successful television advertisers have two things in common: They earmark adequate ad production budgets and they fund media schedules that span at least a multi-month period. If you can do both those things — produce a quality ad and fund an adequate schedule — TV advertising will deliver awareness and credibility for your business.

If your market is limited to a concise geographic area, you can use the ever-increasing number of cable channels to air your ads at a fraction of the price of major station ad rates. But remember that even if the time charge is low, the production value of the ad you air needs to be high enough to represent your business well in this competitive advertising arena.

Overseeing creation of your TV ad

Notice that this section isn't titled "Creating Your TV Ad." *Do not* create your own television ad, your own marketing video, or any other moving-picture product. Ever.

Why the insistence? Consider this: Your ad will play to an audience that has been trained to expect feature-film quality and Nike-style concepts. To compete on a small-business budget, you need a strong, simple ad concept and clean, well-edited visuals. The first step toward making a good impression is to get help from those who deal in television ads daily.

Hiring professionals

As you select a creative partner, rely on the following resources:

- **Advertising agencies:** Big agencies serve major advertising accounts on annual contracts. They often accept large project work as well, but if you want to receive major attention for a fairly small project, interview small agencies to evaluate their talents, expertise, costs, and availability.

- **Video production services:** Look under *Video Production* in the Yellow Pages and you'll find businesses specializing in everything from wedding memories to digital production. Look for a studio that offers creative services, script writing, production, and editing services.

- **TV station production facilities:** Local stations can create your ad for "almost nothing," but get a bid anyway. To those who deal with TV advertising daily, "nothing" could be enough to break your bank.

Airing pre-produced manufacturer ads

High-quality, ready-to-air ads may be available to you through your manufacturers or dealers. The ads feature the manufacturer's products, but they include time to add a tag line directing viewers to your business. If you go this route, consider the following:

- ✔ Run manufacturer ads only for products with major sales potential for your business and for which your business is the exclusive regional representative.

- ✔ The ads are likely to be of higher quality than you could afford to produce on your own. By adding your own tag line, you'll gain advertising visibility while benefiting your business through association with a major national advertiser.

- ✔ When airing manufacturer ads, contact the manufacturer to discuss the possibility of obtaining cooperative advertising support in the form of shared costs for the media placements.

- ✔ Ask your station to add your logo and tag line. In return for your ad buy, they will probably perform the service for free or close to it.

Television ad guidelines

You heard the advice loud and clear in the previous section: Don't even try to conceive, write, or produce your own TV ads. Bring in the pros and then know what to look for as you evaluate their ad concepts and schedules.

The advice in Table 12-1 shows you what to aim for and what to avoid.

Table 12-1	TV Advertising Do's and Don'ts
Do's	**Don'ts**
Do work to stir the emotions and imagination of your audience.	Don't create ads that feature only a lineup of facts about your product or business.
Do focus on the viewer and how your message will change the prospect's life.	Don't keep the entire focus on your product, company, or staff.
Do start strong. You have three seconds to grab the audience.	Don't save your punch line until the end — your audience may be gone by then.

(continued)

Table 12-1 (continued)

Do's	Don'ts
Do get to the point quickly and then use the rest of the ad to back up your point and tell what's in it for the viewer.	Don't go for a slow build-up unless you're confident that your ad will be intriguing and entertaining enough to hold the viewer.
Do present your name visually *and* verbally.	Don't simply flash your logo. Consider leaving it on the screen during most or all of your ad.
Do invest in a quality ad with staying power that you can air for months or even a year, updated with inexpensive tag lines.	Don't go for quantity over quality, creating a lineup of inexpensive ads that fail to create a positive image for your business.
Do place an adequate schedule of at least 150 gross rating points a month.	Don't invest in TV advertising if you can't air a quality ad with adequate frequency.
Do rely on visuals to tell your story and do use your script to support the message.	Don't resort to a talking head, the TV equivalent of a classroom lecture.
Do start with a great idea that can be told visually, and then use words, music, and sound effects as enhancements.	Don't start with a script and then find visuals to fill the screen while an announcer reads the ad.

Infomercials

Infomercials are the program-style ads that you come across when you're channel cruising. They promote housewares, financial and business opportunities, exercise and beauty items, self-help offerings, sports and workout equipment, and such aptitude development products as memory enhancement and reading programs. Oh, and don't forget psychic services. Infomercials involve a direct exchange between the viewer and the advertiser. No retailers, travel agents, or other intermediaries are involved.

Infomercials solicit viewer action in two ways:

✔ *Sales-generating* infomercials invite viewers to call toll-free to place COD or credit card orders.

✔ *Lead-generating* infomercials ask viewers to call for free catalogs, brochures, or other offers.

Products featured in infomercials must have markups high enough to absorb the cost of creating and airing the infomercial. Most infomercial products are priced so that when you divide the retail price by your cost of goods, your result is no less than $3 and usually closer to $5. In other words, a product that retails for $19.95 should cost the manufacturer somewhere between $4 and $6.

Infomercials are high risk. There is no other way to put it. Experts in the field warn that the infomercial success rate is as low as one out of four.

The topic of infomercials comes up among small business advertisers in part because they generate direct and measurable results and in part because the ads look fairly straightforward and easy to produce. Looks can deceive, though. As with all other broadcast ads, viewers have been trained to expect a certain caliber of production value.

The average national infomercial production budget is more than $150,000, though you can find video production houses that will create your infomercial for a tenth of that amount or less and you can air the program for dollars per showing on local-market cable channels. Be aware, though, that as you limit your costs, you also limit your reach and frequency, resulting in fewer contacts, fewer sales, and probably a proportionately lower return on investment than the big-budget infomercial advertiser gets.

Big budget or small budget, all infomercials have the following traits in common:

✔ They promote products not available through retail channels.

✔ They present products that are of interest and use to most viewers.

✔ They feature strong testimonials.

✔ They show easy-to-demonstrate solutions.

✔ They offer prices that most viewers feel that they can opt for without great deliberation.

In creating infomercials, follow these ten rules:

1. Feature the product as king.

2. Solve a viewer problem.

3. Focus on selling, not on entertaining.

4. Use short sentences, short words, and short segments, broken at least three times during the program by your call to action.

5. Don't try to be funny.

6. Know your product position, your unique selling proposition, and the customer benefits you deliver (see Chapter 8). Then use your infomercial to give people a reason to believe what you're saying.

7. Use unscripted testimonials. Let customers ad lib their remarks but ask them to be specific with their praise. "It's amazing" lacks the impact of "I stood there watching the fine lines around my eyes fill in and disappear. I stared at my mirror, and then I started laughing with pure joy."

8. Never fake product demonstrations. It's illegal. Enough said.

9. Evaluate the effectiveness of your infomercial the morning after it airs. Unlike other forms of advertising, infomercials don't work better after repeated viewing. Most viewers will respond after watching the program one time if they are to respond at all. If your infomercial lights up your phone lines, re-air it to reach yet more prospects. But if no one calls, don't wait to see what happens next. Go back into the edit booth and start fine-tuning it, starting with the first three-minute segment, which is the portion that either grabs or loses most viewers.

10. Before you invest your budget, study other infomercials, meet with infomercial producers, and read direct marketing publications and Web sites for more advice and ideas.

Part IV
Getting the Word Out without Advertising

The 5th Wave   By Rich Tennant

MARKETING

"Bad news - Buddy flipped the van spilling 8 crates of samples into rush hour traffic. Good news - the van flipped logo side up."

In this part . . .

When small business marketers talk about guerilla techniques, they usually mean low-cost or no-cost efforts that spread their marketing messages without using traditional media outlets, or at least without incurring traditional advertising costs. That's exactly what this part is all about.

The following four chapters detail why and how to put the power of direct mail, promotional literature, public relations, and online marketing to work for your business. If you're interested in generating one-to-one communications, enhancing media coverage, staging promotions, or building online traffic, the chapters in this part tell you how.

Chapter 13

Mailing Direct to Your Market

- -

In This Chapter

▶ Building relationships using one-to-one marketing

▶ Creating and maintaining a mailing list

▶ Creating effective direct mailers and direct mail offers

▶ Setting realistic direct mail expectations

▶ Navigating the opportunities and landmines of e-mail marketing

- -

irect mail is one-to-one communication that delivers your marketing message to carefully selected prospects and customers one at a time.

One-to-one communication is the exact opposite of mass media advertising. *Mass media advertising* uses the shotgun approach — that is, you create an ad and use newspapers, magazines, and broadcast media to spread the message far and wide. *One-to-one communications* aim your message only at specific and well-defined individuals.

Most marketers believe that the two approaches work best as a tag team effort: You use mass media advertising to build awareness, desire, and perceived value for your products and then use one-to-one marketing to call for the order and to form the basis of a lasting customer relationship.

If you can only afford to do one or the other, however, consider placing your bets on one-to-one marketing so that each dollar you spend is aimed straight at a qualified prospect, and not scattered through mass media to reach prospects and nonprospects alike.

One-to-One Marketing

When you employ one-to-one marketing, you bypass mass media vehicles and take your ad straight to the mailboxes, telephones, and computer screens of individuals who are prime prospects for your product or service. You may hear the terms *direct marketing, database marketing, direct-response advertising,* and *direct mail* used interchangeably in discussions about one-to-one marketing, but they each represent different roles in the direct marketing field (see Table 13-1). For the record, here are the definitions:

- ✓ **Direct marketing** involves a direct exchange between a seller and a buyer — without the involvement of retailers, agents, or other intermediaries.

- ✓ **Direct mail** is a primary means of direct marketing communication that involves sending ads in the form of letters, postcards, or packages directly to targeted prospects.

- ✓ **Direct-response advertising** includes ads that invite consumers to respond directly to your business to take immediate action, such as making a purchase or requesting additional information.

- ✓ **Direct sales** means a sales transaction that occurs over a distance and directly between the buyer and the seller. Mail order and e-commerce are the primary vehicles for direct sales. (See Chapter 16 for information on e-commerce.)

- ✓ **Database marketing** entails compiling detailed information about customers and prospects and then using it to create and send marketing messages that are focused on the specific needs of these unique consumer groups.

- ✓ **Telemarketing** involves communicating with prospects and customers over the telephone — via *inbound calls* made by consumers to toll-free numbers that they see in ads, sales materials, or online, or via *outbound calls* made by a business to the homes or offices of target prospects.

Table 13-1	Differences between Direct Mail and Mass Media
Direct Mail	*Mass Media*
You target your prospects and send your ad only to those consumers.	You reach all consumers who read a publication, tune in to a broadcast, or see an outdoor ad.
You can personalize each marketing message.	You can target your message, but it is very difficult (and expensive) to personalize it.
You determine your format and length, and can include samples, reply cards, or any other item you feel will inspire a response.	You fit your message into available ad units.

Direct Mail	Mass Media
Your cost per contact is higher than with mass media, but your cost per response is lower than with any other medium.	Your cost per contact is very economical, but many unqualified or uninterested consumers are included in your audience.
Has a predictable response period, with most responses occurring within ten days of a mailing.	Has a slower and less predictable response period, especially when using magazine or outdoor advertising.
Response rates are easily measured.	Response rates are difficult to measure.

Direct Sales: The Do-It-Yourself Distribution Channel

Just as you'd guess, marketers who employ direct sales strategies sell to consumers directly, without involving middlemen, retailers, agents, or other representatives. Instead they use direct response ads, direct mailers, catalogs, and e-commerce (see Chapter 16) to communicate one on one with prospective buyers. Following are three examples of how direct marketing tools can generate direct sales:

- ✔ **Direct response advertising:** A jewelry maker advertises his wares by placing small black-and-white magazine advertisements. But instead of aiming to build general awareness, the ads invite readers to call toll-free to purchase the featured item or, alternatively, to visit the jeweler's Web site to view and order from his complete line. Either way, the instructions in the ad lead straight back to the jewelry maker and not to any retailer or other intermediary.

- ✔ **Direct mail:** The self-publisher of a book featuring lists and ratings for summer youth camps promotes the book by sending direct mailers to a subscriber list rented from a major parenting magazine.

- ✔ **Catalog distribution:** A kitchen accessories company generates direct sales by mailing its catalog to the households of current and past customers, ad respondents, and subscribers of gourmet magazines.

Managing an ethical direct sales program

The Direct Marketing Association warns against the two biggest direct sales landmines: nondelivery of merchandise and misrepresentation of offers. Every year a few direct marketers hurt the reputation of all by implementing programs that fail to communicate honestly or to deliver the products as promised. If you sell directly, protect your own reputation and the reputation of all who participate in direct marketing by following this advice:

Be clear, honest, and complete in your communications. Your ad *is* the shopping experience for direct buyers, so make it thorough and consistent with what the customer will see upon receipt of his or her order. Be accurate in the way it describes your product and represents your price, payment terms, and extra charges. Don't make outlandish claims and don't make promises that defy belief or that you can't live up to.

Describe the commitment involved in placing an order. Decide how you will handle returns and communicate your policy in your marketing materials. Be aware that there are laws enforcing honesty in direct mail marketing. If you promise "satisfaction guaranteed" (or if you make a money-back guarantee), Federal Trade Commission regulations mandate that you give a full refund without question and for any reason. If you offer a risk-free trial, then you can't charge the customer until the product is received and met with satisfaction. If you do not plan to refund a customer's money under any circumstances, your marketing materials must state, "All sales are final."

State the estimated lag time between order receipt and product delivery. If the average order takes four weeks for delivery, avoid complaints and concerns by informing customers in your marketing materials and at the time they place their orders.

Get good customer data. Your ability to deliver relies on good customer input. In your marketing materials, ask respondents to use ink on the order form and to print clearly (especially the name and address to which the order will be shipped).

Describe payment options. Require that payments be made by check, credit card, or money order. Do not allow cash transactions. Credit card privileges increase response rates, so plan your policies accordingly.

Log consumer questions and complaints. If — in spite of your best efforts — your ads still result in misunderstandings, pull and revise them.

Marketing with Direct Mailers

All direct mailers, regardless of look, message, or purpose, are alike in one way: They go straight to your prospects' mailboxes rather than reaching them through broadcast and print ads. For a look at the differences between direct mail and mass media communications, see Table 13-1 earlier in this chapter.

Direct mail success factors

Direct mailers are among the easiest of all marketing communications to monitor for success. With each mailing, you know exactly how many pieces you're sending and therefore how many prospects you're reaching. And because direct mailers almost always request an easy-to-track direct response (in the form of a sale, an inquiry, a visit to your business, or some other prospect action), within weeks you can count the responses to learn the effectiveness of your direct mail effort.

To increase your chances for success, consider that the most successful direct mailers all rely on these three important factors:

- **A targeted list:** To be great, a list must reach genuine prospects for your product or service. (See Chapter 2 for help in creating a prospect profile.)

- **A compelling offer:** The *offer* is the deal — the catalyst to which the consumer reacts.

- **An attention-getting format:** Some mailers involve nothing more than a regular or oversized *(jumbo)* postcard. Others involve only a good sales letter in a white envelope. Some are elaborate packages that contain samples, and other enclosures (including brochures, CDs, or product samples). Just be sure that your approach is consistent with the brand image of your business (see Chapter 7) and capable of meeting your advertising objectives (see Chapter 8).

Building your direct mail list

Direct mail programs are successful only when they involve mailing lists full of names of people who match your prospect profile to a tee (see Chapter 2). With all other forms of advertising, you match media selections to your market profile in general, but with direct mail, your marketing investment is aimed precisely at those prospects who possess the exact characteristics that make them likely to buy from your business:

- **Demographic lists** include addresses for people who match the age, profession, household income, and so on of those most apt to purchase your products.

- **Geographic lists** include addresses for people who live in the cities or ZIP code areas that match your market area.

- **Geodemographic lists** include the addresses of individuals in your targeted geographic market area who also match the demographic attributes of your prospect profile. For example, a geodemographic list might target prospects in a specific ZIP code area who live in homes assessed at $500,000 or more.

You can create your own list or you can obtain lists from outside organizations:

- ✔ **House lists** are lists that you create on your own by using your customer contacts as well as the names and addresses of prospects that you collect from other sources.

- ✔ **Outside lists** are available from mailing service businesses and organizations, professional associations, magazines, or other list owners.

Creating your own house list

If you market in a local or very clearly defined market area, you'll probably want to create your own list rather than buy one from outside your company. As you go about assembling the names for your list, follow these steps:

1. **Start with your established customer and prospect base.**

   Begin with the names of current customers. Then add the names of those who have expressed interest by responding to your ads, entering contests, or in other ways sharing their names with your business.

2. **Turn to local business and community directories.**

   For example, a golf club that's seeking to build its membership roster might create a mailing list that includes golfers in the target market area who have golfed as guests or in tournaments at the club, along with names of all target market business CEOs.

3. **Segment names according to past purchasing patterns or interests.**

   By segmenting your list, you can send tailored messages that match the interests of people in portions of your overall list.

4. **Enter the names into a database.**

   You can buy and learn to use database software, you can use the mail or data merge program in your word processor, or you can employ the resources of a professional database manager to keep your mailing list organized. (See the sidebar "Using mail specialists" later in this chapter.)

Where to find good lists

Mailing services and list brokerage businesses can assist with list development or list rental.

Before you contact outside resources to discuss renting a list, though, be ready to clarify exactly whom you want to target. Be sure you can define your prospect profile by stating where your most likely customers reside geographically and who they are in terms of age, income, family size, education, and other lifestyle facts (see Chapter 2). For help on honing your prospect profile, turn to industry and regional media ad reps, the *SRDS Direct Marketing List Source,* and the *SRDS Lifestyle Market Analyst* — each described in the following sections.

Magazine subscriber lists

Many magazines make their subscriber lists available for rent by businesses with approved product offers. Contact an ad representative at the leading publication that serves your industry or market area to learn about list availability, prices, and terms. Ask whether the magazine breaks its subscriber list into specific interest or geographic segments. You may learn that you can rent a portion of the list to reach only those subscribers who are most likely to be in the market for your product.

Say you're marketing a great new travel bag and you'd like to acquire a list of people who would be apt to buy it from you. You start by contacting a major travel magazine to inquire about buying access to its subscriber list. Because you know that your bag won't appeal to *all* subscribers, you ask about the ways the list can be *segmented.* If you want to target your mailer geographically, you'd ask about obtaining names only for subscribers in, say, the Midwest. Or maybe you want to send your mailer only to subscribers who list home addresses. (This eliminates the names of travel agents and others who receive the magazine in their offices.) Chances are good that the magazine ad representative will tell you that the publisher can indeed segment its list geographically and by home versus office addresses. Furthermore, it may be able to segment by subscriber income level — even by the type of travel the person prefers. You're on your way to a list tailored to your prospect profile!

The SRDS Direct Marketing List Source

This guide, published by the Standard Rate and Data Service, is available on the reference shelves of public libraries. It features data on thousands of mailing lists in hundreds of categories.

An hour or so browsing the catalog will help you focus on the kinds of lists available — useful information to know before you enter discussions about list rentals with magazine publishers or mailing service professionals.

The SRDS Lifestyle Market Analyst

Also available at public libraries, the *Lifestyle Market Analyst* provides consumer profiles for the following categories:

- ✔ **Cities:** Target your geographic market areas and then use the available data to confirm (or redirect) your plans.

  If you looked up the profile for our hometown of Bend, Oregon, in the *Lifestyle Market Analyst,* you'd find that the average resident skis nearly three times more often than the average American. (You'd know this because you'd see an *index number* of 282 alongside the word *Skiing,* which means Bend residents ski 282 percent the rate of average Americans.) They also outperform national averages when it comes to using recreational vehicles, camping and hiking, horseback riding, hunting, fishing, bicycling, and real estate investing.

But according to the statistics, the average resident of Bend, Oregon, ranks below average when it comes to buying fashion clothing (with an index rank of 65 on a scale of 100). Translation: If your product serves a customer with outdoor recreation interests, Bend could be a great market for your business. But if you market Chanel handbags or Versace gowns, you'd do well to concentrate on a market other than this one!

✔ **Lifestyle interests:** This section tells about the lifestyles of those who participate in the interest area your business serves.

The marketer of a new sewing product would want to know facts about those who participate in sewing. By turning to the "Sewing" section in the *Lifestyle Market Analyst,* he would learn that the average participant is 55.6 years old. Most are married and also participate (at above-average rates) in needlework and knitting, crafts, gardening, collectibles, and sweepstakes. (Hint: Use large type — and drop any idea of an MTV marketing theme.) The statistics also name the top U.S. market areas for per capita participation in the field of sewing. If an entrepreneur wanted to know where and how to target a product promotion, this information would be like gold — don't you think?

✔ **Consumer profiles:** Here, the *Lifestyle Market Analyst* reveals details about the people who fit your target demographic description.

Say that most customers served by your business happen to be between 35 and 44 years old, married, and with no children at home. By flipping to the section "Married, 35–44 Years Old, No Child At Home," you'll see that those who fit your prospect profile outperform other Americans when it comes to traveling for business, horseback riding, snow skiing, reading science fiction, owning a pet, riding motorcycles, drinking wine, working on their cars, and joining frequent flyer clubs. They are *not,* however, into entering sweepstakes, participating in civic activities, or playing video games. Armed with this information, you might decide to consider a direct mail offer that involves a frequent customer program rather than a sweepstakes or contest.

Renting a list

To rent a list, you can work directly with magazine publishers, mailing service businesses, and others who compile lists for use by marketers — or you can contact a *mailing list broker,* a business that provides preassembled or customized lists for use in direct mail programs. Two large brokers are Experian (www.experian.com/business_services/) and InfoUSA (www.infousa.com).

When renting a list, be aware that the list owner will have set prices and minimum requirements. Expect to take all or some of the following steps:

✔ Pay from 50 to several hundred dollars for a one-time use of 1,000 names — with higher prices for targeted industry and business lists.

✔ Rent a minimum number of names (usually the minimum number is well into the thousands).

✔ Allow the list owner to conduct your mailing, or arrange for the list to be released to a bonded mailing house, if required. Some list owners insist on handling the mailing from within their own operations or through a recognized mailing service to protect the value of their list and to ensure against multiple use or resale of names.

✔ Let list owners review and approve your mailer before it is sent to the names on their list. This allows them to protect their contacts.

Consider obtaining two lists that reflect your prospect profile and then combine them (called a *merge/purge* operation) to see which names appear on both lists. Those are your best prospects.

A destination resort might obtain the names of golfers aged 35 and over living in a targeted metropolitan area *and* the names of homeowners of properties assessed at $750,000 or more. After merging and purging the lists, the resort would have a better chance of reaching people with the interests *and* the financial abilities to match the resort's customer profile.

Using mail specialists

Mailing services go by many names: direct response specialists, bulk mailers, database managers, mail processors, and list managers. They provide professional assistance in the following areas:

✔ Merging, updating, and maintaining databases

✔ Deleting duplicate addresses

✔ Standardizing addresses

✔ Inserting ZIP+4, carrier route, and delivery point bar code information

✔ Presorting your list by computer to qualify for the lowest possible postal rate

✔ Addressing envelopes with inkjet technology

✔ Bar-coding

✔ Folding, inserting, and sealing direct mail packages

✔ Label printing and affixing

✔ Packaging and sacking

✔ Generating postal reports and certification reports

✔ Delivering mailings to the post office

For the names of direct mail specialists, look in the Yellow Pages under *Mailing Lists* and *Mailing Services*, or visit the Mailing and Fulfillment Services Association Web site at www.mfsanet.org. Click on *Find a Mailing or Fulfillment Company* and enter your home state to see names of mailing service businesses in your area.

Remember that when you purchase labels from a list owner, you are *renting*, not buying, the names. You are not allowed to use the list beyond the scope of your agreement or to duplicate the labels for additional mailings. Once you conduct your mailing, however, individuals from the rented list will respond to your company for more information. From that point on, you may market to these respondents: By responding to your mailer, the individuals have basically given you permission to do so.

Deciding on your offer

A successful offer must relate to — and build credibility in — your product or service. It should also be unique, valuable, and interesting to your prospect.

Don't use your existing promotional materials or items emblazoned with your company name or logo as your offer. People get promotional material (for free) daily — they certainly don't want to take the time to write and ask for it unless it is extremely unique or exclusive.

So what is a good offer?

Table 13-2 shows how a public relations agency that's seeking to build relationships with CEOs might weigh offers as bad, better, and improved.

Table 13-2	Examples of Direct Mail Offers	
Bad Example	*Better Example*	*Improved Example*
Invite the CEO to request a free brochure featuring case histories of some of the agency's recent public relations success stories.	Invite the CEO to request a free guide featuring advice on "How to Write News Releases and Manage Media Interviews."	Invite the CEO to specify how many free copies of "How to Write News Releases and Manage Media Interviews" she would like you to deliver.
Why?	*Why?*	*Why?*
This brochure is a promotional piece, and this "offer" asks the CEO to take time to request the kind of thing that other companies send out on routine basis. The CEO's response will likely be, "So what?"	This guide is a free resource that can benefit the recipient. It contains advice that public relations professionals usually sell by the hour. It also addresses the needs of the CEO.	The CEO has a good reason to respond to this offer. It promises a valuable and unique item, and because only the CEO knows how many copies her company can use, the response request has meaning.

A good offer contains the following elements:

- ✔ **A great deal:** This might be a free sample or gift, a trial offer, a special price, or special payment terms — depending on the objective of your mailer and the nature of your product. In crafting your offer, be aware that the word *free* pulls more responses than discounts or other price offers. If possible, offer something free of charge (for example, a free sample, free catalog, or an offer to buy one, get one free).

- ✔ **A guarantee:** To improve results, offer an assurance that working with your business is risk-free and reliable. For example, extend a money-back guarantee, a delivery guarantee, or a service guarantee. And keep your promise — for good business purposes and for legal reasons.

- ✔ **A time limit:** This will increase interest and response — even if the deadline is only implied (such as *Please reply by December 15*).

Although every direct mailer wants a strong response rate, remember that your goal is to receive *quality* responses. If your offer is *too* great, it will generate responses from people who simply want your gift. So don't go overboard.

Creating your mailer

Mailers come in all shapes and sizes, but the best ones are, above all, *personal.* (The opposite of a personalized mailing is one addressed to Occupant.)

You can personalize your mailer in a number of ways. You can use what looks like hand-written addresses. (Computers and mail house technology make this seemingly arduous task pain-free.) If you're enclosing a letter (see the following section on writing direct mail letters), you can increase your mailer's effectiveness by personalizing the salutation line and adding a paragraph that mentions the consumer's past purchasing patterns to boost response rates even further.

No matter what, don't use a catch-all greeting such as the dreaded *Dear Friend* or, worse, *Dear Valued Customer.* If your mailing is too extensive to allow for personalized greetings, replace the salutation with a headline.

The best mailers also

- ✔ **State your offer clearly.** Repeat your offer on the envelope, the letter, the letter's postscript, and any additional enclosures. Reiterating your offer on the reply card will provide a last-minute reassurance regarding the request or commitment that respondents are making.

✔ **Make the reply mechanism free to the consumer.** Include a toll-free number or a postage-paid card or envelope so that the customer can respond at your expense.

✔ **Include a reply card in addition to a toll-free number.** Many people prefer to mail in their responses — even if you provide a toll-free number or Web address. On your reply card, give people a chance to say yes or no. Believe it or not, giving them the chance to decline your offer increases the chances of them accepting it. To save money, contact your post office or a mailing service for help obtaining a Business Reply Postage Number to print on your reply cards. That way you'll pay only for the responses you receive — rather than paying to place a stamp on every reply card you enclose.

Writing direct mail letters

First things first: If your mailing is any larger than a postcard or self-mailer, *enclose a letter.*

People may tell you that no one reads the letter or that the letter just gets in the way of other enclosures — but they're wrong. The letter is an essential ingredient of direct mail: Enclose one in every package.

In your letter, follow each and every piece of advice for writing advertising copy (see Chapter 11), taking the following steps:

1. **Start with a short, clear, strong first sentence.**

   Your opening line is your chance to establish rapport, focus your message, and entice the recipients to continue on to the next sentence. It should make readers want to go on to the following sentence and right through to the all-important P.S.

2. **Tell your prospects what's in it for them.**

   Don't use your letter to talk about yourself or your company or why you think your product is so great. (Never ever begin your first sentence with *I, we,* or your company's name.) Write your letter imagining that you are the consumer — not the advertiser. Ask yourself, "So what's in it for me?" If the letter delivers a compelling answer, you've hit the bull's-eye.

3. **Get to the point quickly.**

   Introduce your offer and explain in clear terms how easy it is to take advantage of your invitation. Keep your words short, your sentences short, your paragraphs short, and your tone casual.

4. **Talk in terms that matter to your market.**

   Emphasize the benefits your consumers can count on. They don't need a line-up of facts or features that matter more to you than to the market. (See Chapter 8.)

5. **Use as much space as you need to communicate your offer.**

   Multi-page letters can work beautifully — *if* they are superbly written. If you decide to go with a long letter, use headlines and bulleted or high-lighted text to catch and hold reader attention.

6. **Finish with a P.S.**

   An astonishing number of direct mail recipients glance only at the open-ing line and the P.S. (postscript) of the letter. Some studies show that as many as three-quarters of readers actually read the P.S. first. Use it to sum-marize your sales message, reiterate key benefits, make a pitch for and reinforce the value of your offer, remind the reader of the time-sensitivity of your offer, and tell how to contact you.

Sending your mailers

Know before you go is the rule when creating direct mailers. For mailers origi-nating in the U.S., start at the U.S. Postal Service Web site at `www.usps.com/directmail` — it is full of how-to instructions, advice, resources, postal rate information, and free downloadable direct mail templates. You can also order or download the free Postal Service brochure called "Simple Steps" which details five steps to a successful direct mail campaign.

Meeting regulations

Mailers must match precise dimensions in order to be processed by post office equipment. Use the templates available at `www.usps.com/directmail` or visit your post office or a mailing professional to make sure that your mailer conforms. Do so while your project is still in the design stage — not when it's printed and ready to be sent.

Take particular care when it comes to the address panel of your mailer. Postal equipment reads addresses using high-tech postal character-recogni-tion equipment. If your recipient address doesn't appear in the correct place on the envelope or if other design elements intrude on the space, your mail-ing piece may take longer or cost more to process.

Taking advantage of discounts

If you prepare your mailers to meet processing and delivery regulations, the post office rewards you with reduced rates, called *Standard Mail (A)* or *bulk* rates. To take advantage of these discounts, you must

- ✔ Obtain a mail permit and pay an annual bulk mail fee.

- ✔ Include a mail permit imprint, called an *indicia,* showing that postage has been paid.

- ✔ Send at least 200 pieces in each bulk mailing. To qualify as a bulk mailing, all 200 pieces must be identical except for the address, and none can contain checks or bills (these must be sent using first-class postage).

- ✔ Include the correct ZIP code on each piece.

- ✔ Presort the mail. *Presorting* means sorting and bundling mail to postal specifications before delivering it into the post office in trays or bags.

- ✔ To simplify presorting, use a list that has been CASS (Coding Accuracy Support System) certified. When you purchase outside lists, ask to see the CASS certificate that the U.S. Postal Service provides.

You can receive further discounts by using ZIP+4 codes and adding bar codes that support the postal service's automated systems. Various kinds of bar codes earn different discounts. Inquire at the post office or ask a mail consultant about the requirements that you must meet in order to receive reduced rates on your bulk mailing.

Specifying Postal Service instructions

When you send bulk mail, you can include instructions, or *endorsements,* that tell the post office what to do with mail that is undeliverable as addressed. Without an endorsement, returned items will be thrown away.

An endorsement reading *Return Service Requested* instructs the post office to return the piece with the corrected address or the reason the mail was undeliverable. The item won't be forwarded, but you will have the information you need to update your list. You can also instruct the post office to discard the piece but notify you of the new address *(Change Service Requested)* or to forward the piece *(Forwarding Service Requested).*

Each endorsement will result in an additional charge. Base your instructions on how much you want to pay for the service, the value of your mailer (if you're sending a valuable gift in each mailer you'll probably want to request return service), and your confidence in the accuracy of your list.

Following up

Half of all responses arrive within two weeks of the date that people receive a direct mailing.

How many replies should you expect? Brace yourself: 1 to 3 percent is considered a home run with a purchased or outside list. If you use internal lists that are full of highly qualified names, you can hope for a 5 to 10 percent return, or sometimes higher.

Responding quickly

Don't wait even one week to get back to your direct mail respondents.

If you don't think you can handle the volume of responses in a timely manner, send your mailers out in *flights* — groups of several hundred every three or four days. This ensures that the responses will be staggered as well. In your response

- ✔ **Enclose a letter thanking the respondent for the inquiry.** Many people forget that they sent in a card — so refresh their memories.

- ✔ **Enclose the item that you promised in your initial mailing, along with a description.**

- ✔ **Introduce your business in terms of benefits that matter to the consumer.** See Chapter 8 for advice on how features and customer benefits are different.

- ✔ **Offer the next step in the buying process.** Include an introductory offer, invitation, coupon for service, or some other means to heighten interest in an effort to convert the prospect into a customer.

Creating a database of respondents

After fulfilling the request, enter the respondent's name into a database for timely follow-up. Within eight weeks, contact prospects a second time via a mailing, phone call, or — if they've invited you to do so — an e-mail newsletter or update. (See the following section for information on the detrimental effects of sending unauthorized e-mail messages.)

As you enter each name into your database, be sure to include

- ✔ The source of the lead.

- ✔ The date of the first and each subsequent contact.

- ✔ The respondent's name, mailing address, and e-mail address.

- ✔ Any information that can help you customize future contacts (such as the answers to questions that you asked on your reply card).

- ✔ Additional space in which you can log follow-up activity.

If your business has a limited number of prospects, you can keep this database manually. But if you are managing a larger number of leads, use a computer program or a database management company.

Sending a second mailing to nonrespondents

Within 30 days of your first mailing, contact all recipients who have not yet responded. (If you are using an outside list, rent the list for two-time usage and obtain a duplicate set of labels for this purpose.)

Research proves that follow-up with nonrespondents increases your overall response rate dramatically. It also gives you much more value for the cost of the list rental, because the second-time usage is usually at a fraction of the cost of the initial usage.

Scouring your list

Every time you receive word of an address change, update your list immediately. And from time to time poll the individuals on your list to be sure that they are still in the market for your offering. The following sections tell you how.

Keeping addresses current

Address lists go bad at a rate of almost 2 percent a month. To keep your list current, follow these steps:

- ✔ Request address correction information from the post office. Make the request by including an endorsement on your mailer (see "Specifying Postal Service instructions" earlier in this chapter).

- ✔ Take advantage of the *National Change of Address (NCOA)* file, a compilation of change-of-address records. When renting mailing lists or using mailing services, ask if the lists provided have been updated against this file, which is licensed by the U.S. Postal Service.

Confirming prospect interest

On either a 12- or 18-month basis, send a mailer that includes the opportunity for prospects in your database to opt out of their relationship with you. It may sound crass, but the fact is that disinterested prospects aren't prospects at all — they're simply a marketing expense.

To determine the validity of the names on your list, you can occasionally add an opt-out option as one of the choices on your reply cards. For example:

- ✔ *Yes, send me whatever great offer you are making in this mailing.*

- ✔ *I'm not interested at the moment, but please keep my name on your list for future invitations.*

- ✔ *No, I'm not in the market right now. Please remove my name from your list with the promise that you'll welcome me back in the future if my needs change.*

Direct mail — or junk mail?

Direct mail becomes junk mail when consumers feel that the offer isn't personal. For example, if a college student lives in an apartment and gets a mailing for landscaping services, she automatically determines that it's junk mail — especially if she has received the same offer three times already. Timely and targeted messages that communicate information and offer good value, however, are not considered junk mail. As a direct mail marketer, it's your job to tow the line.

E-mail Marketing

It's only partly coincidental that the preceding section on junk mail is followed by this part on e-mail marketing. The sequence isn't meant to imply that e-mail mass mailings *are* junk mail, but a good many of them spiral into the junk mail category, and for legal and marketing reasons you'll want to be sure yours don't.

Opt-in e-mail

The unanimous advice from reputable online marketers regarding unsolicited e-mail is this: *When in doubt, don't.* Commit to an opt-in policy instead and limit your e-mail marketing messages to the following recipients:

✔ Those who have *opted in* by providing their e-mail addresses and asking for more information. In fact, many e-mail marketers now use a double opt-in system that allows a person who opts in to confirm his decision by responding positively to a first e-mail that provides the recipient the opportunity to restate interest or opt out immediately.

✔ Those who are friends, colleagues, suppliers, customers, or prospects who have requested similar information in the past.

✔ Those who were referred to you by a colleague or by a group related to your business with the assurance that they will appreciate receiving your information.

Before clicking Send, see that you can answer yes to at least one of the following questions:

✔ Did the recipient ask you to provide information?

✔ Is the recipient a friend, colleague, supplier, customer, or prospect who has previously requested related information from your business?

Spam — Is it or isn't it?

Spam is the term for electronic junk mail that is sent to a large number of e-mail addresses — none of whom requested the information and most of whom feel invaded when they find the messages in their in-boxes. Spam, the opposite of opt-in mailings, is something to avoid at all costs.

What's more, it's illegal. In 2003, the U.S. federal government passed the CAN Spam Act,

requiring, among other things, that unsolicited e-mail be clearly identified as such, provide a valid physical postal address, present a means to opt-out or unsubscribe, and honor unsubscribe requests within a specific time frame. For a good explanation of the CAN Spam ruling and ways to comply, visit the Web site `www.wilsonweb.com/wmt9/canspam_comply.htm`.

✔ Are you confident that this person is interested in your message because an associate asked you to send the information? If you're promoting a 10K race by using an e-mail list provided by the local running group, you can be pretty sure that your message will be welcomed. Still, to be safe, include a line in your message associating your business with the referring source — just as you would if you were making a telephone cold call based on a referral from a mutual friend.

Don't publish lists of your carefully collected e-mail addresses on your site. You've probably seen company sites that include customer lists, event sites that post participant lists, or athletic event sites that post finish results, including names and e-mail addresses. Opportunistic spam mailers cruise the Net looking to cherry-pick from lists like these.

Also protect your customers by hiding their addresses when you send the same e-mail to a number of recipients. To maintain the privacy of each recipient, enter your own address in the "to" line of your e-mail, and enter all recipient addresses as *blind carbon copies* by using the *BCC* address option.

Writing e-mail that gets read

Once you are confident that your e-mail will land in welcome mailboxes, use these tips to make each mailing effective:

✔ Keep your message quick, to the point, and casual.

✔ Use a short subject line (maximum of five to seven words). Remember:

• If your mailing is based on a referral, use the subject line to say so. Doing so will help keep you out of the spam category — and get your message opened. Think of your subject line as your e-mail headline. Use it to draw attention and lead the recipient into your message.

- Create a subject line that alerts recipients that the message is aimed specifically at them. For example, *Calling All Sausalito Mac Users* is far more targeted than *Closeout Computer Prices.*

✔ Limit your message to ten lines if possible. Rather than making a comprehensive sales presentation in an e-mail message, link the consumer to your Web page or invite the consumer to request your electronic newsletter. This allows you to offer far more information — to an already engaged prospect.

✔ Write your e-mail so it can be quickly scanned. Rely on an attention-getting subject line, a great opening sentence, and a P.S., which is nearly as important in e-mail as it is in hard-copy direct mail letters. Eliminate long blocks of text in favor of three- to four-line paragraphs, separated by double spacing to create white space. Use dashes or bullets to create easy-to-scan lists.

✔ Include an e-mail signature file at the end of every message (your e-mail Help function will provide details for establishing a signature). Use the signature to present your business information, physical address and phone number, Web site address, e-mail confidentiality statement, and promotional information such as a newsletter subscription invitation.

✔ Write your note in plain text. HTML lets you add graphics, formatting, color-coded text, and clickable links, but about half of all recipients prefer to open plain-text notes. Also, on mobile phones or PDAs, plain text is easier to interpret and download. HTML is especially effective, though, for newsletters. When recipients subscribe to your newsletter, let them choose which format they prefer to receive.

Few marketing arenas are less tolerant of intrusion than the e-mail in-box. Tread cautiously and build successful relationships.

Chapter 14

Brochures, Promotions, Trade Shows, and More

In This Chapter

▶ Producing brochures and marketing literature

▶ Choosing and using advertising specialties

▶ Producing printed and electronic newsletters

▶ Preparing for trade shows and sales presentations

▶ Launching promotions that work

Mass media advertising and direct mailings are the most obvious ways to promote your business, but the communications toolbox also includes a long list of other effective (and often far less expensive) communication vehicles to consider.

Brochures and fliers, free giveaway items known as *advertising specialties,* product promotions, trade show appearances, and sales presentations are all means of bypassing traditional advertising as you carry your message into the marketplace.

Most of these alternatives come with low price tags, and for that reason many small businesses use them with a nothing-ventured-nothing-gained-or-lost attitude. But even though large sums of money are rarely at risk when you print a stack of fliers or order pens imprinted with your name, your reputation may be on the line instead. This chapter offers advice so that every marketing investment — however large or small — works to your advantage while contributing to a favorable image of your business.

Producing and Using Marketing Literature

People who aren't professional marketers consider *collateral* to be something you pledge when you're trying to get a bank loan. To marketers, though, collateral means brochures, fliers, fact sheets, sales folders, posters, and all the other forms of printed material that carry your logo, message, and reputation into the marketplace.

When, why, and how to produce brochures

Designers make a handsome living off all the small business marketers who say that they need a brochure but can't say *why* they need one. To many small business owners, getting a brochure is like getting a Web site. They think they need one because everyone else has one. But here are five more sensible ways to decide.

You need a brochure if

- Your prospects aren't easy to contact in person or by phone but would likely respond to literature about your business.

- Your business would benefit from a printed piece that could be sent ahead of sales presentations to pave the way for your visit, or left afterwards to reiterate key points.

- You're trying to communicate with individuals who aren't easily or affordably reached by mass media but who are likely to pick up literature at information kiosks or other distribution points.

- Your service or product is complicated and involves details that your prospects need to study in order to make informed decisions.

- The price of your product is high enough or the emotional involvement is such that prospects will consult with others before making the decision, in which case they will benefit (as you will, too) from a brochure that conveys your message in your absence when your prospects consult with advisers, associates, or spouses.

Before you decide to produce a brochure or any other form of sales literature, see that you can answer yes to these questions:

✔ **Do you have an adequate budget?** Can you allocate enough money to create a brochure that makes a favorable impression for your business?

✔ **Will the brochure strengthen your image?** Can you commit to designing and writing a brochure that enhances your company's image?

✔ **Do you have a distribution plan?** Do you know how you will use the brochure? The literature will do no good sitting in a back closet.

Types of sales literature

Sales literature runs the gamut from elaborate folders filled with sets of matching fact sheets to laser-printed cards that sit on countertops or in *Take one* racks. The following sections help you sort through the opportunities:

Capabilities brochure

A *capabilities brochure* is an "about our business" piece that tells your story, conveys your business personality, and differentiates your offerings from those of your competitors. Especially if you're marketing a professional service business (such as a law or accounting firm, a financial services firm, or some other consulting business) or a business that offers high-emotion products (such as a homebuilder), this type of brochure is a marketing necessity.

Capability brochures are among the most expensive kinds of brochures to produce, so give yours a "keeper" quality. A financial planner might include a net worth asset worksheet, or a homebuilder might include a checklist for how to get the most value out of a homebuilding budget. The goal is to include some reason for prospects to hold onto and refer back to the piece.

Product brochure

A *product brochure* is a piece that describes a specific offering of your business. This kind of brochure is important when marketing products that require more than spur-of-the-moment consideration, such as high-ticket products, products purchased with input from more than one person, and products that involve cost and technical comparisons before a buying decision takes place.

Modular literature

Modular literature involves a number of sheets or brochures that all use the same or a complementary design. This format allows you to assemble a quality package of easily updated sheets that can be mixed and matched inside the folder or handed out individually, depending on the impression you wish to make on your prospect.

A modular format is a great approach if your business offers a range of products that can be represented on separate marketing pages, if your price lists or other information changes frequently, or if your prospects have widely differing interests or needs.

Rack cards

TIP

Rack cards get their name from the fact that they fit into 4-x-9-inch brochure racks. Some rack cards involve a single, folded sheet that opens up to a multi-panel brochure. Others include a number of pages folded and stapled down the middle (called *saddle-stitched*). Many businesses create inexpensive rack cards by printing the same image three times on an 8½-x-11-inch sheet of paper (*3-up* is the printing term), which they then cut into three cards of 3⅔ x 8½ inches.

The most important thing to remember about rack cards is that only the top few inches are immediately visible to the consumer — the rest is hidden under the brochure that sits right in front of yours in the rack, covering all but the top portion of your brochure. So be sure that your name and a message announcing your customer benefit appear in that small top space.

Fliers

The least expensive promotional piece you can print is a flier, which usually takes the form of an 8½-x-11-inch sheet of paper printed on one side or both to announce a sale, open house, limited-time event, or low-cost product that doesn't rely on a high-quality presentation for its success. In producing a flier, write copy that can be understood at a glance (remember, a flier is a throw-away piece, so don't expect people to hang on every word). Design it following the advice for creating a print ad in Chapter 11. Then take it to a quick-print shop and for as little as $50 you can walk away with a thousand copies printed on white or colored paper.

Fliers usually look like what they are — low-cost handouts — but the caliber of design and copy, the quality of paper and printing, and how you get them into circulation can enhance the image they make.

Planning and writing brochures

The best brochures talk directly to the prospect, anticipating questions and providing answers before the person even thinks to ask. As you develop brochure content, refer to these copywriting tips:

- **Include a headline.** Simply putting your name on the cover is wasteful and too *I-oriented*. Customers care about what's in it for *them*. Use your brochure cover to present a benefit-oriented headline (see Chapter 11 for headline-writing tips) that grabs your prospect's attention.

- **Use subheads.** By placing secondary headlines throughout the brochure, you can communicate your message quickly to those who aren't inclined to read it all.

✔ **Write directly to your prospect.** Know your prospect profile (see Chapter 2) and write copy that delivers the same benefits and reasons to buy that you would describe in person if you could be there yourself.

✔ **Avoid technical jargon, long feature descriptions, and clichés.** Clichés would include *committed to excellence* and *dedicated to your needs.* Turn every selling point into an easy-to-understand, unique, and believable customer benefit. (See Chapter 8.)

✔ **Don't boast.** Aim to write a brochure that informs, inspires, and establishes a friendship with prospects. You wouldn't (or shouldn't) brag if you were presenting in person, so don't do it in your sales literature, either. Avoid hyped-up superlatives (the *best,* the *biggest,* and all those other *est* words). Trying too hard to impress almost always backfires.

✔ **Let satisfied customers do some talking.** A convincing way to tout your excellence is to feature customer testimonials or client lists. When featuring endorsements, see that the customers are credible and clearly identified, that their comments are honest and believable (nothing is worse than testimonials that seem scripted), *and* that you get permission in writing to use the customer quotes with attribution.

✔ **Tell what to do next.** A brochure is a marketing tool. It needs to compel prospects to take the next step. Do you want them to call to make a reservation or to schedule an appointment or demonstration? Should they return a reply card to request more information? Should they come to your business to take advantage of a special offer? Know what action you're trying to achieve and use your brochure copy to lead the consumer to the desired decision.

✔ **Make the next step in the buying process an easy one.** If you're asking for phone calls, include your toll-free number on every page. If you're encouraging the consumer to request information (perhaps a demonstration or an appointment), provide a phone number and a postage-paid reply card. Make your address, phone numbers, and e-mail and Web site addresses easy to see and read, and if you're inviting visits to your business, give office hours and a locator map, too.

✔ **Revise and proofread.** Ask a colleague to read your copy for accuracy and understanding. Then revise it, read it out loud, make final revisions, and, finally, proofread it a few more times before turning it over to the printer. Your brochure will stand in for your business when no actual person can be present to tell your story, so tailor it accordingly.

Brochures are read most carefully by those who are ready to buy or who have just purchased and who now want to validate their decisions. Write your brochure with those committed consumers in mind. By doing so, you will minimize the tendency to oversell and instead focus on the benefits and promises that customers can count on when they work with your business.

Designing brochures

Before designing your brochure, know your budget. If you're operating on a shoestring, limit your use of photos and colored inks and opt instead for a simply designed, standard-sized brochure that can be printed on a small, economically priced press.

If you don't have design skills within your company, don't resort to desktop publishing, as the results almost always look like they were fashioned in a basement. Instead, invest in the talents of a graphic artist or choose a print shop that provides design assistance and backs the offer with a portfolio of good-looking samples. (See Chapter 9 for help when hiring professionals.)

As you proceed, keep the following tips in mind:

- ✔ **If color photos are essential to your story, budget accordingly.** Color increases response to a brochure, but it also increases production and printing costs.

- ✔ **Keep your brochure quality in line with the nature of your offering.** A laser-printed brochure on neon-colored paper may be ideal for a rental shop featuring the least expensive Halloween costumes, but it will never do for a restaurant striving to be *the* place to spend anniversary evenings. Avoid rich embossing and foil-stamped headlines unless you want your literature to look upscale and exclusive. Similarly, save the do-it-yourself, quick-print handouts for when you want to communicate bargain-basement offers.

- ✔ **Know your type and color guidelines.** Designers love to be creative. That's their job. It's your job to give them parameters to work within. See Chapter 7 for guidance in making type, color, and logo usage decisions so that all materials present a uniform image for your company.

- ✔ **Make your company name visible.** If your brochure will sit in a rack display, position your name on the top part where it will be visible. For multi-page brochures, consider including your name and contact information (phone, address, and Web site) on every panel.

Getting your brochure into the marketplace

Printers will rightfully tell you that printing the first brochure is the most expensive. After that, you're paying only for ink and paper, so print enough brochures to ensure that you won't feel a need to save your supply. Then get them into circulation by using these ideas:

- ✔ **Announce your brochure to your business mailing list.** Send copies to customers, prospects, suppliers, and associates. Include a cover letter thanking them for helping you achieve the business success that you're

proud to portray in your new brochure. Tell them that you want them —
your most valued business friends — to be the first to preview the
brochure. Enclose extra copies that they can share with others who may
be interested in your offerings.

✔ **Send copies to editors at local and industry publications.** A new
brochure isn't a news item, but it presents an opportunity to make media
contacts and to provide information about your business. When sending
it to editors (and with luck you've established editorial relationships —
see Chapter 15), attach a cover note — not a news release. A homebuilder might say *I thought this updated background on our company might
be useful. As you continue your coverage of growth in our area, please feel
free to contact me. Our firm has records of the changing tastes of homeowners over the past decade, along with information on regional and industry
statistics and trends.*

✔ **Carry brochures with you at all times.** Encourage your staff to do the
same. Don't hoard them. On the other hand, don't hand them out like
Halloween candy. Target your distribution so that your literature ends
up in the hands of qualified prospects who will value your message and
who can make referrals or buying decisions in your favor.

✔ **Send a brochure ahead of your arrival at meetings** so that your prospect
has a sense of you before meeting you.

✔ **Contract with a brochure distribution service.** If you want to make your
literature available to consumers who stop at high-traffic brochure racks
such as those in visitor welcome centers, for example, contract with a
distribution service for regularly scheduled delivery and supply maintenance. For the names of services in your area, contact the International
Association of Professional Brochure Distributors at www.apbd.org and
click on "Find A Distributor."

✔ **Use your brochure as a step in the buying process.** When qualified
prospects leave without buying, follow up by sending your brochure
along with a cover letter that provides additional information that
relates to the consumer's concerns or interests. Also, keep a list of pending prospects and use your brochure — along with copies of recent publicity, news announcements, or other timely information about your
business — as a reason to stay in touch on a regular basis.

Launching and maintaining newsletters

Newsletters are informal, friend-to-friend communications that deliver newsworthy information, useful updates, reminders of what your business does,
and ideas of interest and use to newsletter recipients.

Newsletters can accomplish the following for your business:

- Build credibility and reputation
- Provide a means of frequent communication
- Deliver news from your company and your industry
- Answer questions, usually through a question-and-answer column
- Offer tips that enhance the credibility of your business while also building customer confidence and loyalty
- Share profiles of employees, customers, and success stories
- Convey industry information (with permission, of course)

Newsletter planning advice

Newsletters work only when they're produced and distributed on a consistent basis, which means you have to commit to the long haul before you undertake the first issue.

As you make your decision, consider the following:

- **Define the purpose of your newsletter.** Is it to keep an open line of communication with customers? Is it to share promotional offerings? Is it to enhance your reputation by sharing company news and success stories? You may have one or several objectives. Know what you expect from your newsletter before you design or write the first issue.

- **Establish how often you will produce and send your newsletter.** Weigh two considerations: How often are you and your staff able to get a newsletter assembled and distributed? How often is your customer interested in hearing from you?

- **Decide who will receive your newsletter.** You might start with a list that includes customers, prospects, suppliers, and other business friends. Grow your list by featuring a free newsletter subscription invitation in direct mailers and other direct-response marketing efforts.

- **Set your newsletter budget.** How many will you send — and how often? Will you handle the task in-house or hire outside writing, design, and mail service help? Tally the costs and be sure you can afford to commit to the project for at least a full year.

Writing and designing newsletters

Here is good news for small-budget marketers: The most effective newsletters look newsy and current rather than expensive and labored, which translates to the fact that newsletters are among the most economical of marketing materials.

In creating your newsletter, consider the following points:

- ✔ **Include many short items rather than a few long ones.**

- ✔ **Establish a simple format and stick with it issue after issue.** The more your newsletter looks like a brochure, the less it looks newsy. If you use Microsoft Word, you'll find about a dozen newsletter templates available for free download at `http://office.microsoft.com/en-us/templates/CT063469341033.aspx`.

- ✔ **Invite reader responses to help you gauge the effectiveness of your newsletter.** If you've launched a new product offering, summarize the news in an article and offer to send information or samples on request. Find ways to inspire responses to verify that your newsletter is being read.

- ✔ **Include valid dates when presenting time-specific offers.** Newsletters may be read well into the future, long after your offer has expired.

- ✔ **Use your newsletter to promote your Web address** and give readers an incentive to visit your site. A resort might include this item:

> Our new online reservation service is already doing a brisk business. More than half of our site visitors click to view room photos and floor plans, and 38 percent of those who view our property online go on to make a reservation request. If you haven't visited our site lately, go to `www.[ourhotel].com`. On our home page, be sure to click to enter our Web-only sweepstakes for a free weekend stay. Also, if you'd rather receive our newsletter electronically than by mail, just click on the newsletter request icon, enter your e-mail address, and we'll transfer your mailing information into our confidential electronic file. Either way, we look forward to sending you our quarterly updates, special packages, and resort event news.

- ✔ **Combine sales messages with news updates** so that readers will view your newsletter as more than a promotional mailing. For example:

> Rocky Mountain vacations are more popular than they've been in years, based on the number of toll-free reservation calls and Web site visits. Calls in April 2004 were up a full 22 percent over April 2003, with Thanksgiving and Christmas reservations already coming in at a brisk pace. Call us at 1-800-555-5555 just as soon as you know your vacation dates so we can reserve your stay.

- ✔ **Include your company identification** — your logo, phone number, mailing address, e-mail address, and Web site address — on every page of every issue to encourage communications.

Publishing opt-in electronic newsletters

Opt-in is a term that refers to promotional e-mails that have been requested by recipients, unlike dreaded (and often illegal) *spam* e-mails that are sent to people whether or not they want to receive them.

Opt-in e-mail is the only way to assure that your mailing is both legal and capable of retaining the recipient's goodwill. One of the most successful ways to invite people to opt in is by offering to e-mail them a free newsletter with information on good deals, useful tips, and advice.

Why e-newsletter readers subscribe

People subscribe to online newsletters because they want highly targeted, immediate solutions to their needs, problems, or situations. They aren't looking for general, chatty information. Nor do they want newsletters that go on and on, or arrive too often.

Instead, they want

- Work-related news from their employer or business organization, or news pertaining to their personal interests and hobbies.
- News about prices, sales, and special offers.
- Advance notice of upcoming events.

The key word is *news*. Keep your newsletter current, informative, relevant, timely, and to the point, and readers will look forward to its receipt.

E-newsletter writing etiquette

People expect online messages to speak to them in a one-to-one voice.

As you write your newsletter, write like you talk — clearly, with good grammar, and to the point. Be casual but not overly informal; be relaxed yet still businesslike. (Think of the difference between boardroom and Friday-casual office attire. One is relaxed, and the other is buttoned-down, but both are still appropriate to the business environment.)

In terms of length, keep daily or weekly newsletters to a screen or less, and allow biweekly, monthly, or quarterly mailings to run only as long as the content is interesting and newsworthy.

Designing and publishing your e-newsletter

Design your newsletter for readers who skim.

As e-mail volume continues to swell, readers spend less and less time reading individual messages thoroughly. Instead, they glance through content, reading headlines for an overview and spending only a few extra seconds on information that stands out as worthy of extra attention.

As you get ready to publish, follow these tips:

- ✔ **Know the purpose and frequency of your newsletter** and stick to what you promise to provide.

- ✔ **Decide on your newsletter format.** Plain text is easy to assemble and send, but may not allow you to show URLs as clickable links. HTML is more complicated, but allows you to present workable hyperlinks as well as color, fonts, and graphic images, while also allowing you to track the rate at which recipients open your mail or click through to links. You may want to set up your newsletter so that subscribers can choose the format they want to receive at they time they subscribe. If you opt for an HTML format, consult a Web designer to set up at least your first issue or contract with an e-mail marketing service such as Constant Contact (visit www.constantcontact.com for information and a trial offer).

- ✔ **Include a link to your Web site.** If your newsletter refers to a specific part of your site — for example, the page for a new product — then link directly to that page.

- ✔ **Include your address and phone number** so people can reach you after they've logged off.

- ✔ **Provide a subject line** that flags prospect interest. Consider using a bulk e-mail program that lets you add the recipient's name to the subject line to help get it past those with a trigger-ready finger on the delete key.

- ✔ **Begin with a first line**, such as *Thank you for subscribing to our newsletter* to remind recipients that they opted-in to your mailing. If your newsletter covers a number of screens, provide a table of contents so readers can scroll straight to parts of interest. Throughout the newsletter, use headlines, bulleted or numbered lists, and boldface, benefit-oriented statements to catch attention as eyes sweep over the screens.

- ✔ **Add an issue number to each edition.** Expect people to keep and refer to your newsletters. Be clear about the valid dates on limited-time offers. And provide links to your site only if you're sure they will work well into the future. (If they don't, a customer trying to link to your site a year from now may think that you've gone out of business.)

- ✔ **Test your newsletter** by e-mailing it to a few e-mail accounts before sending the full distribution. Use the test to check the formatting and to be sure the links all work.

- ✔ **Send the newsletter in batches if your distribution list is large.** By sending a portion of the list each day over, say, a weeklong period, you can better manage the responding e-mails and phone calls.

Building and protecting your opt-in newsletter e-mail list

Don't send unsolicited newsletters, ever. Instead, take the time to inform people about your newsletter and invite them to become free subscribers. See the "Opt-in e-mail" section in Chapter 13 and follow these guidelines as you build your electronic mailing list:

- ✔ Make it easy to sign up.

- ✔ Follow each subscription with a reply message that welcomes the subscriber, describes the purpose and frequency of the newsletter, and provides an easy way for the recipient to confirm interest or unsubscribe.

- ✔ Don't reveal the names on your distribution list. Your software should allow you to send bulk e-mails so that each recipient can't see who else is on the same list.

Converting Business Material to Marketing Opportunity

For all the money that small businesses spend on marketing, they often look right past the free opportunities that exist to coattail marketing messages onto their own business materials.

Following are several tactics that deliver excellent return on their almost nonexistent investments.

Using your packages as advertising vehicles

Every time you package a product for a customer, you're creating a vehicle that can give your marketing message a free ride. You'll incur practically no cost when you add an on-pack or in-pack advertising message that's certain to reach a valid prospect, because the recipient has already made a purchase.

Manufacturers can affix or print ads right onto product cartons, or they can enclose materials in the box to invite the purchase of accessories, warranties, service programs, or other offers.

Retailers might drop into each shopping bag a tasteful invitation to join a frequent customer club, to request automatic delivery of future orders, or to receive a special offer on a future purchase (called a *bounce-back offer* because it aims to bounce a customer back into your business). For example, a pool or hot tub chemical supply company could enclose a flier offering a monthly service program, automatic twice-a-year chemical delivery, or an annual maintenance visit. A shop that sells infant and toddler clothes could enclose a form inviting participation in a baby shower registry program.

Building business with gift certificates

It's astonishing how many small businesses make a gift certificate request seem like an inconvenience, when actually it is the sincerest form of customer compliment. If someone wants to give your business as a gift, roll out the red carpet. Here's how:

- ✔ **Create a gift certificate form.** This form can convey the details of the gift while also enhancing the gift's perceived value simply by its creative presentation. Use quality paper, a professional design that matches your company image, and a look that is appropriate to the nature of your business offering.

- ✔ **Deliver it to the buyer in an envelope or a gift box.** The gift certificate buyer is a current customer making an effort to bring a new person into your business. Reward the effort with a package that flatters both the gift giver and your business.

- ✔ **Keep track of the names of both the gift buyer and the gift recipient.**

- ✔ **When the gift is redeemed, be in touch with both parties.** Reinforce your relationship with the gift buyer by sharing that the certificate was redeemed and that you and your staff were flattered by the gift choice. Send a separate mailing to the gift recipient, welcoming that person to your business and enclosing an offer, perhaps an invitation to a free subscription to your newsletter, a special new customer invitation, a frequent-shopper club membership, or some other reason for the person to become a loyal customer of your business.

- ✔ **If the deadline is nearing on an unredeemed certificate, contact the gift recipient.** Offer a short extension or invite a phone or online order to build goodwill rather than let the certificate lapse.

Papering the market with business cards

Even the highest-quality business cards cost only a few cents each. You'll be hard-pressed to find a more economical way to get your name and brand image into your marketplace.

To create a business card that makes a quality statement for your business, use a professional design, careful type selection, quality paper, good printing, a good straight cut (nothing looks cheaper than a card with a crooked cut), and good ink colors. Unless you're certain of their design talents, don't ask staff members or quick-print shop designers to create your card. Invest a few hours with a graphic designer to achieve a distinctive, professional design that enhances your company image.

Be sure that the card features your business name and logo, your phone number and contact information in a type size that can be easily read, and either a slogan or tag line or a short list of your business offerings.

Use your cards liberally, following these tips:

- **Print a supply of business card *masters*.** These can be quickly imprinted with the names and titles of new or promoted staff members. Doing this isn't necessary if you have an inexpensive single-color card, but if you invest in specialized ink colors, embossing, or foil stamping, print a large supply all at once, dramatically reducing your unit cost as a result. Leave the excess supply uncut and in storage at the print shop, to be imprinted in small quantities as needed.

- **Give a stack of cards to every employee.** First of all, it's great for staff morale. Second, employees can use their cards to introduce your business to their friends as well as to their business contacts, and you'll reap the cost of the cards many times over.

- **Consider printing a map to your business on the back of your card.** Maps are especially important if you're an out-of-the-way retailer or a service business with drop-in clients.

- **Add value to your card by imprinting the flip side with useful information related to your business.** For example, a mailing service company might include a schedule of postal rates. A retail outlet or visitor attraction might print open hours. A fine-dining restaurant might imprint the dates of the current year's holidays, so patrons won't forget Mother's Day, Father's Day, and even local events such as the high school proms or regional festivals.

If you print both sides of your card, keep the most pertinent information — your logo, name, title, and contact information — on the front. Many people keep business cards in files in which only the front side is visible.

Weighing the Benefits of Advertising Specialties

Advertising specialties are ubiquitous little mind-joggers for your business. They include a wide range of giveaways including pens, pencils, refrigerator magnets, mouse pads, matchbooks, notepads, paperweights, pocketknives, calendars, calculators, T-shirts, golf towels, and a long list of other items that can be printed, engraved, embossed, or emblazoned with a business logo.

They're also called *tsotchkes* or *SWAGs,* which stands for "Souvenirs, Wearables, and Gifts," or (to trade show attendees) "Stuff We All Get."

Most specialty advertising items are cheap — and often they look it. Before investing in an advertising specialty, consider the following advice:

- Select only items that relate to your business and that are capable of advancing a reminder of the benefits you offer.

- Choose items that your prospective customers will want or need and things that they will notice, pick up, and keep for at least a short time.

- Opt only for items that will add to — and not detract from — your business image.

- Decide how you will feature your name on the item. The more exclusive your clientele and offering, the more discreet you'll want to make your name. If the item is targeted for prospects or clients who value quality and exclusivity, present your name so that it is subtle and scaled to the item rather than in a gaudy design that monopolizes the item and assures its quick trip to the trash can.

- Know how you'll distribute the items before you place an order for advertising specialties.

For information on ordering from the unbelievably wide range of specialties available, start in the Yellow Pages, looking under *Ad Specialties* or *Promotional Products.*

Choosing and Using Trade Shows

Trade shows are industry gatherings that bring together businesses, suppliers, customers, and media representatives in a given field for a daylong or multi-day extravaganza of selling, socializing, entertaining, product previewing, and competitive sleuthing.

Attendance at trade shows is a great way to maintain customer contacts, introduce products to your business, develop and maintain media relations, and stay on top of industry and competitive developments. The only drawback — and it's a big one — is that even in the most targeted industry, you have a lineup of trade shows from which to choose.

Because attendance at even one show costs a significant amount of time, money, and energy, invest cautiously, using this checklist:

- Choose shows carefully. Track the number of presenters and attendees over recent years (if the number is going up, it probably indicates a well-regarded show). Also see if leading media outlets are among the sponsors, another indication of the show's reputation.

✔ Decide whether you need to invest in a booth or whether you can achieve visibility by buying an ad in the show guide, making a presentation, hosting a reception, or simply working the floor.

✔ If you host a booth, know whom you want to attract to your booth, what you want to communicate, and what action you want to inspire.

✔ Know how you will capture trade show visitor information and how you will follow up with your trade show contacts.

Table 14-1 offers suggestions to guide your trade show planning.

Table 14-1	Trade Show Do's and Don'ts
Do	*Don't*
Do prospect before the show, using personal letters, direct mailers, and phone calls to invite and encourage prospects to visit your booth.	Don't count on prospects to seek you out or even to find you on their own. Big shows, especially, simply have too many distractions.
Do arrive at the show with preset appointments for meetings with your top-choice media reps, journalists, customer prospects, and vendors.	Don't expect to simply catch time with key contacts at the show. Take the time in advance to introduce yourself and establish scheduled appointments.
Do use your staff well. Be sure they wear business identification or, better yet, logo shirts or uniforms. Have a staffing schedule that lets you present with your best presenters, turning other team members loose to meet with suppliers and do competitive research.	Don't let your whole team hang out in your show booth — it gives the impression of a dull spot. Aim instead to have ongoing client or media meetings underway, a greeter visiting with passersby in the entry area, and other staff members out working the show.
Do have moderately priced handouts and logo items available for distribution, along with a means for collecting prospect names for follow-up. After the show, send a thoughtful letter and gift to prospects who were serious enough to complete a short form to qualify their interest.	Don't set up for "trick-or-treaters." You don't have to give something to every visitor, and you shouldn't waste money (or weight down your prospects) by giving out expensive or heavy literature or catalogs at the show. They'll appreciate the information more if it arrives by mail.

Do	Don't
Do invest in a professionally designed booth that reflects your business image, your advertising, and your current message.	Don't try to do it cheap by using a self-designed booth plan and do-it-yourself graphics.
Do use lights, banners, moving displays, bright colors, floor carpeting, and counters to break your booth into parts, and other devices to draw attention and make your booth look like a hub of activity.	Don't be bland and don't expect a banner with your logo to double as a booth design. You need huge colorful photos, ad enlargements, and graphics that shout *New!* to passersby.

Building Sales through Promotions

A promotion aims to increase sales over a short time period by offering an incentive that prompts consumers to take immediate action.

Businesses stage promotions for a number of reasons, such as

- ✔ To increase activity by existing customers.
- ✔ To entice the attention of new customer prospects.
- ✔ To urge customers to adopt new buying patterns, such as greater dollar volume per transaction, more frequent purchases, or purchases via a certain payment method.
- ✔ To stimulate sales during slow seasons by offering limited-time special pricing or added-value offers.

Choosing your promotion incentive

The whole purpose of a promotion is to create a desired consumer action over a short period of time. The objective is accomplished by offering one of the following types of action incentives:

- ✔ **Price savings:** Incentives include percentage discounts, two-for-one offers, buy-one-get-one-free deals, and other appealing reductions. The bigger the incentive, the more attractive to the consumer, of course. But be careful to come up with an offer that can inspire customers without giving your store away.

✔ **Samples:** Businesses introducing new products or trying to win over competitors' customers offer samples or free trials to prove their advantage and get their products into circulation. First, be sure that your product will show well in comparative tests. Second, accompany the sample with a bounce-back offer that prompts the customer to make an after-sample purchase or to take a follow-up action (for example, subscribing to your newsletter) to cement the new relationship.

✔ **Events and experiences:** Events draw crowds, spurring increased sales and sometimes even attracting media coverage. (See Chapter 15 for advice on getting your business information to the media.)

✔ **Coupons and rebates:** A *coupon* provides an offer that a customer can redeem at the time of purchase. A *rebate* provides an offer that a customer can redeem following the purchase, usually by filling out and sending in a form. Fewer than 2 percent of coupons in circulation are ever redeemed, and yet coupons remain a popular promotion staple. They catch reader attention when placed in ads, and they provide a measurable way to reward customers with price reductions. When using coupons, protect your profitability through small-print advisories stating expiration dates and that the coupon *is not valid with other special offers.*

Promotions are especially important to restaurants, hotels, retailers, and consumer product businesses. They are less appropriate for service professionals or for business-to-business marketers who may lose a degree of esteem and dignity by sending out pricing or other buying incentives.

Staging cross-promotions and cooperative promotions

Promotions benefit from critical mass — which is why businesses team up to participate in cooperative promotions or cross-promotions that bring together the media budgets, consumer incentives, customer corps, and staff energy of not one but two or several businesses or organizations.

Before forming a promotional partnership, be sure you can answer yes to the following questions:

✔ Do your businesses operate without directly competing with each other?

✔ Do your businesses serve customers with the same or very similar profiles?

✔ Are your businesses equally respected by your customers?

✔ Do you trust the management of the partnering company?

✔ Have you put the strategy, budget, timeline, and fiscal responsibilities in writing, and have all parties agreed to the responsibilities?

✔ Can you explain the promotion in a sentence that will make sense to and motivate consumers — and do all parties agree to the description?

Promotion planning checklist

When staging a promotion, know your objective in advance, including exactly the end you're working to achieve and how you will measure success. Use the following checklist as you make your plans:

✔ **Know the target market that you intend to influence with the promotion.**

✔ **Know what incentive you'll offer and be sure that it is capable of motivating your target prospect.**

✔ **Inform your staff.** Nothing is worse for a consumer than to arrive at what was billed as a promotional event only to learn that no one at the host business seems to know anything about it.

Keep the promotion description simple. If you can't explain the promotion and the incentive in a single sentence, the idea almost certainly won't fly.

Chapter 15

Public Relations and Publicity

In This Chapter

▶ Generating publicity

▶ Writing, distributing, and following up on news releases

▶ Preparing for media interviews

▶ Staging news conferences

▶ Handling crisis communications

*L*et's smash two notions right up front:

First, public relations is not simply whitewashing.

Second, publicity is not free advertising.

Whew! That was quick. With those two misconceptions out of the way, count on this chapter to confirm what public relations *is,* what publicity *is,* and how you can use each of them to increase your company's visibility, supplement and reinforce your advertising, and enhance your reputation in your market and industry.

If you wait to launch a public relations program until you face an image problem, you will have waited too long. Use public relations and publicity to *enhance* your image, not to right a wrong or fix an image disaster.

The following pages tell you how.

The Relationship between Publicity and Public Relations

The same people who think *marketing* is a dressed-up word for *sales* will tell you that public relations is a way to get publicity — and that publicity is a way to get free media coverage. That's like saying fashion is about hem lengths. There's a shard of truth in there, but it's hardly the full story.

The wide-angle view of public relations

The Public Relations Society of America defines *public relations* as activities that "help an organization and its public adapt mutually to each other."

Other professionals say that public relations involves activities that aim to establish, maintain, and improve a favorable relationship with the public upon whom an organization's success depends.

In *Small Business Marketing For Dummies* terms, public relations means doing the right thing and then talking about it — using publicity and other nonpaid communication opportunities to inform those whose positive opinions favorably impact your business.

The field of public relations consists of the following:

- **Media relations:** Establish editorial contacts, distribute news releases and story ideas, and become a reliable and trustworthy news source. Publicity is part of media relations, and media relations are part of — but not all of — public relations, as this list aims to prove.

- **Employee or member relations:** Use newsletters, meetings, events, and programs to develop communications and rapport with internal audiences and to demonstrate that your company's interest in doing the right thing starts at home.

- **Community relations:** Build ties to your local market area by joining groups, serving on boards, spearheading charitable endeavors, and donating time, products, services, or funds to support projects that benefit your community. As you undertake efforts for community causes, above all do so because you believe in the cause. Second, do it because you and your business benefit by the association and from the visibility you receive as a good community citizen.

- **Industry relations:** Join industry associations, attend industry events, and serve as an officeholder in groups that represents your business arena. A strong industry role keeps your business in the forefront and establishes your credibility with consumers and editorial contacts.

- **Government relations:** Build relationships with elected officials. Acquaint them with your company so they have a favorable impression should they be asked to comment on your business or should you need their help in the future. (Just as with bankers, it's good to make friends with politicians long before you need to enlist their help.)

✔ **Issues and crisis management:** Sometimes your news will be confusing, and once in a while, it may even threaten your image. One function of public relations is to explain and build support for complex issues and to manage crises when they arise.

Focusing on publicity

When you get mentioned in the media, that's *publicity.* It sounds so simple, and yet a surprising amount of planning and effort goes on behind the scenes before a company gets a "free" mention in a newspaper or magazine, a television or radio station, online, or even in another company's newsletter.

Those who spend much time generating publicity know that *valuable* is a much more appropriate descriptor than *free.* Costs are involved to develop news releases, make and maintain media contacts, stage events, and implement programs worthy of editorial coverage. But when the effort results in editorial coverage for your business, the benefit outweighs the investment many times over.

Each time you succeed in generating positive publicity, you score a triple victory. First, you win valuable editorial mentions in mass media vehicles. Second, you win consumer confidence, as people tend to find information they receive through the editorial content of mass media more believable than they find paid advertising messages. And third, you can use reprints of the coverage you obtain through your publicity efforts to add credibility to your other marketing communications by enclosing copies in direct mailings, sales presentations, and press kits.

Orchestrating Media Coverage

To generate publicity, start with a news item of interest. If an editor thinks his audience won't care about your story, it will never make it into print or onto the airwaves. But if your story conveys timely and useful information — if it tells something new, or a different or easier way to do something — then package it up and get it to the media, applying the process described in this chapter. Be prepared to proceed with both tenacity and patience, however, because the art of getting your name into the news requires both.

Getting real with your expectations

The fable about the oil driller who tossed in the towel just feet before reaching liquid gold is a good analogy for what most small businesses term their *failed publicity programs.* They send out five, maybe even ten, news releases, nothing happens, and they quit — disappointed and without a clue of how close they came to achieving the result they so badly desired.

To generate publicity for your business, commit to a long-haul program and keep the following in mind:

- ✓ **Don't expect instant or even consistent results.** Most news releases never make it into the media. Don't expect to bat 1.000, or .500, or even .250.

- ✓ **Tailor your story to individual editorial contacts.** Universal news releases — the same exact releases sent to all media — are less apt to be picked up than releases that are customized to specific audiences and news vehicles.

- ✓ **Don't try to get news coverage as a perk for your advertising investments.** To obtain news coverage, submit newsworthy information and avoid anything that smacks of editorial arm-twisting. Your advertising investment will help your publicity effort only in that it will pave the way by building awareness, so that when your release arrives, your editorial contacts will be familiar with your name and brand.

- ✓ **Don't peddle hype as news.** If the focus of your story is why you think your product is better than that of a competitor, that's hype. But if your story announces a major change of importance to the public, that's news. Newsworthy releases announce financial results, special events, awards given or received, staffing or management changes, reactions to legal or financial difficulties (see "Dealing with bad news" later in this chapter), and announcements of new products, technology, or industry updates.

- ✓ **Don't hound the media.** Never demand an explanation for why a release hasn't run. If you are concerned that your releases are being ignored, buy an hour or two of a publicist's time to receive a professional assessment of your efforts and to obtain guidance for presenting your news in the future. Also see the section on "Establishing media contacts" for help in establishing editorial relationships.

- ✓ **Aim for quality — not quantity.** Don't try to get publicity by papering the world with releases and don't write releases that are even one sentence longer than they need to be. Send releases only when you have news of interest to readers or viewers. Keep each release hype-free and to the point. Follow a standard or electronic news release format (see the following sections), and get it right in terms of grammar and typing.

Circulating your news

There are three main ways to circulate your news:

- **Distribute it yourself.** You can deliver news releases by hand, mail, fax, or e-mail. Mail delivery is still a widely used distribution approach, but, especially for time-sensitive news, the more immediate options win hands-down. Before faxing or e-mailing (see the following section for advice), call the assignment or story editor to obtain instructions. The extra effort will increase the chances that your release will reach and be read by your editorial contact.

- **Hire a public relations firm.** You can hire professionals to distribute your news to a select media list or, if your story has broad-reaching market impact, to appropriate wire services and the Associated Press.

- **Use a news distribution service.** Business Wire (www.businesswire.com) uses electronic services for simultaneous release of time-sensitive material to newspapers, magazines, news bureaus, television and radio stations, online networks, and investment and research departments in the business and financial world. PR Newswire (www.prnewswire.com) provides the same service but isn't limited to business press.

In addition to media distribution, leverage your news release by using it in the following ways:

- Post your release on your Web site.

- Distribute your release to those of influence to your business, including clients and those in a position to refer business your way.

- Post it within your company. Employees should never have to learn their own company's news through the media.

Writing news releases

News releases summarize stories appropriate for coverage in the editorial portion of news media. They are the main tool used in the effort to generate publicity. News releases are also called *press releases,* but with the ever-growing impact of broadcast and Internet news, the term *news release* provides a more appropriate and all-encompassing label.

News releases for delivery by mail or fax

News releases that are mailed, faxed, or hand-delivered to media follow a standard format as described in the following list and illustrated in Figure 15-1.

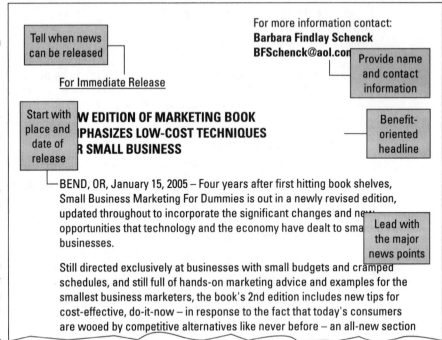

Figure 15-1:
This sample shows a standard format for news releases that are mailed, faxed, or hand delivered to media. Electronic releases differ slightly, as explained in this chapter.

The hard-copy, printed release is still considered the standard format, although increasingly news is submitted electronically using e-mail, as described in the following section.

Develop your release by first deciding on an *angle* from which to present your news. This involves deciding what makes the facts you are sharing timely, interesting, and worthy of media interest. Often the same news will be presented from a number of different angles — one for the local media, one for distant or national media, one for industry media, and so on.

Once you know your angle, begin writing your release in this order:

- ✔ **Whom to contact for more information:** At the top of your release, include the name of a knowledgeable person who can be contacted for information, along with a telephone number for reaching that person directly and without any time-consuming voice mail interfaces.

- ✔ **When the news can be released:** In rare cases, releases are sent with a line describing an *embargo*, or an instruction not to release the news until a certain date or time. Embargoes are unnecessary for all but the most sensitive news announcements, which probably require the help of a publicity pro. Instead, notify the media that the news is *For Immediate Release* by typing those words above your headline.

- ✔ **A headline:** Your headline should be active (in other words, it should include a verb), succinct (it should fit on no more than two lines), and benefit-oriented (it should tell what's in the news for the media audience — not what's in it for you).

- ✔ **A dateline:** The meat of the news release begins with the name of the city and the abbreviation of the state from which the release originated, followed by the date the release was issued.

- ✔ **Clear presentation of the facts:** Journalism 101 prevails in news release writing. Tell who, what, where, when, why, and how (called the *five Ws plus how*) in what is known as an *inverted pyramid* style. Here's what that means: Tell your news in the first sentence and pack your most important supporting facts into the first few paragraphs. This allows an editor to chop the entire end portion, if necessary to save space, and still retain the vital information.

- ✔ **Quotes:** Simple announcements don't require quotes, but if your news benefits from meaningful comments from top management or credible customers or industry leaders, include and clearly identify the sources for one or two quotes.

- ✔ **Boilerplate information:** End your release with a short paragraph, called a *boilerplate,* that summarizes information about your company. This paragraph should tell your business name, what your business does, a few points about how your business is unique, a line about your history (when your business was founded, your ownership, and other key facts), and a few words about the size and scope of your business. A release from a fictional private school might end with the following paragraph:

  Amazing Preparatory School is a private academy graduating 100 college-bound students annually. Founded in 1975, the school is located on the grounds of the historic Smith Estate, where students from throughout the world live in dormitories or commute from the nearby metropolitan area. The school is a member of the Private Schools Association and the International Study Institute.

- ✔ **No more than two pages:** Print your news release on 8½-x-11-inch white paper. (Advice for electronic news releases follows.) Use wide margins and one-and-a-half or double-spacing. If your news runs more than one page, don't print both sides of the same sheet, as editors frequently tear off and forward only the first part of the release for production. Type the word *More* at the bottom of the page if the release continues on and start the next page by identifying the release in the top left-hand corner (for example, *Small Business Marketing For Dummies, Page 2*). Following the final sentence of your release, center three pound symbols (# # #) to indicate that the release has ended.

  ✔ **Supporting materials:** Include only news in your release. Then attach separate fact sheets to detail price and availability information, lists of features, company background summaries, and frequently asked questions and answers. But don't go overboard. Attach only information that will assist the editorial staff in compiling a story.

  ✔ **Graphics:** When submitting news by mail or hand delivery, enclose photos in the form of prints, slides, or on disk. For prints, submit in a 5-x-7-inch or 8-x-10-inch glossy format. For illustrations, charts, or other artwork, submit camera-ready, black-and-white reproductions (this means first-generation, high-contrast reproductions on bright white paper). Accompany graphics with clearly labeled captions.

As you write news releases, test them against the information in Table 15-1.

Table 15-1	Spotting the Good and Bad in News Releases
Attributes of Releases That Get Results	*Attributes of Releases That Get Tossed Out*
Feature timely news about your products or services, your staff, recent legal or legislative actions, industry changes, or other items of interest to the public.	Contain promotional messages, recycled stories that have already been covered by competing news media, or self-serving puff pieces.
Are customized messages tailored to the audience of a specific news vehicle, often accompanied by a brief note written to an established editorial contact.	Are blanket mailings that relay the same exact news to competing media with no unique angle, no offer for interviews, or no other ways to customize the story.
Contain crisp, clear, accurate, and factual language.	Rely on superlatives (biggest, brightest, strongest, and so on), opinions, and hype.
Describe benefits to the reader or viewer.	Emphasize product features rather than benefits and use insider terminology.
Make a clear point regarding why the news is important and how and when readers or viewers can take action.	Fail to answer the fundamental question, "Who cares?"
Use management quotes plus quotes from customers and industry leaders.	Fail to make a clear point about how the news impacts your industry, your business, or especially your market.
Are intriguing and believable.	Are boastful or stretch the bounds of credibility.

Sending releases electronically

E-mailing news releases is immediate and cost-efficient. It's also effective — *if* you take a few extra steps first.

First, check media Web sites to learn news submission preferences and to obtain editorial e-mail addresses. *Or* call the assignments editor at your target media outlet, or better yet, the editor of the section in which you hope your news will appear.

Explain that you have a news release you believe will be of interest and ask if the editor prefers to receive submissions by e-mail. It's likely that the editor will ask the nature of your news, in part to provide accurate delivery directions, so be ready with a one-sentence answer.

If the editor prefers electronic delivery, confirm the e-mail address. Also ask whether the editor prefers the release as an attachment or typed right into the e-mail message box. Don't make assumptions. Most editors won't open attachments, so never send them unless requested.

If the editor requests your news as an attached file, you can simply e-mail your standard news release document.

If not, prepare your news in an e-mail message following these guidelines:

- ✔ **Type your subject line** in uppercase and lowercase, presenting a succinct headline for your release content. For example, *Hometown Landscaping: Hosts Free Pond and Waterfall Workshop.*

- ✔ **Write and send your e-mail in plain text.** Don't use HTML or other markup languages, as they can reduce the readability of your news when it reaches other networks.

- ✔ **Include the following items:**

  - Start your message with the words *FOR IMMEDIATE RELEASE.*

  - Double-space and then type your headline in uppercase and lowercase, keeping it to one line if you can, or two lines at the most.

  - Double-space after the headline and then type the name of the city and the abbreviation for the state from which the news release originates, followed by a dash, and then the month, day, and year of the release.

  - Type another dash after the city, state, and date line, and begin typing your release, following instructions for standard releases but single-spacing within each paragraph and editing content down to 500 words or fewer.

- End the body of your release with instructions *For additional information* or, if appropriate, *To schedule interviews* or *For demonstrations,* or whatever other next step you think editors might be willing to take to cover your story.

- End your release with company background information (see "Boilerplate information" in the preceding section).

- Close your e-mail with your contact information, in this format:

  CONTACT INFORMATION:

  Contact Person's Name

  Company Name

  Phone Number with Area Code

  Contact Person's E-mail Address

  URL for Your Company Web Site

✔ Don't attach files unless the reporter or editor specifically instructs you to do so. And don't attach photos or artwork unless requested. (See the nearby sidebar "Preparing and submitting artwork digitally.") Instead, include a link to your Web site where high-definition artwork is available.

✔ Print a copy of your e-mail release so that you have a reference copy handy when editors follow up to request additional information.

Establishing media contacts

Create a list of media contacts that serve your geographic and industry arena, including the following outlets:

✔ **Your local daily newspaper:** In making contacts, keep in mind that general and "hot" news goes to the city or news desk. News that relates to feature sections of the paper — sports, home, business, entertainment, and so on — goes straight to the department editors. Study the paper or go to the paper's Web site to see which reporters cover which beats — education, small business, and technology, for instance. Call the person who covers your field to learn whether you should deliver releases to the news desk, the section editor, or directly to the beat reporter.

✔ **Regional weekly and business publications:** Study back issues and media kits to familiarize yourself with the standing columns and upcoming special focus topics. Think about angles for stories that you can discuss with the editor. Then call to introduce yourself and discuss ways that you can assist in providing information for news stories.

✔ **The radio and television stations that broadcast in your area:** Include those in adjacent cities whose signals come in via cable.

> ✔ **Your industry publications:** Make a list and then find out the names of the writers who cover the kind of news you generate and include them on your news release distribution list. Begin by looking at the magazine's *masthead,* which is the editorial staff listing that's normally listed on one of the early pages of each issue.

Preparing and submitting artwork digitally

Increasingly, newspapers emphasize art in their page designs. They need good images to accompany stories, which presents a great opportunity for businesses that submit photos or graphics in easily usable formats.

Follow these steps as you make digital art submissions:

✔ Start with a clear, well-exposed image that has good composition, good focus, and interesting subject matter.

✔ Submit an image that is at least the size you hope it is going to run in the paper or, better yet, the size the editor has requested. Most newspaper columns are approximately 2 inches wide, so if the photo is to run 2 columns wide, for instance, you'd want to submit an image that has a width of at least 4 inches.

✔ Prepare your photo or art for adequate digital resolution before sending. Nearly any paper can use your image if it is submitted at a resolution of 250–300 PPI, which means pixels per inch. (You'll also hear the term DPI, which means dots per inch.)

✔ Obtain permission to submit artwork before attaching your file to an e-mail message. When writing the e-mail, type your caption into the subject line (for example, Photo: *Small Business Marketing For Dummies* book cover). In the message box, type your cutline, which is a detailed description of the photo or artwork. If your photo includes people, include in the cutline the complete names of all people who are recognizable. (Keep in mind that photos featuring groups of more than four are rarely used.) Close your e-mail with your name and contact information.

✔ Most papers can receive your image if you compress and send it in JPEG format. Even compressed, however, the file may exceed the size allowed by your e-mail provider. Check your system capacity before sending. If it is inadequate, locate a different system or burn the file to a disk and send it by overnight delivery.

✔ Transmit your image in RGB (Red, Green, Blue) color format if possible. Most images originate in RGB; it is the most common color mode for viewing digital images on-screen and the default setting in photo software.

✔ If you are submitting a digital photo, change the filename designated by the camera (which is probably something like DSCN0015. JPG) before submitting. Do this by bringing the image up on your computer monitor and using the Rename file function to change the filename from the default to your photo caption.

✔ One last step: Be patient. Your image may not be used this time, but if you are a good, reliable source, in time your efforts will pay off. Keep at it!

As you compile your media contact list, count on the resources of your local library. The reference desk should have copies of the *Bacon's Publicity Checker* and *Bacon's Radio/TV Directory,* which provide information on editorial contacts at U.S., Canadian, Mexican, and Caribbean media outlets.

Maintaining media relationships

Before e-mailing your first news release, call editorial contacts to introduce yourself. Or, if you're sending your release by mail, attach a note explaining that along with your release you're enclosing a kit of information about your business and that you stand by to answer questions or to be a resource whenever you can be of assistance. After the first contact, earn a reputation as a business that sends only newsworthy releases, passing on any item that isn't timely, doesn't announce a major milestone, or has no unique angle or hook.

Other advice: Be a good source and make yourself available to the media. Alert those who answer the phone to route media calls to you immediately. If you aren't the owner or president of your organization, do all that you can do to get the top person to be available as well. Nothing is more damaging to your efforts than to have the most powerful person in your company say "No comment" or refuse to be interviewed by news writers when they call.

Promptly return media calls and be sensitive to deadlines. Don't call near deadline and don't take more time than you need. Offer to e-mail or fax summaries of lengthy or complex material.

Finally, always assume that you're on the record. See the following section, "Managing media interviews," for more information on this topic.

Managing media interviews

When you hit the publicity jackpot and a reporter calls for an interview, be ready!

Before the interview

Get the details. In advance of the interview, confirm the publication or station name and deadline, along with the interview topic, the angle of the story, and the type of questions you will be asked. Ask whether others will be interviewed for the same story. This will give you an indication of the nature of the story and allow you to prepare your remarks accordingly.

Then take time to prepare yourself. Unless the reporter is on a deadline or calling in response to a release that you put out (in which case you should have talking points prepared and by your phone), buy a couple of minutes' time by asking if you can wind up a meeting or project before returning the call — and then do so, preferably within a half hour. But before hanging up, ask whether the reporter has specific questions in mind so that you can have information available when you call back.

Once you know the scope of the interview, jot down the two or three most important ideas that you want to convey about the topic. Grab any appropriate reference materials that will help you make your points clearly. Consider negative issues that might arise and develop short responses. And think about what photos, charts, industry statistics, or other materials you'd like to offer to the reporter to enhance the coverage.

During the interview

Proceed with confidence — and caution — during media interviews. Answer questions clearly and then stop talking. If you try to fill time with additional comments, you run the risk of saying something you don't want to see in print or hear on-air. Follow this list of advice and warnings:

- ✔ Do ask how much time the reporter has scheduled for the interview. Then watch your clock and make all important points within the allotted time.

- ✔ Do admit that you don't know an answer rather than make a guess. And if you can't disclose information due to legal or regulatory reasons, say so. Avoid saying *no comment,* which tends to taint the words of even the most credible news source.

- ✔ Do speak slowly and in clear terms and take the time to explain your point if the reporter seems confused.

- ✔ Do make your most important points in the beginning and again at the end of the interview.

- ✔ Do keep your comments brief so that they make good quotes.

- ✔ Do confirm the spelling and pronunciation of your name and business name, your title, and other vital information.

- ✔ Don't respond if you don't know the answer. Or, if the answer should be provided by a more qualified person such as a legal or financial professional, say so and provide that person's name and number.

- ✔ Don't say anything you don't want to read or hear later. You can ask not to be quoted by stating that your comments are *not for attribution,* and you can say that a comment is *off the record.* But there are no guarantees. The best idea is to bite your tongue before saying anything negative or potentially harmful or embarrassing.

- ✔ Don't take a jab at the competition.

- ✔ Don't pick a fight with the reporter.

- ✔ Don't stonewall. If a negative issue arises, provide a brief answer. If you avoid the issue, the reporter is apt to follow up by talking to someone who is far less apt to protect your position.

✔ Don't mention your advertising investment in the reporter's publication or station unless the point is relevant to the news story — which likely it isn't.

✔ Don't let your guard down or assume the slant of the story.

✔ Don't swear or make colorful comments that you don't want to see in a large quote above your name.

✔ Don't try to fill silences. You're most apt to get yourself in trouble when you start rambling. Answer the question and then wait for the next one, unless you choose to use the idle time to advance one of the major points you want to make in the interview.

Following the interview

Following the interview, thank the reporter and ask when the article will run or air. Don't demand prior review of the story, but do offer to be available to assist in confirming any facts or quotes.

Realize that sometimes, even after interviews, stories get canceled or they don't run on the date you were told they would. Also realize that you may notice discrepancies between they way the story is worded and what you thought you said. Request corrections only for actual and important errors, not for differences of opinion or approach. Instead, look for a positive aspect of the coverage and highlight that point in a thank-you note to the reporter. Good words will get you further than nitpicking or criticizing.

Guidelines for broadcast interviews

In preparing for and conducting radio or television interviews, follow all the preceding interview advice and then add these items to your checklist:

✔ Ask whether the program will be live or taped. The good *and* bad news about live shows is that they can't be edited.

✔ Ask the name of the program and host and then watch the show to acquaint yourself with the style.

✔ Confirm the interview site and length. If the location is out of town, ask whether the studio pays transportation and lodging costs.

✔ Ask whether other guests will be part of the same show. If so, ask the producer who they are and what point of view they represent. The interviewer may be setting up a battleground — in which case, you'll want to arrive at the interview with a bulletproof strategy.

✔ Ask whether submitting a biography and list of possible discussion topics in advance would be helpful.

✔ Confirm the interview in writing.

✔ Try to visit with the host before tape rolls to relax a bit.

✔ For TV, avoid patterned clothes or jangly jewelry. Accept makeup assistance if it is offered.

✔ Acquaint yourself with the locations of the camera, microphones, and monitors, and, whenever you're in the studio, protect yourself by assuming that you're on-air.

✔ Think and speak in sound bites no longer than 20 seconds.

✔ On radio shows, use commercial breaks to learn from the host what topic you will discuss next.

✔ Avoid any effort to be promotional and don't hog the microphone.

✔ Smile, show confidence, and be thoughtful with your answers.

✔ Don't take notes, don't answer if you don't know, and don't hesitate to build a bridge to a point you want to make by tagging a statement such as *by the way* onto an answer.

Staging news conferences

Companies like the concept of news conferences a lot more than editors and reporters do. In fact, many media organizations, including many small-town newspapers and stations, simply won't attend ribbon-cutting and ground-breaking events, considering them promotional and easily described in simple news releases. Even the most newsworthy conference (in your view) can be eclipsed by late-breaking news. Stage a news conference only for a huge and time-sensitive announcement and only in the following cases:

✔ When important news should be announced simultaneously to all media.

✔ When news is best told in person, backed by displays, and followed by the chance for reporters to ask questions.

✔ When you are presenting important speakers or celebrities.

Watch your words

People pay a big price for attacking someone's reputation in the media. To stay out of trouble in media interviews, steer clear of negative opinions about others.

For the record, here are two terms you don't ever want to hear again:

✔ Libel: Printed statements that are untrue, defamatory, and harmful

✔ Slander: The verbal form of libel

Schedule and announce the news conferences well in advance. Send invitations in the form of brief letters or announcements that are formatted like news releases but with the words *Media Advisory* replacing the words *For Immediate Release.*

Here are some additional tips:

- ✔ Schedule the time with sensitivity to media deadlines. Most conferences start at 10:30 a.m. to best suit as many media schedules as possible.

- ✔ Start on time and hold speakers to their allotted schedules.

- ✔ Be sure that speakers can be seen and heard. Plan in advance to have a well-placed podium (situated with photo opportunities in mind), microphones, speakers, extension cords, and other supporting items.

- ✔ Place a company logo behind the speaker or on the front of the podium.

- ✔ Minimize speeches in favor of demonstrations that provide the basis for good photos and footage.

- ✔ Distribute news packets that feature a news release on the day's event, background company information, and the name and number of the spokesperson to contact for more information. Following the event, deliver packets to major media not in attendance.

Dealing with bad news

Chalk it up to bad decisions or just plain bad luck, but sometimes bad news happens. When it does, work fast to first find out what went wrong and to fix the problem if possible.

Waste no time preparing a news release telling what happened and, if possible, what actions are being taken to see that it won't happen again. As much as you'd like to run and hide, don't. Almost certainly your company will fare better if you show a concerned face and release a truthful explanation. The last thing you want is for those who care a lot less about your reputation than you do to be speculating or spinning the story for you.

Public relations strategists have complete scenarios to use in what are called *crisis communications.* If your event is apt to have negative ramifications that continue for more than a few days, and if the bad news seems likely to reach out farther than your local market area, call in a pro to help you manage the story. Look in the phone book under *Public Relations* or ask business leaders in your area for references.

Chapter 16

Tapping the Internet's Marketing Power

....

....

*T*oday — with the world sending 35 billion e-mails a day, the Internet hosting 10 million Web sites, and e-commerce ringing up retail and travel sales in the billions and growing steadily — it's hard to remember that the Internet didn't even enter business conversation until the mid-1990s, and back then most discussions ended with more questions than answers.

Well, here we are barely a decade later and the issue is no longer whether small businesses *should* dive into the field of online marketing, but rather, *how* they should plan and implement their online presence.

The issue is hot because small businesses are just beginning to tap the Internet's marketing power. Research shows that eight of ten small businesses have computers, and two-thirds have Internet access, yet only one-third have Web sites. If you're among those testing the air in cyberspace, this chapter defines the terms, weighs the opportunities, and outlines the steps to take to put the Internet to work for your business.

Who's Online and What Are They Doing?

Most forecasts project that during 2005 the number of people with Internet access worldwide will soar close to 1 billion.

- Users currently divide almost evenly between men and women and disperse into every age group from early teens up, with those 65+ showing the greatest usage increase.

- English is the official language of two-thirds of Web pages, but more than half of Web users are native speakers of languages other than English. Companies serving global markets increasingly view multilingual options on their sites as necessary rather than optional.

- Most users are sending e-mail, but they're also logging on to shop or to research products. They study options online before making purchases. Whether they buy online or make the purchase from a bricks-and-mortar establishment, if your business isn't one they can access via the Web, you may not make it onto their list for consideration.

- They're online for recreation and entertainment. (E-gambling is expected to rake in $15 billion annually by 2006.)

- They are informed consumers. They walk into doctors' offices, car dealerships, and other major decision-making situations armed with unprecedented levels of facts and figures. Be ready!

- They expect Web sites to deliver customer support and information with a high level of service. They want an easy and obvious way to contact your business (online *and* through your physical location) and they expect prompt inquiry responses.

Using the Internet with or without a Web Site

Most businesses equate using the Internet with building a Web site, but even without a site you can take advantage of opportunities to use e-mail, keep an eye on your competition, and connect with networks of business consultants and management resources, as described in the following sections.

Once you create a Web site, your opportunities expand even further. You can:

- Use your site like an extension of your business lobby. Increasingly, instead of walking into or phoning your business, your prospects meet you online. Design and use your site to make a good first impression with a clean look, efficient service, easy-to-access information, and quick response to prospect needs.

- Use your site the way you'd use a toll-free phone number. In the same way that ads and mailers traditionally sent prospects to a phone line, e-mail and ads now send people to the information-rich environment of your Web site.

- Use the Web as an advertising vehicle by getting your site ranked in search engines and directories and achieving links from other sites in an effort to drive new prospects to your business. (See the section titled "Driving Traffic to Your Site.")

- Use the Web to background and pre-sell prospects, job applicants, and suppliers, who frequently do a Web search to find your business online before pursuing a personal contact.

- Use your site to sell your products to current and new customers, as detailed in the sections titled "Advertising Online" and "Is E-Commerce Right for Your Business?"

Communicating via e-mail

Few small business owners need to be convinced that e-mail is a great way — and increasingly the preferred way — to communicate one-to-one or with many customers at the same time. And hitting Send is free, everyone's favorite price.

On the chance you don't yet have e-mail capability, here's all you need to do:

- **Contact an Internet Service Provider (ISP)** to arrange Internet access and set up an e-mail account. Your ISP doesn't need to be in your local area so long as you can access the Internet and your e-mail account using a local number or cable connection. Comparison shop. Begin with listings in the Yellow Pages under *Internet Access Providers*. Or use a computer at your local library to sign onto an ISP locator site such as www.ispfinder.com or www.thelist.com.

- **Establish your e-mail address,** preferably as part of your own domain name (see "Establishing Your Online Identity" later in this chapter). The Internet is a giant equalizer that allows small businesses to establish credibility by looking larger than they actually are, yet too many small businesses use e-mail addresses that give away the potential online advantage. Think about it: Which looks like a major company, yourname@hotmail.com or yourname@yourbusiinessname.com?

- **Establish a routine for checking and responding to e-mail.** People expect rapid e-mail response and will judge your customer service accordingly. For advice on writing e-mail and managing your company's e-mail impressions, see the "Online encounters" section in Chapter 6.

✔ **Use e-mail to send one-to-one or one-to-many messages**, which are the online equivalent of direct mail — but without the costs of printing and postage. See Chapter 13 for advice on sending opt-in versus *spam* or unsolicited junk e-mail. Then see Chapter 14 for information on publishing opt-in electronic newsletters — one of the most effective ways for building your mailing list and sending direct mail to your customers.

The language of cyberspace

The online world is evolutionary. With the constant debut of applications and opportunities comes a continuous string of new words and phrases. Here are definitions for key terms you're sure to hear in any online marketing discussion. Also, watch for the Technical Stuff icon in the margins throughout this chapter. It flags explanations for additional terms that apply to Internet usage.

✔ **The Internet, or Net:** The global network that links networks worldwide. The Internet allows users to send and receive e-mail and browse the World Wide Web.

✔ **World Wide Web, or Web:** The graphical, multimedia aspect of the Internet that uses *Hypertext Markup Language* (HTML) and browsing software to allow users from around the world to enter through a linked server and navigate the Internet by accessing and jumping between documents called Web pages.

✔ **Web page:** A document with its own address that is accessible through the World Wide Web. The address is called a *Universal Resource Locator* or URL. An example of a URL is www.dummies.com. The *http* part specifies which protocol the computer will use to access the document, and *www.dummies.com* is the address or domain name. Together they tell your computer how to find a Web page.

✔ **Web site:** A Web page or group of pages that contains text and graphics that can be accessed by anyone with an Internet connection. The *home page* is the site's first page.

✔ **E-mail:** Short for electronic mail, e-mail uses the Internet to send and receive computer-to-computer messages worldwide. E-mail is the main reason most people use the Internet, sending literally trillions of messages each year.

✔ **Browser:** Software used to access and display Web pages. Microsoft Internet Explorer, Mozilla Firefox, and Opera are commonly used browsers.

✔ **Search engine:** A program that allows Web users to search and access sites containing keywords or phrases. Each search engine keeps a catalog of millions of Web sites. Following a user request for information, the search engine returns lists of matching sites presented in order based upon the search engine's proprietary relevancy algorithms.

Keeping tabs on your competition

Go online as if you were a customer searching for services or products like the ones you sell. Find and monitor your competitors' sites in the same way that you watch the activities of bricks-and-mortar competitors to evaluate how they might impact your business. Here are some suggestions:

- ✔ Go to directory and search engine sites and enter combinations of words that people might use to define your offering. The results reveal the competitive options that prospects see when they shop on the Web.

- ✔ Look through publications that you know your customers read. Make note of Web site addresses in articles and ads and visit the sites to see how competitors are working to reach your customers online.

- ✔ Sign up for electronic newsletters offered on competitors' sites.

- ✔ Buy products online and rate your purchasing and delivery experience.

Accessing free business advice

The Web is rich with sites that can help you write business and marketing plans, address challenges faced by your business, hire employees, get legal advice, and find research and information to aid in business and marketing decisions. Start with the small business Web sites listed in the Appendix that follows Chapter 22. Each one is packed with advice and information, and each features links to dozens of other sites you'll find useful.

Putting a Web Site to Work

If you're trying to reach prospects outside your current market area, if you want to enhance customer service by offering 24-hour access for those wishing to place or track orders, if you want consumers to find the latest news about your business, then you're probably in the market for a Web site.

Follow these steps as you weigh the decision to launch a Web site:

- ✔ **Define how prospects and customers will use your site.** Will they want general information, answers to frequently asked questions, product details, the ability to request quotes or customer support, maps to your location, or other information? Will they want to buy online? Will job applicants want to apply online? The answers help determine how your site will work and what features it will need to include.

✔ **Define your goal for the site.** Determine your goal in terms of lead generation, online sales, customer support, or other expectations. This will help you weigh site development costs against the value you expect the site to deliver to your business.

✔ **Commit to the cost,** including site construction, hosting, and support.

✔ **Be ready to market your site.** Building a site is similar to opening a business. You need to commit to marketing for the investment to pay off. (See "Driving Traffic to Your Site" later in this chapter.)

Types of Web sites

Defining the purpose of a Web site is just like defining the purpose of any other business communication. You need to know whom you're trying to talk to, what people currently know or think about your business, what you *want* them to know or think, and, most of all, what action you want them to take after encountering this communication with your company.

Most Web sites fall into one of the following categories.

Contact and brochure sites

These are promotional sites that tell who you are and what you do.

Company Contact Sites: These are the easiest and most economical to create and maintain. They allow prospects, who increasingly seek business information through search engines or online local directories rather than through printed Yellow Page directories, to find your business on the Web.

A simple contact site includes your business name, a description of who you are and what you do, the products and services you offer, your open hours, and how to reach you online and at your physical location.

For online contact, provide your e-mail address or include a contact form on your site. The contact form is less convenient for users but protects your address from spam harvesters who collect addresses to use in ways you'd like to avoid.

Brochure Sites: Just like printed brochures, good online brochures educate prospects about your products and services in a way that convinces them that they want to do business with your company or at least that they would like to receive more information about becoming a customer. (See Chapter 14 for tips on writing brochures and other company materials.)

This type of site requires a design that incorporates your brand look (see Chapter 7) while delivering information that is clear and easy to access. Costs depend on the complexity of your design, amount of content, number of pages, and whether the site can be built using an existing template.

Support sites

Support sites provide online customer service and communication. They offer information about product installation, usage, and troubleshooting; share industry trends and product update news; and help customers put products to use. Sometimes support sites include e-commerce components as well.

If you're thinking of including support and training as a purpose of your Web site, begin by asking yourself the following questions:

- ✔ **Do your customers all seem to ask the same questions?** If so, a support site could provide this information in the form of a *frequently asked questions* (FAQ) page. But if your customers need a wide range of information, you may need a more customized service approach.

- ✔ **Do you have a great number of customers?** If so, a support site is apt to pay off. But if you have only a few big customers, the investment to build and maintain a support and training site may not make sense.

- ✔ **Will your customers go to a Web site?** Or will they continue to call you directly? Unless you believe they will embrace the Web site as their contact point, skip the cost of building support into your site.

- ✔ **Are you a reseller or a merchandiser of branded items?** If so, maybe you can simply send your customers to manufacturers' Web sites for support, therefore avoiding the cost of building one of your own.

- ✔ **Are you ready to commit to serving online customers?** Web users expect site content to be fresh and up-to-date, and they expect their online queries to prompt immediate response.

E-commerce sites

The primary purpose of an e-commerce site is to sell goods online. Site visitors can view products, make choices, place orders, and submit payment.

Building an e-commerce site is complicated because of the many features that must be included. Customers need to learn about your products, place orders, pay in a secure way, and submit customer information to allow delivery. Although software products assist with the task, e-commerce site creation falls outside the realm of the computer novice.

Price tags for professional creation depend on the technology and complexity involved. Before venturing into the arena, study the section titled "Is E-Commerce Right for Your Business?" later in this chapter.

Blogging 101

Blogs, short for *Web logs,* are online chronicles of news, ideas, facts, and opinions. They are part editorial, part journal, and part dialogue. Easy-to-use blogging software became available in 1999 and millions of blogs have been launched since, most by individuals, but a growing number by businesses who use them to share expertise and information with colleagues, suppliers, customers, and employees.

The topics of blogs vary widely, but all share common elements:

✓ **They are graphically simple sites** full of short entries or *posts* that are updated frequently and arranged chronologically with newest items listed first and most prominently.

✓ **They advance a distinct point of view** or focus on a particular interest area.

✓ **They use *RSS* (Really Simple Syndication) or other file formats** that allow one blog to distribute and share posted items with others, allowing third-party Web sites to post excerpts along with a link back to the originating site.

Before launching a blog, be sure you can commit to keeping content fresh by updating it daily or at least weekly, that you are set up to receive and respond to reader feedback, and that you are prepared to promote your blog through ongoing marketing efforts and by registering it with blog directories.

For a good overview on blogging basics, visit the Technorati Web site at `www.technorati.com/help/blogging101.html`.

For free step-by-step set-up assistance and instructions, visit the Google-owned Blogger Web site at `www.blogger.com/start`.

Building your site

Chapter 9 includes a section on "Hiring Help for Web Site Design." Unless you're a computer designer, turn to the pros for assistance in building a custom site for your business. This approach will cost you time and funds — that's the downside. The upside is that you'll end up with a site that conveys your unique brand image, with a viewing and navigation system precisely tailored to your unique business offering, all built on a platform that can grow with your business. Look in the Yellow Pages under *Internet Web Site Development* for names of consultants and site-building specialists.

Using site-building services

If you decide to create your own site, you can use templates provided by Internet hosting and site-development resources.

Yahoo! offers starter, standard, and professional site-building tools, along with domain name registry, e-mail addresses, and a hosting service for a low monthly fee (see Figure 16-1). For information, visit `http://smallbusiness.yahoo.com` and click on "Web Hosting."

Network Solutions also provides one-stop packaged services, starting with a free online site-building trial, followed by a free 30-day test drive. Go to `www.networksolutions.com/en_US/build-it/` for information.

Using Web site design and management services

If you don't have expertise to do the job yourself and you want a site that is more custom-tailored than the template solutions offered by site-building services, use the services of a Web site design and management company (see Figure 16-2). These companies offer site hosting and management along with development of a site uniquely designed for your business. To find a nearby firm, go to the *Internet Web Design Developers* section of the Yellow Pages for your hometown and the larger cities in your state.

Figure 16-1: Web hosting services such as Yahoo! provide economical packages to help small businesses launch Web sites.

Figure 16-2:
Web site design and management companies like Alpine Internet Solutions provide easy-to-run, quick-start, and uniquely tailored sites, along with site hosting and management services.

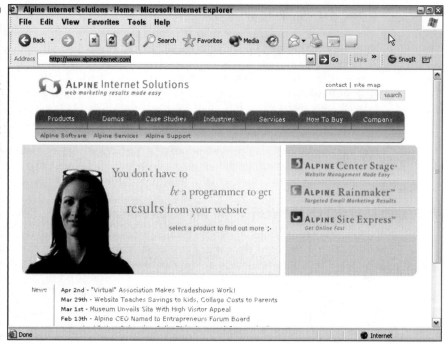

Center Stage is a registered trademark of Alpine Internet Solutions, Inc.

Using software tools

To build your own site, you need software and at least intermediate computer skills, as well as expertise using word processing or publishing software, a good knowledge of your operating system, and an eye for design.

Macromedia Dreamweaver, Adobe GoLive, Microsoft FrontPage, and Fireworker are a few of the most frequently used software tools. Before investing, get advice from the company that will host your site. Software resellers can also help you make a selection.

Using HTML to build your site

HTML is the code that underlies most Web pages and the common language of the Web. HTML tells your browser what's what in a Web page — what's a heading, where a picture goes, and everything else you see on your screen. Part of the appeal of the software tools and Web development solutions mentioned in previous sections is that they eliminate the need to learn HTML by building the code for you. If you do decide to use HTML, the bookstore or library offers plenty of titles to guide your effort, among them the different incarnations of Ed Tittel's *HTML For Dummies* (Wiley Publishing).

Creating content

Content is the term used to describe electronically delivered information. *Documents (copy), photos,* and *graphics* are all part of *content*.

Keywords are words or phrases that describe the content of your page. When people seek information online, they enter keywords into search engines. If the search request matches your keywords, your pages will appear in the search results. How high on the list your site appears is a topic unto itself. See "Optimizing your site for search engines," later in this chapter, for information.

As you prepare content, use the following guidelines:

- ✔ **Organize content by the page.** Rather than writing your site as a unit, think in modular terms. Focus each page on a single topic with unique keywords, which you should place in the headline and several times in the page copy. By using unique keywords on each page, you'll cast a broader net for catching Internet users seeking information under various keyword searches. Be aware, though, that this approach may send people not to your home page but to an internal page of your site. So that they aren't disoriented, be sure that each page carries clear identification for your company along with a link to your home page.

- ✔ **Limit your words.** Know what you want to communicate, prioritize your objectives, and keep your message to the point. Go for visibility over volume. Online, people demand clarity and easy of use.

- ✔ **Make it easy to skim.** Use short, bold headings, bullets, lists, or other devices to make your pages easy to scan.

- ✔ **Talk directly to your customer.** Use short paragraphs and sentences.

- ✔ **Make the visit worthwhile.** From the first moment users arrive, give them a reason to stay on your site. Use quotes, testimonials, headlines, graphics, or other quick-to-grasp methods to telegraph the message that they will find what they're looking for on your site.

If you write your own Web site content, ask someone who is good at editing *and* unfamiliar with the technicalities of your business to review your material. This will help eliminate jargon and keep content focused.

Site navigation

Navigation is the way users move around a Web site to find and access information. Sites use menu bars and colored or underlined text or icons to help users find and link to designated pages.

To help visitors get around your site, present them with clearly labeled selections. For example, labels such as *Technical Support, Our Products, Our Customers, News, Contact Us,* and *Frequently Asked Questions* tell people way more about what to expect than labels like *Features, Information, What People Are Saying* or other more ambiguous descriptions. Keep these tips in mind as you develop your site:

- ✔ Start with a home page that tells visitors exactly what you want them to know about your company — clearly and immediately.
- ✔ Let visitors jump from section to section with ease.
- ✔ Provide a link back to your home page from every page.
- ✔ Keep choices clear and to a minimum.
- ✔ Provide a site map so users can see how your site is organized.

Attributes of a good site

Good sites have some common strengths:

- ✔ The purpose of the site is clear.
- ✔ The visitor can tell who the company is and what it does.
- ✔ The site is organized so visitors can easily find and access information.
- ✔ Visitors can quickly learn how to contact people at the company.
- ✔ The site comes up on all computers quickly and reliably.
- ✔ The site is easy to read and use.
- ✔ The look of the site makes a good impression for the company.
- ✔ The site doesn't crash or give error messages.
- ✔ Content is well written, clear, and directed at visitors' wants and needs.

As you build your site, aim for the following three attributes:

- ✔ **Speed:** Your site must be quick because most visitors are only willing to wait five to ten seconds for a page to load. Ask your site-hosting service to provide response-time measurements. If you host your own site, connect to the Web with a dial-up modem and time how long it takes each page to load.
- ✔ **Graphics:** A picture's worth a thousand words only if it appears before the user tires of waiting for it to download. Reduce the dimensions of

your graphics and use compression software to save time. Or economize by changing the quality level or file type.

✔ **Accessibility:** Hire someone who really knows computers to test your site, including how it works with all the major Web browsers.

Table 16-1 offers advice to follow and mistakes to avoid.

Table 16-1	Site Design Considerations
Do	*Don't*
Do consider that your online customer may need personal assistance when you aren't available to offer it. Include contact information and promise a prompt reply.	Don't assume that customers who need personal assistance will be satisfied to wait until your business is open and someone is available to receive a phone call.
Do treat your Web site like all other marketing materials. Launch it when it is ready and not a second before.	Don't launch with site pages labeled *Under construction* — just as you wouldn't print a brochure with parts headlined *This part wasn't done when the presses rolled.*
Do protect ownership of your site. Add a copyright notice followed by the year at the bottom of your home page, for example, ©2005, *Your Business Name.*	Don't make assumptions about site owner-ship. The U.S. Copyright Office permits registration of graphic and text elements. If you use an outside site developer, be sure you retain the copyright.
Do be moderate with your use of graphics. Design your site so that someone with a dial-up modem can download each page within five to seven seconds.	Don't overlook factors that slow download: size of your site and graphics, computer that your site is hosted on, speed of the host's connection to the Internet.
Do visit sites such as www. useit.com and www. wilsonweb.com to keep up with Web design principles and technologies.	Don't steal content from other sites. Seek permission from the site owner or author before using material you see online.
Do keep your site clear, clean, usable, and easy to navigate.	Don't use your organization chart as your navigation plan.

Is E-Commerce Right for Your Business?

Because of the Net, consumers can buy from literally all over the world. This presents a huge opportunity for your business *if* you offer great pricing on high-ticket items or *if* you sell high-demand, hard-to-find products, and *if* your product lends itself to online sale and distant delivery. This section helps you assess your odds for success.

Be aware that even a moderate foray into the e-commerce arena involves competitive research, site construction, and administrative retooling to serve an online market. And once you decide to open your business to online customers, you incur costs for merchant account set-up, service and transaction fees, security systems, marketing, fraud management, refund and return policies, fulfillment, order tracking, and site update and maintenance.

Contact Web site design and management companies for individually tailored e-commerce sites and service packages. Or check out ready-to-customize site templates and hosting packages, such as these:

- Microsoft Small Business Center Commerce Manager Package:

    www.microsoft.com/smallbusiness/products/online/cm/detail.mspx

- Yahoo! Small Business Merchant Solutions:

    http://smallbusiness.yahoo.com/business_services/

E-commerce green lights/yellow lights

To decide whether e-commerce is for you and your business, consider the following questions. *Yes* answers are e-commerce green lights. *No* answers are flashing yellow lights — indicating obstacles you'll need to overcome before selling your product over a distance.

- **Can you explain your product easily via written descriptions and photos?** Or do you have a *high-touch* product, such as clothing, that requires greater effort to describe thoroughly so that customers really understand what they are buying.

- **Is your product easy and affordable to package and ship?** Perishable, fragile, and hard-to-package products present special handling needs, and some products are simply too heavy to ship over long distances. Also, e-commerce sites serve a global marketplace, so be prepared for the realities of shipping over international borders.

✔ **Is your customer willing to pay for shipping?** Or are you willing to include shipping in your product price? Especially if your product is available locally, you may need to include shipping to win the business.

✔ **Does your product require only limited after-the-purchase support?** In other words, if assembly, installation, or usage training is required, can your customers handle the task on their own?

✔ **Is the risk relatively low if a customer makes an ordering mistake?** For example, if your customer meant 10 and typed 100 on an order of packaged goods, correcting the error involves only shipping costs. But if the mistake involves an order of custom-made windows, you're talking about absorbing a serious after-the-fact expense. Use this guideline: If your product involves more than a few simple steps for configuration to the buyer's specifications, it is likely too complicated for online sale.

✔ **Is your product or service unique or difficult to find?** If not, your online offer has to include competitive pricing or other enhancements to tip the decision in your favor.

✔ **Are you ready for the administrative and marketing realities of online sales?** E-commerce requires intensive marketing to drive prospects to your site, and systems that allow customers to input data, select products, make payments, and trigger shipping and billing — promptly, efficiently, without error, and, with luck, on a repeated basis.

Selling online using auction sites

Auction sites allow you to sell products just like you would in a live auction, only online. Auctions at sites like Yahoo! Auctions, Amazon Marketplace, and eBay sell surplus inventory, creative or unique items, used products, and products available only in a limited supply.

To sell in an online auction, you don't need to have or use your own site. You don't need to set up an online payment process. You don't even need to find customers; you just wait for them to come to the auction site.

Your role is to pay the transaction fee (and sometimes a setup fee as well), set the lowest acceptable price for your item, write a marketing blurb, upload a few pictures, and ship out the product.

When using online auctions, include a link to your Web site in your product description to increase traffic to your own site.

Online payment options

One-fifth of the adult population doesn't own a credit card. Of those who do, many have spending limits that preclude online buying, and others simply won't use cards for fear of online fraud. Credit cards are still the most popular form of online payment, but the following payment alternatives are steadily gaining in popularity:

✔ *PayPal* is a money-transfer system that allows online buyers to establish an account to pay anyone with an e-mail address. See www.paypal.com.

✔ *Bill Me Later* invoicing provides instant credit to the consumer and delivers

payment within 24 hours to the merchant. See www.i4commerce.com.

✔ *iChecks* allow customers to provide a bank account and check routing number to pay for purchases. For information visit www.paybycheck.com.

Protect yourself from fraud before handling online sales transactions. In the United States, consumers pay the first $50 of fraudulent bankcard charges. Merchants pick up the rest of the tab. Visit the Internet Fraud Watch site, www.fraud.org/intinfo.htm.

Establishing Your Online Identity

The first step toward establishing your online identity is to obtain a *domain name,* which is the string of characters a Web user types to reach your site, such as yoursite.com. If you don't already have one, think about getting one — the sooner the better. Follow these steps:

✔ First, see if you can register your business name plus *.com*. Sounds easy, but it isn't because nearly every word in the English dictionary is already taken, so unless your business is named for *you,* and unless you have an unusually unique name, your business name is likely not available. Try anyway, but realize the odds are against you.

If the domain name you want isn't available, here's what *not* to do:

• Domain names involve two parts, your name on the left and a three-letter *top-level domain* (such as *com, net,* or *org*) on the right, separated by the now-famous "dot." If www.yourname.com is already taken, don't try to use www.yourname.net or www.yourname.org. Out of instinct, most people enter *.com* at the end of a business Web address, which means they'll go straight to the other site, which is likely a competitor of your business.

• You can use hyphens or unusual spellings to get to a domain name very much like the one you want, but again, don't. They're hard to remember and type correctly.

✔ Get creative and come up with a name that describes your business offerings. For example, the Hawaii Visitors and Convention Bureau site is www.gohawaii.com.

✔ Try to purchase your first-choice name from the existing owner, but understand that this process is typically expensive and time-consuming.

A good place to begin your domain name search is Network Solutions (www.networksolutions.com). This site (see Figure 16-3) can tell you

✔ Information about how domain names work and how to choose one

✔ What domain names are already registered

✔ How to register your name

Expect to pay $25 to $75 to register a domain name for a standard three-year period. Be prepared to renew when the registration period is up. If you forget, someone else can purchase your domain name. For a complete list of domain name registrars, go to www.internic.net/regist.html.

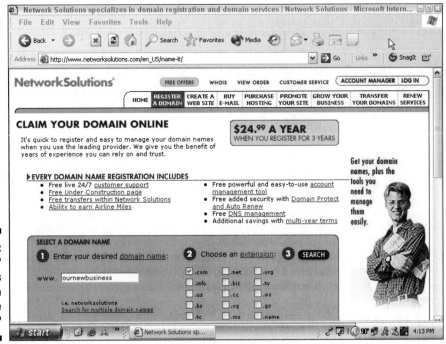

Figure 16-3:
Let's see?
Is this
domain
name
available?

Driving Traffic to Your Site

The big myth is that millions of people are cruising the Net looking for your business online. The truth boils down to something more like this: Opening a Web site isn't all that different from getting a toll-free phone number. It is a huge convenience — but only if people know about it. Lead people to your site using the following means:

- ✔ Print your Web site address on letterhead, envelopes, and business cards.

- ✔ Include your address, along with a reason to visit you online, in brochures, ads, and news releases.

- ✔ Prominently present your address on your products and product packages.

- ✔ Post your address on business trucks, trailers, and cars.

- ✔ Mention your Web site and address in your phone voice-mail and on-hold messages.

- ✔ Include your address on each page of printed or electronic newsletters.

- ✔ Include a link to your site in articles that you write for other sites.

- ✔ Optimize your site for search engines and directories (there's more on this topic later in this chapter).

- ✔ Build a *Tell a friend* feature into your site so visitors can refer others to your site.

- ✔ Establish online affiliations to gain links to your site.

How search engines and directories work

Search engines such as Google (www.google.com) and directories such as Yahoo! (www.yahoo.com) are sites where customers go to find what they're looking for online. The difference between a search engine and a directory is the way information is cataloged.

- ✔ **Search engines** collect information using a program called a *spider* that crawls around the Web, reading and indexing Web sites and sending keywords of sites back to the search engine index. Then when someone asks the engine to perform a search, it goes to its database to find the sites with words that match the request and connects those looking for information with sites that best fit their requests.

✔ **Directories** are site listings categorized by people who read the sites and index the information. The most recognized directory is Yahoo! (www.yahoo.com).

Registering your site for online searches

The quickest way to have your site recognized online is to submit and have your URL accepted at directories. Google and other crawlers then pick up your address. For the latest information, go to Search Engine Watch (www.searchenginewatch.com) and click on "Search Engine Submission Tips" (see Figure 16-4).

Minimally, register your site at Open Directory (www.dmoz.org/add.html), the human-powered directory that AOL, Google, HotBot, Lycos, and Netscape use in their searches. Submit your site for free, wait three weeks, and if your site hasn't been picked up, resubmit it. This is an essential link.

Figure 16-4:
Visit www.searchenginewatch.com and click on "Search Engine Submission Tips" for current advice on getting your site recognized by search engines and directories.

Also consider registering at the following:

Yahoo! This is the largest human-compiled directory. To register your site, go to `https://ecom.yahoo.com/dir/express/intro`. Registration involves a submission fee. Response is rapid, and although your listing isn't guaranteed, most sites are accepted. Check first to see if your site is already included.

Google: You can submit your site to `www.google.com/addurl.html`. Google will also find you if there are links to your site, which is what you're building when you gain listings in Open Directory and Yahoo!

All the Web (previously FAST): Lycos uses results from this huge search engine. Submit your main page and two inside pages for free to `www.alltheweb.com/add_url.php`.

Ask Jeeves: An annual fee provides inclusion in Ask Jeeves and throughout the Teoma search partner network, which includes ask.com, Excite, Hotbot.com, and Metacrawler, to name a few. Go to `http://sitesubmit.ask.com`.

To see if your site has been listed, go to each search engine and enter your URL into the search box. If the search engine responds by displaying your link, you're listed.

Optimizing your site for search engines

With Google powering the vast majority of all online searches, the ultimate goal of every site owner is to achieve good Google presence. The outstanding resource for achieving this victory is the book *Building Your Business With Google For Dummies* by Brad Hill. With his permission, the following are some top tips for optimizing your site for Google, which should also serve you well on other search sites as well:

- ✔ Build pages around core keywords that define each page's topical focus.
- ✔ Incorporate core keywords into the page's content.
- ✔ Place core keywords in each page's `<META>` tags, which are the hidden HTML code commands that search engines scan.
- ✔ Fill in the `<TITLE>` tag using core keywords.
- ✔ Use `<alt>` tags, with keywords, on page graphics.
- ✔ Use text, not graphical buttons, for navigation links.
- ✔ Register and use domains that describe the site's business.

✔ Avoid splash (entry) pages.

✔ Avoid the use of frames.

✔ Devote one page to a comprehensive site map.

✔ Keep pages focused; write new pages for divergent subjects.

✔ Don't use spamming, keyword stuffing, or cloaking.

✔ Build a network of incoming links from other sites to your site.

Building your Business With Google For Dummies offers other valuable advice, including the suggestion that you test your keywords at `www.wordtracker.com`. This is a paid service, but it offers a free trial after which you can subscribe for periods ranging from one day to one year.

Another free resource is the Google Keyword Sandbox. Go to `https://adwords.google.com/select/KeywordSandbox`, enter a general keyword or phrase for your business or product, and see a long list of related terms to consider. The tool is for Google AdWords users (see "Advertising Online," later in this chapter), but nonusers can benefit from it as well.

Promoting your site

The launch of your Web site should begin an intensive effort to integrate your site address into all your other marketing efforts.

Start by coattailing on all communications that your business currently sends into the marketplace. Use this checklist:

✔ Your letterhead, order forms, invoices, fax cover sheets, envelopes, and especially business cards.

✔ Your building sign and other promotional signs.

✔ The closing paragraph of news releases (see Chapter 15).

✔ The signature of your e-mail messages.

✔ In ads and brochures. If your marketing includes an emphasis on television and radio advertising, try to choose a Web site address that is easy to hear, understand, and remember. Think about the difference in recall between `www.cookiesncream.com` and `www.cookies.com`.

✔ In your voice mail message.

Building links to your site

Google especially relies on links from other high-traffic sites when it assesses the relevance of your site. By submitting your site to search engines and directories, you begin to establish links. Beyond that, consider exchanging links with other compatible businesses. Also, write articles for online publication to get your site address into circulation.

Establishing link exchanges

Exchanging links with compatible sites builds visibility for your site and leads to increased traffic. Consider taking these steps:

- Locate sites that you think would interest your site visitors and whose visitors would also benefit from information on your site. Ideally, these sites already include links to other sites, therefore demonstrating interest in building reciprocal site visits.

- E-mail Webmasters at each site. Explain that you would like to include links to their URLs on your site and that you would appreciate reciprocal links. Provide your URL and information on linking to your site, including a description of the information visitors will receive upon landing, and how that information is mutually beneficial.

Also check into link exchange organizations within your industry or interest area. Search *link exchanges* through a search engine for ideas.

Publishing articles online

To publish online, start by referring to the section on generating publicity in Chapter 15. Then create a list of Web sites that your prospective customers might frequent and where you might be able to place in-depth, newsy articles.

A florist might write an article full of wedding planning advice for bridal Web sites. To get it published, the florist needs to follow these steps:

- Contact the Web site to obtain the name of the editor.

- Send an e-mail query. Provide a backgrounder on your expertise and a list of topics that you believe would be relevant to site readers — and why. Offer to submit articles for free in exchange for links to your site.

Also, submit articles to *ezines,* newsletters and magazines that are delivered via e-mail to subscribers. Go to www.freezineweb.com for a list of ezines including editorial contacts.

Online referrals

Referrals are the way that marketers warm up cold calls. A referral allows you to contact the friend of a friend instead of contacting a stranger. The Internet is rich with opportunities for cultivating various types of referrals online:

- ✔ **Manufacturer referrals:** If you're a retailer, ask manufacturers of the products you carry to include links to your business on their Web sites.

- ✔ **Professional referrals:** If you belong to a professional organization with a Web site, ask that a link to your Web address be included in the membership roster.

- ✔ **Associate referrals:** If you receive frequent leads from other businesses or organizations, consider swapping links so that a visitor to your site can link to your associate business or organization.

An easy way to increase referrals to your site is to have your Web site designer add a button that allows visitors to send a Web page from your site to a friend. When adding this feature

- ✔ Be sure that the process sends the friend to the exact location on the site, not just to the home page.

- ✔ Include a feature that allows visitors to write brief notes telling friends why they are receiving the message.

Gaining referrals through affiliate programs

Online *affiliate* programs were the brainchild of Amazon.com, where they were created as a way to entice publishers and other businesses to promote their offerings on the Amazon site.

An affiliate program includes two key players:

- ✔ **The fulfillment company:** Becoming a fulfillment company takes computer savvy and retailing expertise. It also requires software to track who visits the site, which merchant referred the visitor to the site, and what the person purchased on arrival. The fulfillment company also recruits, manages, and pays commissions to the reseller companies.

- ✔ **The merchant, or reseller, company:** This company directs customers to the fulfillment site in return for a commission on all resulting sales.

For information, visit www.affiliateguide.com. Also visit the affiliate marketing area on the Commission Junction site at www.cj.com.

Evaluating Your Online Activity

On your own, you can and should keep track of the number of leads generated by your site. Additionally, Web site activity reports allow you to measure the nature and number of visitors or visitor sessions that your Web site is hosting, as well as the pages viewed, files downloaded, dates and times of visits, referral sources, session length, features used, navigation path followed, errors encountered, even the keywords entered to find your site.

Ask the business that hosts your site about the kinds of reports available, costs involved, and ways to adjust your site to allow capture of valuable information about your site visitors.

To evaluate the success of your traffic-building efforts, consider setting up a *redirect*. This is a page where referrals will land before being redirected to the appropriate page on your site. By creating a redirect, you can measure traffic coming to your site from each link.

Use redirects only if people are clicking on a link to reach your site. If people have to type in your address, forget about redirecting them because you may lose them in the process, defeating the purpose of measurement altogether.

Advertising Online

Banner ads. AdWord ads. Click-throughs. Advertising online is expanding at a dizzying rate. Some studies see online advertising revenues surpassing magazine advertising revenues over the next few years. Whether or not the forecast will hold true, advertisers are flocking to online opportunities in large part because they can be so specifically targeted and clearly measured for effectiveness.

Banner ads

These narrow image ads — 480 x 60 pixels or about 1½ inches high and 4 inches wide — run on third-party Web sites. When viewers click on the banner (called a *click-through*), they go directly to the advertiser's site. Interest in banner ads waned largely due to consumer resistance, but a Google program allowing banner ads on sites that participate in the Google AdSense program was announced in mid-2004, inspiring new interest in the format.

Here are some factors that influence the effectiveness of a banner ad:

- ✔ **Creative design** including questions that invite interaction, free offers, and good use of colors.

- ✔ **Targeted placement** on sites where prospects are likely to be visiting.

- ✔ **Frequency:** Place a number of ads with similar messages. Try them out and then quickly — within a day or two — watch click-throughs to see what's working and yank all but the top performers.

A distant cousin to the banner ad is the *pop-up ad,* which appears in your browser window when you open some Web pages. Pop-ups (and *pop-unders,* which hide beneath Web pages) represent a very minor percentage of online advertising, largely due to the fact that consumers rank them among the least popular of all advertising approaches. Pop-up blocking software is in wide use and Google, for one, does not allow pop-up ads on its site.

AdWords advertising program

Each time Google displays results of a search, up to ten all-text ads focusing on the same keywords as those requested in the search are displayed down the right-hand side of the screen.

The ads are part of the AdWords advertising program. To participate, go to `http://adwords.google.com/select`. Once there, do the following:

- ✔ Choose the language for your ad and the countries, cities, or areas you want to target.

- ✔ Write a three-line ad, followed by the URL you want users to land on after clicking on your ad.

- ✔ Select the keywords that you want your ads matched to, choosing words specific to your site or product.

- ✔ Choose your preferred currency and the maximum *cost per click* (CPC) you wish to pay. A traffic estimator will calculate how much your requested program will cost per day. Based on this estimate, you can specify your daily budget and enroll in the program. Google will time your daily ad placements to spread exposures over the 24-hour period.

A companion program to the AdWords is the AdSense advertising program (`www.google.com/adsense`), which allows information sites with reasonable traffic to earn revenue by displaying AdWords ads on their Web pages.

Part V
Winning and Keeping Customers

The 5th Wave   By Rich Tennant

"Snappy ad copy. And it really got my attention."

In this part . . .

When it comes to customers, small business concerns fall into two categories: the revolving door and the slow leak.

The *revolving door* is the problem businesses face when their marketing delivers prospects but no purchases. The *slow leak* is when marketing delivers customers but no repeat business. This part helps overcome both, with chapters dedicated to winning customers and closing sales, developing customer satisfaction, and building the invaluable business asset called customer loyalty.

In a world where competition is at a fever pitch, the chapters in this part serve as a road map to winning long-term customers and achieving business success.

Chapter 17

Making the Sale

*L*et's start with some assumptions about your business:

You have a great product or service.

You've developed a clear business image.

You've honed your marketing premise into a succinct message that matters to consumers.

You've run ads, sent direct mailers, opened a Web site, and driven traffic to your business.

In other words, you've got plenty of prospects. Now what do you do?

If you're like most businesses, you follow the *if it ain't broke don't fix it* rule and you keep doing what's working. You run more ads, send more mailers, create more links to your Web site, and build more interest.

But . . . if you're like the most successful businesses, this is the point at which you shift emphasis. After all, your goal isn't to gather prospects but to gain customers. Prospect generation is a step on the path, but it's not the destination.

That means it's time to focus on making the sale, closing the deal, winning the customer, and getting to yes. That's what this chapter is all about.

Converting Prospects to Customers

Much as you want each ad to serve as a magic wand that causes the cash register to ring, the reality is a little more practical.

The truth is that people become customers over time and usually only after seeing multiple ads, promotions, and personal presentations.

First they need to gain awareness of who you are and why to trust your business. Then they need to hear things about your product that pique their interest. After that, they need to be presented with a deal capable of inspiring action. And finally, they need to be asked for the order in a way that prompts them to actually make the purchase.

Figure 17-1 shows the steps that prospects take as they move from awareness to the cash register. In rare instances, the awareness-to-sale scenario happens with a single communication — sometimes infomercials or direct mailers lead prospects through all the steps in one fell swoop.

Be aware, though, that single-communication, on-the-spot selling usually occurs only with certain kinds of high-appeal, low-cost, low-involvement, and low-risk products.

Figure 17-1:
How marketing moves your prospects from awareness to the decision to buy.

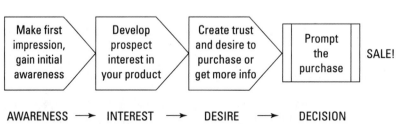

Moving prospects to the buying decision

Plan your marketing communications to move prospects through the steps illustrated in Figure 17-1 and described in this list:

✔ **First, gain positive awareness.** Introduce your business and build a good reputation by using advertising, mailers, publicity, networking, and presentations to reach prospects and those who influence your prospects' decisions.

- ✔ **After achieving awareness, generate interest in your offering.** Present your product as the answer to a need or desire and prompt the prospect to request more information, perhaps by watching a demonstration, visiting a Web site, or requesting a brochure or other information.

- ✔ **After gaining your prospect's interest, convey the value your offer represents.** Set face-to-face meetings, share product samples, offer proposals, or take other steps to let the prospect see how your offering is better and more valuable than other alternatives. (Remember that *best value* doesn't mean *lowest price*. Chapter 3 describes the value formula that customers apply when making buying decisions.)

- ✔ **After establishing value, close the sale.** Present your offer, address questions, help the customer reach a satisfying decision, and make the buying transaction an easy, enjoyable process.

Don't jump the gun. Plan each marketing communication to move prospects to the next step they will be willing to take on the buying decision path.

A brand-new preschool wants to enroll 30 toddlers. With no existing awareness or reputation, the preschool owners would be expecting parents to leapfrog over the decision process if they ran ads saying, *Introducing our brand-new preschool. Call to register children between 2 and 5 years old.*

They would be more apt to succeed if they preceded the enrollment request with a program that builds awareness, interest, and trust. They might begin with a message saying: *Our brand-new preschool and playground is ready to serve 30 lucky 2- to 5-year-olds. Please join us Thursday afternoon for an open house and tour, or call any time for an appointment.*

The first approach calls for the order before the prospect is ready for the question. The second approach seeks to build rapport. Which would you respond to more comfortably?

Prospect conversion guidelines

The number of *people* you reach with your marketing program really doesn't matter. What's important is how many *qualified prospects* you reach and how you move those prospects through the steps that turn them into customers.

Think about the preschool mentioned in the preceding section. Say that the owners run an ad in a newspaper delivered to 20,000 homes in the preschool's market area. If 5 percent of those homes have 2- to 5-year-olds in need of day care, the ad will reach 1,000 prospects. If half of those prospects are qualified prospects, in other words if half of the newspaper's readers with children that age want and can afford preschool offerings, then the ad will reach 500 target market homes.

Of those 500 qualified prospects, some will miss the ad, some won't be interested, some will already have a different solution, and some will convert into customers, as shown in Table 17-1.

Table 17-1	Where Do All the Prospects Go?
Where Prospects Disappear	*Why Prospects Disappear*
The majority of prospects won't get "caught" by the ad.	If the ad reaches 500 qualified prospects, it might gain the awareness of a few hundred. The others, though they fit the prospect profile, aren't tuned in to receive the message, or it doesn't grab them, or they're too busy to notice the offer.
Many who become aware won't have interest.	If 200 prospects notice the ad, only a portion will have interest. The others may be committed to a competitor, they may not be in the market for the offering, or the message may not motivate them.
Of those with interest, only some will look further into the offer.	If 100 prospects are interested, a portion of that number will take action by starting the buying process. The others may decide, based on the specifics of the product, price, offer, or presentation, not to part with their time or money at that moment.
Of those with desire, a rare few will decide to buy.	In other words, a handful of the 1,000 prospects reached by the ad will become customers. That's why marketers need to communicate frequently using multiple forms of communication to keep the pump primed for success.

Increase your prospect-to-customer conversion odds by following these steps:

1. Establish market awareness and a good reputation among prospects and those who influence their decisions.

2. Create a pool of qualified prospects by projecting marketing messages frequently and on an ongoing basis.

3. Convert prospects to customers via a sales program that makes the buying decision easy and the purchase transaction efficient and pleasant.

Winning at Sales

The cost of your marketing program is the price you pay to play in the business arena, and the sale is your first point of investment return. Weigh your efforts well and you'll end up with a trifecta payoff.

> ✔ Make the sale and you'll win a new customer and immediate revenue.

> ✔ Exceed the customer's value expectations and you'll reap repeat purchases — each at a fraction of the cost of recruiting a new customer.

> ✔ Develop loyalty and you'll achieve word-of-mouth leading to prospect referrals, starting your chance at the three-way payoff all over again.

Figure 17-2 illustrates a *marketing cyclotron* within the marketing process — a circle within the marketing cycle where sales and service efforts intensify to convert prospects to customers, customers to loyalists, and loyalists to ambassadors who recruit new prospects to your business.

That's how to leverage your marketing investment!

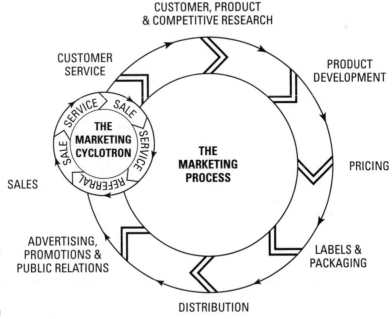

Figure 17-2:
Intensify
sales and
service
efforts to
create
customers,
win repeat
business,
and gain
referrals.

Selling redefined

Forget terms like high-pressure, low-pressure, hard-sell, or soft-sell. For that matter, forget about *selling* and concentrate on helping your prospect to *buy*.

Your role in the process is to know and believe in your offering, to persuasively communicate the value your product provides, to lead the prospect through the decision, and to facilitate a satisfying transaction.

Preparing for the task

Selling is the art of matching product benefits with customer needs or desires. Before you start, be ready with the following information:

- ✔ **Know your product.** Imagine every question a prospect might ask and arm yourself with answers, linking each product fact to a customer benefit. Remember, people don't buy features. They buy benefits or, better yet, the personal outcomes that benefits deliver (see Table 8-1 in Chapter 8).

- ✔ **Know how to explain your offering in a sentence.** Condense everything you know into a brief explanation that will grab interest and cause the prospect to think, "Hmm, this will benefit *me*." Don't resort to jargon. Think of the difference between *We offer aesthetic laser services* and *We restore the look of youth and health using the most advanced laser, medical, and therapeutic treatments.*

- ✔ **Know your prospect.** Visit Web sites, read company brochures, talk to mutual associates, and do any research necessary to arrive armed with prospect knowledge, including who in the organization has the authority to say yes to your proposal.

- ✔ **Know what message your prospect is ready to receive.** Especially if yours is a new or unusual offering, you may need to help the prospect see the need before asking for the order. (In the 1960s, Wisk detergent built a success story by establishing *Ring around the collar* as a personal embarrassment before suggesting the purchase of liquid soap as the solution.)

  Or maybe your prospect is aware of the need but doesn't see your offering as the best solution, in which case you'll want to present your advantages before asking for the buying decision. Or perhaps the prospect requires information to share with those who will influence the decision. Or maybe some incentive is necessary to spur action. Determine your prospect's mindset and tailor your presentation accordingly.

- ✔ **Know your sales presentation goal.** Sometimes your goal will be to make the sale and launch a celebration. More often, your aim will be an incremental step — to prompt the prospect to request a proposal, to schedule a meeting with a higher-level decision maker, to arrange a demonstration, or to take some other step to move the process toward its final step. Be aware that if your product involves significant cost and deliberation, it may take half a dozen tries before you achieve the sale.

✔ **Know how to dress for success.** The general rule is to project your own business image well (see Chapter 6) while dressing at least as formally as those to whom you'll be presenting.

Establishing contact

Closing a sale begins with opening a relationship, and the first step involves meeting your prospect either in person or via phone, mail, or e-mail.

Welcoming walk-in prospects

Here's an amazing fact: Even in the retail environment, fewer than half of all people who enter the door make a purchase. The percentage is higher (way higher) in supermarkets and convenience stores, and far lower in exclusive boutiques and galleries. But across the board, the *conversion rate* — the number of prospects who become buyers — is ripe for improvement.

Calculate your conversion rate by inconspicuously counting the number of people who enter your business and the number who walk out with shopping bags or other purchase indicators. Divide the former number by the latter one to benchmark your current situation. And then set a goal for improvement.

The fastest route to sending retail conversions on an uphill climb is to increase the number of prospects who have staff contact. It sounds too simple to be true, but retail scientists (there *are* such things) have validated the fact. They've also proven that staff contact increases the time a prospect spends in a retail setting, which directly affects spending levels.

Follow these tips:

✔ Use displays and personal contact to intercept shoppers upon arrival.

✔ Offer a shopping basket, explain a current special offer, or give a quick store orientation to increase involvement.

✔ Enhance comfort by pointing out refreshment and sitting areas, play areas for children, and fitting rooms for shoppers.

✔ When you see signs of prospect uncertainty, step in to reinforce decisions, suggest complementary items or alternative choices, or make other suggestions to both facilitate and increase the sale.

✔ Don't prejudge prospects. Watch, listen, and respond to prospect cues rather than letting first impressions limit your sales expectations.

Warming up cold calls

Those who make them and those who receive them seem to share an equal aversion to cold calls. Prepare for a warmer reception by turning your next cold call into a referral call or a networking follow-up.

Try breaking the ice by mentioning a previous encounter with the prospect (I appreciated the ideas you shared when I met you at the Chamber after-hours event last Thursday. . . .).

Or open the door via a referral from a mutual acquaintance, as shown in the sample script in Figure 17-3.

As an alternative, try making a research call or visit before initiating prospect contact. Explain to the person who answers the phone or greets your arrival who you are, that you're just collecting information for future use, and that you'd like to learn the name of the person who handles purchases of whatever kind of product you're selling. Collect the information, along with the name of the person you're talking with. Then when you contact your prospect you can approach the call as a referral: *Bob Jones shared your name when I visited your office last week. . . .*

Each time you initiate contact by telephone (or for that matter, via e-mail or in person), know your goal and stick with it. Most likely you're calling to ask for an appointment, not to make a sale.

Keep your aim in mind and don't derail the effort by launching into a product pitch. Keep the call short. Be friendly and professional. Make your message clear. And keep calling until you get through — not just to voice mail but to your actual prospect.

Figure 17-3:
Using a referral warms a cold call and paves the way for an appointment request.

SAMPLE PHONE SCRIPT: Mr. Smith, this is Jan Jones with Neighborhood Bank. Jim Brown of Brown & Black Accounting is a customer, and he suggested we meet. ← **Use of Reference**

Perhaps he's already shared my name with you. We've just introduced a comprehensive business banking package that lets you earn interest while receiving a wide range of benefits and services. ← **Convey Customer Benefit**

I'd like to set a 20-minute meeting to explain the offering. Would later this week work for you... ← **Assumptive Approach**

Writing letters to introduce your business

The point of an introductory letter is to make the impression you'd like to make in person if you could. Almost certainly in a face-to-face meeting you wouldn't use blustery language or spend the whole time talking about yourself. You'd shift the focus to your prospect, engage his or her interest, and launch a conversation rather than a lecture.

Do the same exact thing when you write letters, following these points:

- ✔ **Open with a sentence that grabs interest** and establishes a reason to keep reading.

- ✔ **Introduce yourself in terms that matter to the prospect.** If you can, refer to a previous meeting or mutual acquaintance. For instance, *After hearing your name from so many good friends, it was great to meet you at Rotary . . .* or *I've just learned that we have a mutual friend in Jack Smith. . . .*

- ✔ **Explain your offering by conveying benefits the prospect can count on** rather than simply reciting a list of the features involved.

- ✔ **Keep your letter short.** Keep sentences short. Keep paragraphs short. And limit the length to a single page.

- ✔ **Make a clear point.** Maybe you just want to say thanks. Maybe you want to tell the person that you'll be calling next week. Maybe you want to set an appointment. Or maybe you want to announce a good deal (*Our first 2006 model will arrive mid-month. As soon as the schedule is set, I'll call for an appointment so you can be the first to see it. . . .*).

- ✔ **Edit and proofread.** Delete as many *I's* as you can. Then read the letter for accuracy, double checking that you've spelled the recipient's name and address perfectly.

- ✔ **Sign your letter.** Amidst all the junk mail, a personally worded letter with an original signature on good stationery can make a great impression. Don't let an assistant sign for you, reducing your letter's impact with the subliminal message that *I'm too busy to sign this but I hope you're not too busy to read it.*

Presenting your product

The presentation is your chance to present your proposal, product, or concept in person, summarizing key points, responding to questions or concerns, explaining benefits, and providing facts that will help the person before you to either make the purchase or introduce you to the ultimate decision maker.

Successful presentations share three attributes:

- ✔ They describe the product or service by showing how it will deliver benefits, solve problems, or provide opportunities for the prospect.
- ✔ They focus on a few major points that the prospect can relate to and remember.
- ✔ They are appropriately entertaining — grabbing and holding the prospect's interest while reinforcing rather than detracting from the sales message.

Translating your message into prospect benefits

People buy benefits, not features. They don't buy all-natural, algae-based facial moisturizer; they buy the promise of firmer skin in four weeks. They don't care about lists of ingredients as much as they care about the benefits those ingredients will deliver.

To keep your presentation focused on benefits, stay tuned at all times to your prospect's station WIII-FM: What Is In It — for *me?* Prepare a presentation that clearly answers that question and you'll be on your way to closing the deal.

Ask, then listen

The more your prospect is talking, the more likely a sale will occur. Make your introductory remarks and then ask questions that elicit more than yes or no answers. Nod to validate points, but don't interrupt. Wait until the prospect is done talking before you begin to respond, share additional information, or present another question.

Show, don't tell

People start to *own* a product when they hold it in their hands, take it for a test drive, carry it into a fitting room, or in some other way get involved in a tactile manner.

Realtors take home buyers onto a bedroom deck to deliver a sense of waking up in the home. Restaurants put menus in phone books to involve diners while they're still deciding where to make reservations. Service businesses encourage prospects to gain a sense of their offerings by calling other clients for testimonials or by accepting speculative presentations.

To accelerate the buying process in your business, figure out ways to let your prospects touch or sample your offering.

Realize this: People *buy in* before they *buy.* Help them do so by letting them acquire a sense of ownership long before the money changes hands.

Pre-empt objections

People raise objections as a delay tactic, as a means to gather information to pass along to decision influencers, and as a way to accumulate facts to justify the buying decision. Often, objections are questions in disguise. Encourage them, because if the prospect is asking questions, he's engaged in the process.

Get the conversation going by presenting objections on your prospect's behalf, saying something like, *Nearly all our customers asked the same few questions before buying, so let me share a few quick facts. . . .*

When the prospect follows with his or her own questions or concerns, validate input by saying things like, *That's an important point. . . .*

Probe to learn more, paraphrase to show you understand, and then present a positive response, as described in Table 17-2.

Table 17-2	Responding to Prospect Objections
Objection	*Positive Response*
Lack of belief or trust in your business	Share testimonials.
Preference for a competitor	Never badmouth. Instead present unique added-values included with your offering and show how the prospect will receive greater benefit and cost-effectiveness from your business.
Concern over cost	Present pricing options, volume discounts, payment terms, or other incentives to address the concern. Then move quickly from emphasis on cost expended to emphasis on value received, including warranties, service, reliability, convenience, and quality.

As long as you dwell on price, you're letting the conversation focus on what's in it for you. Shift the focus to a discussion about value to move the conversation to a discussion of what's in it for your prospect.

Closing the Deal

There's a moment that many salespeople miss, and that's the moment when the seller needs to quit selling and give the prospect a chance to buy. Instead, too many salespeople keep talking. They unconsciously undo the sale by raising issues that confuse rather than comfort the decision maker. As a result, they miss the moment when the prospect was ready to become a customer.

The minute your prospect begins to agree with your responses to her objections, or as soon as you pick up buying signals, move from selling to affirming your prospect's good choice and get ready to close the deal.

Buying signals

When a prospect indicates he's ready to buy, *stop selling.*

Table 17-3 shows the signals to watch for.

Table 17-3	Buying Signals
Examples of Nonverbal Cues	*Examples of Verbal Cues*
Relaxed demeanor	Increased questions about product details
Increased eye contact	Requests to see features demonstrated a second or third time
Leaning forward, uncrossing arms or legs	Questions about customization options
Nodding, agreeing, showing enthusiasm	Questions about delivery schedules
Making calculations, studying sales tags or contract, reaching for pen, billfold, or handbag	Questions about payment plans or options

Asking for the order

More than half of all sales presentations drift to a finish without an order request. Don't let yours be among them.

Follow one of these closing approaches:

- ✔ **Ask for the order.** Don't rush it or you'll race the customer to the word *no,* which is a hard place to make a U-turn. Wait for buying cues, and once you receive them, present one more summary of benefits before moving toward closure with questions like, *How many would you like?*

and *When would you like it delivered?* Gain positive responses to those gateway questions and then close the deal.

✔ **Make a buying assumption.** For service or major-investment products, you may choose to replace the outright order request with a buying assumption. Using this approach, you paraphrase your prospect's needs, reiterate how your offering provides a cost-effective solution, and explain when you can deliver or begin work, ending with a question such as, *Will that schedule work for you?*

✔ **Gain agreement to a delivery plan.** This approach is similar to making a buying assumption, but it goes one step farther in involving the prospect in the closing process. By presenting a detailed, written schedule, you convey your readiness to do the job, your ability to do it well, and your willingness to adapt your plans to your prospect's wants and needs. By providing input to the plan, your prospect begins to take ownership, an important prerequisite to actually making the purchase.

Make buying easy

So your customer said yes. Now it's time to complete the transaction, get the contract signed, collect the money, and begin to deliver all the promises you made as you presented the attributes, benefits, and values of your offering.

This is the point at which loyalty *or* dissatisfaction begins to grow. Opt for the former by doing the following:

✔ **Make the transaction flawlessly easy.** In professional service businesses, see that the contract is professionally produced, error free, easy to understand, and delivered in a manner that reinforces the caliber of your business and product. In retail settings, be sure the cash/wrap area is clean, adequately sized, efficient, and well staffed with people trained to affirm the buyer's decision and ready to begin the process of customer service. (Customers literally abandon the product in their hands and make a quick exit when they see long lines at a cash register.)

✔ **Add unexpected value.** Package your offering well and include an unexpected enclosure, be it a sincere thank-you note (*not* a one-size-fits-all preprinted card), a thank-you gift, an invitation to a new-customer event, a next-purchase certificate, or some other offer that inspires customer commitment to your business.

✔ **Make the purchase your first step in developing customer loyalty.** The next two chapters tell how.

Chapter 18

Enhancing Customer Service

. . . .

. . . .

*G*reat businesses know whom they serve best, attract those people into their businesses, convert them to customers, and lock them in with a level of service and appreciation they can't find elsewhere.

On the other end of the business spectrum, too many companies let their customers get lost in the workload shuffle where they get overlooked, treated like intrusions, asked to wait too long, imposed upon, and confronted with rules that send them right out the same door that the business worked so hard to get them through in the first place.

Put your business on the winning side by recognizing and leveraging the value of your customers and with a customer service program that permeates every aspect of your business.

This chapter describes how.

The Fundamentals of Customer Service

Services and *service* are not the same thing.

▶ *Services* are what you provide to customers as part of your product.

▶ *Service* is how well you do what you do — how well you deliver your product to your customer.

Companies renowned for their customer satisfaction levels have great services *and* great service, as described in Table 18-1.

Table 18-1	Examples of Services and Service
Services	**Service**
Customer parking	Clean, well-signed area with the most convenient spaces reserved for customers
Public restrooms	Immaculate and well-equipped area
Complimentary refreshments	Fresh, unique offerings provided in a clean, accessible, inviting setting
Children's play area, spouse sitting area, customer waiting area	Convenient and inviting areas supplied with interesting, enjoyable entertainment
Delivery service	Well-identified, friendly, and reliable

The Service Cycle

Customer service involves a cycle of activities that starts before the sales presentation and continues well past the time the purchase is complete. See that your business has a plan for each of these steps:

- ✔ **Step 1: Establish contact** with a prompt, friendly greeting. Whether the prospect arrives via e-mail, phone, mail, or in person, your first response establishes an impression upon which all other contacts build.

- ✔ **Step 2: Build rapport.** A marketing truth goes like this: *People don't buy because you make them understand. They buy because they feel understood.* They also buy from people they like and feel they know. In the first few minutes with your prospect, establish a friendly relationship.

- ✔ **Step 3: Present your product.** See Chapter 17 for ideas on how to present your product as a high-value solution to your customer's needs.

- ✔ **Step 4: Make the sale** following advice for reading buying signals and closing the deal in Chapter 17.

- ✔ **Step 5: Complete the sales transaction,** making the process of payment completely efficient, a reinforcement of your company service, and a confirmation of the customer's decision to buy from your business. This is not the time to conduct lengthy customer research or to make promotional pitches for additional products. If you introduce options at this point, be sure they are clear and easy to explain, and that they contribute to the value and satisfaction the customer will receive from the product being purchased. Don't complicate the moment of payment or you'll risk losing the sale.

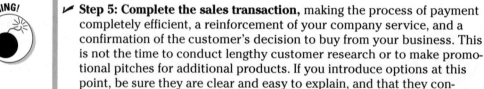

✔ **Step 6: Deliver the product,** reaffirm the buying decision, offer to be of ongoing service, and invite future business.

✔ **Step 7: Monitor customer satisfaction** and troubleshoot any issues that cause customer concern.

✔ **Step 8: Follow up after the sale,** completing these important three steps:

- **Assess service satisfaction.** Ask the customer: *How was your experience?* If the answer is less than positive, request ideas for improvement, avoiding questions that require yes and no answers in favor of open-ended input. If the customer reveals reasons for discontent, address the concern immediately, following the suggestions in the upcoming section on "Handling complaints."

- **Confirm complete satisfaction.** Ask outright: *Were you completely satisfied?* If the answer is no, learn more and work to move the customer into the "completely satisfied" category. You will increase your chances for repeat business and positive word-of-mouth as a result.

- **Ask for future business.** Once you have confirmed complete satisfaction, don't miss the opportunity to cultivate the customer's repeat business. Issue an invitation to join a frequent buyer or other customer program (see Chapter 19), share information on upcoming special offers, and in all cases provide a business card along with the sincere offer to assist with any future needs.

Improving your service

Products lead to sales, but service leads to loyalty. To improve your service, consider the following:

✔ **Make a service guarantee.** Assure customers that promises will be met or exceeded. Make the guarantee straightforward and liberal (no small print), relevant and substantial (worth the effort it takes to request it), available immediately (no management approvals required), and easy to collect.

✔ **Notice and immediately overcome dissatisfaction.** Compensate dissatisfied customers on the spot by offering upgrades, discounts, or premiums when something goes wrong. Don't wait for a complaint. Most people never register dissatisfaction verbally. Instead, they quietly slip out the door once and for all, perhaps politely saying thanks as they exit your business for the final time. See the section on "Reading unstated customer clues to dissatisfaction" later in this chapter.

✔ **Accompany every operational decision with the question,** *How does this help our customer?* Unintentionally, many business decisions add management layers and cumbersome processes that complicate rather than contribute to customer service.

✔ **Spend time monthly or at least quarterly evaluating your service** and brainstorming ways to improve it further. Use the worksheet in Table 18-2 as you conduct your self-evaluation.

Table 18-2	Customer Service Self-Evaluation
Yes *No*	
	Are you and your staff committed and trained to enhance satisfaction at each step of the service cycle?
	Do you make a special effort to help customers feel important?
	Do you bend rules and tailor services to individual customer needs?
	Do your customers feel comfortable to share concerns or complaints with you and your staff?
	Do your services exceed those offered by your competitors?
	Do you and those on your staff genuinely like your customers?
	Do you communicate with customers frequently to understand their needs and to learn how they think you could offer even better service?
	Do you deliver high-quality products accurately, on time, on budget, and with friendly service?
	Do you follow up when customers make suggestions or share concerns?
	Do you address and resolve customer concerns promptly?
	Do you implement loyalty programs that keep customers committed to your business?
	Do customers feel that doing business with you is a pleasure in their day?

Tally your yes answers. If they total 11 or 12, your business excels at service. If they total fewer than 8, get ready for serious improvement in order to enhance customer satisfaction.

Benchmarking your customer service performance

At its best, customer service is a way of business life. It affects every business decision and every customer encounter.

Bring your staff together to brainstorm the questions in Table 18-3 and to make a plan for service enhancements.

Table 18-3	Benchmarking Your Customer Service
1. How is our overall service right now?	Give yourself a 1–12 rating based on the Customer Service Self-Evaluation in Table 18-2. Then set a goal for improvement.
2. How does this compare to how we were doing in the past?	Service levels rise on good morale. Give praise when praise is due.
3. How does our service compare to that of our competitors?	Find a couple of areas where competitors exceed your service and commit to improvement by defining specific actions you will take.
4. How extensive are any problems being experience by our customers? Are they one-time problems or recurring issues that point to operational problems?	Bring front-line staff into the discussion because they hear concerns first-hand. Also ask some of your best clients and suppliers for input.
5. How well are we handling customer concerns?	Analyze some recent specific complaints. What was the issue? How was it handled? How do you evaluate the outcome? How do you think the customer might evaluate the outcome?

(continued)

Table 18-3 *(continued)*

6. Which customers are most satisfied, most dissatisfied, having most problems, and so on?	Look for common traits in each customer group. Evaluate the chances of pleasing each customer and weight efforts accordingly.
7. What do our most satisfied customers appreciate about our offerings?	Know what you're doing right and telegraph your strengths in marketing communications.
8. What are we doing to reward, thank, and reinforce our most satisfied customers?	Initiate loyalty programs that deliver customized and unexpected gestures of thanks while steering clear of anything that looks routine, promotional, or like a bribe.
9. What are the most frequent requests or complaints that we receive?	Requests point to opportunities; complaints point to problems. Act on both.
10. What can we do to address customer requests or to reduce concerns we're hearing about our business?	Define up to five actions you'll take over upcoming months. Assign responsibility for implementation. Monitor progress.

Cultivating "best customers"

Every person who buys from your business is an important asset deserving of your total courtesy and best service.

But as you tailor unique solutions and extend special services for customers, it's important to direct the extra investment toward the kind of customer that is likely to become a loyal, repeat client and speak well on your company's behalf.

Some customers will never be satisfied by anything other than the very lowest price. And others may never be satisfied even if you provide your offering for free. Be aware of the following three customer categories, and weight your efforts toward developing relationship customers in your business.

Relationship customers

Relationship customers value loyalty and commitment. Recognize them, remember them, do them favors, offer them gifts, bend your rules, anticipate their needs, and win their trust, and they'll become loyal customers for life.

Transaction customers

Transaction customers are interested primarily in price. They represent sales and generate word-of-mouth for your business, but they'll leave you for a deeper discount in a split second, so gauge your efforts to meet their high demands accordingly.

Toxic customers

Sooner or later, you'll encounter an excessively negative customer. When you do, you have two choices.

One is to get defensive, trying to prove why your business is right in spite of the bad opinion held by the person standing in front of you. This route almost certainly leads to an argument, which erodes your customer service standard and leaves you in a losing position.

The better approach is to use the same friendly service style for which your business is known — listening, trying to solve the customer's complaint, and working to arrive at a mutually agreeable outcome. Many times, this service approach will calm the customer and lead to a positive outcome.

But . . . some customers demand concessions you shouldn't make, and those customers are simply not a good match for your business. Catering to their demands risks the financial stability of your business and threatens your ability to retain your good employees.

When you encounter an overly negative or abusive customer, make a choice in favor of your business. Forego the customer's business — in other words, let the customer go

- ✔ If the customer is acting abusively to you or your employees

- ✔ If the customer is abusing your systems or otherwise taking advantage of your business

- ✔ If the customer ignores your payment policies or refuses to pay what you know is the fair price for your offering

Keeping good customers

Ask yourself

- ✔ Why do our customers leave?
- ✔ What would it take to get them to stay?

Throw out the names of a couple recent departures to help focus the discussion. Write down every reason you can come up with for why they moved their business elsewhere. What will emerge is information that will help as you analyze your competitive arena, your pricing policies, your customer service, and your product offerings.

Be prepared for your first response to be, *We're too expensive,* but don't allow your thinking to stop there. Price alone is rarely the reason that good customers move their business. More often, service is the issue.

In a sentence: Customers leave because of mediocre service.

A widely-cited Rockefeller Foundation study concluded the following facts:

- ✔ 14 percent of customers leave because their complaints aren't handled.
- ✔ 9 percent are baited away by competition.
- ✔ 9 percent move away.
- ✔ 68 percent leave because they are treated with indifference.

Other research helps define what customers mean by *indifference*. Among the findings: Customers feel they are served with indifference if they have to return to a business repeatedly with the same problem, or if they have to wait longer than they think necessary to be served. And as soon as they think they are being treated with indifference — in the way they are greeted, in the time it takes to serve them, in the way their complaint is handled, or in the quality of the product they receive — they begin the defection process.

Eliminating service indifference

Eliminate service indifference — and the dissatisfaction that follows — with these tips:

- ✔ Fill special requests.
- ✔ Go beyond the ordinary.

✔ Offer special, customized favors and follow through with exceptional delivery.

✔ Keep records on customer wants, needs, special requests, and past favors so you can surpass your service efforts in the future.

✔ Increase communications with customers, lapsed customers, and service staff.

✔ Polish your first impression (see Chapter 6) by improving the way you greet customers by phone, mail, e-mail, online, and in person.

✔ Be open to new ideas. If customers ask for something, get it. If they complain, fix it.

✔ Create a customer service environment. Put pens where people need them, chairs where they want to sit, reading material where they're apt to be waiting, courtesy phones in convenient, quiet areas, supply after-hour contact options, and on and on.

✔ Go the extra mile — and empower your staff to do the same.

Nurturing Concerns and Complaints

Use customer complaints to lead your business to service improvements and satisfied customers. Follow these tips:

✔ **Talk with customers.** Listen for direct and indirect complaints along with suggestions for how you can improve your service.

✔ **Encourage complaints.** A complaint handled well leads to loyalty.

✔ **When you receive a complaint, first deal with the customer, then deal with the problem.** Let the person talk, hear the full story, listen to the degree of disappointment and the level of anger, and then make amends — quickly. Don't make excuses or blame others and don't simply complete a complaint form. Resolve the issue with a refund, an alternate product, or whatever feels like a fair trade for the customer's inconvenience. Then, once the customer is calmed down and out the door, take actions to see that the problem doesn't happen again.

✔ **Treat returned products as nonverbal forms of customer complaint.** If products are coming back, either they're faulty or your communication was unclear and the product was misrepresented. Similarly, watch what's backlogged as an indicator of unmet consumer demand.

✔ **Encourage customer pickiness.** Businesses that win customers for life create discerning and demanding customers with expectations so high that no other business can rise to the occasion.

Why customers don't complain

The Direct Selling Educational Foundation reports that for every complaint received, the average business has another 26 customers with problems — at least six of which are serious. Here's why disgruntled customers stay mum:

- ✔ They don't think that anyone in the company cares.
- ✔ They don't know where to register their dissatisfaction.
- ✔ They're embarrassed to say anything because they know the owner.

You can't fix it if you can't hear it.

Encouraging input

Invite customer comments and study them well:

- ✔ **Talk with current customers.** Learn their opinions and their ideas about how you could better be of service. Watch for unstated clues to dissatisfaction (see following section).
- ✔ **Talk with past customers** to learn why they left, where they took their business, and what differences they were seeking.
- ✔ **Talk with employees.** Ask what kinds of concerns they're hearing. What needs do they sense? What do customers ask for that you aren't currently delivering?
- ✔ **Create a dialogue.**
  - • Opt for ongoing conversation rather than a one-time survey.
  - • Don't assume that you understand the concern. Give customers the chance to explain themselves fully.
  - • Respond to input promptly.
  - • Show appreciation for input. When changes result, tell your customer and offer your thanks for the idea. If a change is in the works, explain your plan and listen for further input.

Reading unstated customer clues to dissatisfaction

Many customers consider small business owners and employees their friends. For that reason they hesitate to complain, criticize, or directly share service complaints.

That means small business owners need to watch for unstated clues to dissatisfaction, including the following:

✔ Listen when they share compliments about other suppliers.

✔ Take note when they reminisce about how things *used to be.*

✔ Especially be aware if compliments they used to offer quit coming.

Hidden in your customers' comments may be concerns or complaints about your business, so listen carefully.

Handling complaints

Treat complaints like concerns. When a customer is dissatisfied, stop whatever else you're doing and give your full attention, following these steps:

1. Listen to the problem.

✔ Let the customer rant, preferably out of earshot of others.

✔ Don't argue. Don't make excuses or blame others.

✔ Don't make the problem seem routine by pulling out a form to complete.

✔ Empathize. Paraphrase the problem and offer to help.

✔ If your company is at fault, apologize. If you're not sure, give the customer the benefit of the doubt, within reason. Protect the relationship, the possibility of future business, and the chance for future positive word-of-mouth.

2. Take action.

✔ Offer options to allow the customer some control over the outcome.

✔ Say what you can do, not what you can't do. Opt for *I'll see that the refund is ready by 10 a.m. tomorrow* rather than *We can't cut a check today.*

✔ If your product or company is at fault, a refund or replacement isn't enough. Provide a no-strings-attached add-on that delivers value with no additional spending requirement.

✔ Refunds or exchanges may fix the problem, but only personal service will repair a relationship.

3. Follow up.

Call the customer to see that the problem was adequately resolved to the customer's complete satisfaction.

- ✔ Ask if the customer is completely satisfied with the outcome and whether there is anything else you may do to help further.

- ✔ Thank the customer for voicing concern and letting your company make things right.

4. Fix your business. Revamp systems if necessary. Ask:

- ✔ Is this the first complaint of its kind or one of many?

- ✔ Did we oversell the product?

- ✔ Can we eliminate this fault?

- ✔ Did we address the customer concern promptly and well?

Turn complaints into loyalty springboards

Dissatisfied customers complain to dozens of friends and post disparaging messages that reach thousands of others online, but you'll find it comforting to know that a complaint well handled repairs itself, circumvents potential damage, and results in an even stronger customer relationship.

McKinsey & Company has conducted research showing that when a complaint is resolved, more than half of initially dissatisfied customers will buy again, and when it is resolved rapidly, the number rises to 80 percent.

Best of all, if you resolve a complaint on the spot, the chance of keeping the customer's business — even inspiring the customer's loyalty — soars above 90 percent.

Developing Positive Word-of-Mouth

It may not be fair, but bad news travels faster than good news.

Someone who is dissatisfied with your business will share the tale of woe with three times more people than a person will who is highly satisfied with your offerings.

Stack the odds in your favor by handling every customer exchange with a view as to how that person will describe the encounter to a friend.

Show care, competence, and concern; anticipate and exceed expectations; provide great service; and send each customer away from your business with only good words to share with others.

Building a Customer Service Environment

Make customer satisfaction a core value of your company.

Insist on customer respect and courtesy. Don't air dirty laundry about customer disagreements. And don't speak poorly about your employees, your competition, or your customers — ever.

Empower employees to do the right thing for customers. Give rewards to great employees and to great customers. Treat employees and customers like VIPs by following these ten surefire tips:

- ✔ Get to know your customers, recognize them as individuals, and treat them like friends, insiders, and valued partners.

- ✔ Create a team of great service people within your business and reward their efforts with frequent and sincere gestures of recognition and appreciation.

- ✔ Anticipate customer needs.

- ✔ Communicate often.

- ✔ Thank customers for their business.

- ✔ Encourage customer requests and respond with tailor-made solutions.

- ✔ Bend your rules to keep loyal customers happy.

- ✔ Provide extra services and favors to high-volume and long-time customers.

- ✔ Make dealing with your business a highlight of your customer's day.

- ✔ Teach your customers to expect your company's service and keep your standard so high that no other business can rise to the level you set.

Chapter 19

Fortifying Customer Relationships

· ·

In This Chapter

▶ Retaining customers through defensive marketing

▶ Knowing and delivering what customers want

▶ The difference between satisfied and loyal customers

▶ Nurturing your best customers

· ·

*E*specially during times of competitive or economic threat, developing unshakable customer relationships is the smartest — and most economically efficient — way to proceed.

Strong customer relationships protect your business from competitive assault. What's more, they lead to customer loyalty, and loyal customers allow you to generate repeat sales at a fraction of the marketing cost and effort required to find, inform, interest, and sell new prospects.

Plus, loyal customers spread good will for your business, bringing along a tide of new customers with their positive words.

Creating loyal customers is essential to business success. This chapter shows why and how.

Why Customer Loyalty Matters

The U.S. Department of Commerce confirms that it costs five times more to get a new customer than it does to retain a current one. Research from Xerox Corporation shows that customers who claim to be "totally satisfied" are six times more likely to become repeat purchasers than customers who claim to be only "satisfied." Other studies show that a loyal customer is worth ten times the value of a single-purchase customer.

Defensive marketing

In war and sports, defenders are the ones who protect from threats, withstand attacks, and prevent opponents from gaining an advantage. Defenders protect the goal. They place more emphasis on preventing an opponent from gaining an advantage than on winning new territory or scoring new points.

There's a marketing lesson in the analogy.

When sales are down or the balance sheet is under siege, many businesses go on the marketing offensive — reducing prices, launching promotions, and increasing advertising to win new customers.

Defensive marketers place greatest value on keeping existing customers and protecting ongoing relationships by providing unrivaled service and communication. They fortify themselves against competitive attacks by training customers to expect service levels other businesses can't meet. They build customer loyalty — and reap the resulting benefits — by delivering consistently enhanced value to customers who grow ever more loyal as a result.

Why else does loyalty matter?

Consider this list:

- ✔ Loyal customers account for higher buying rates and lower marketing and service costs than other customers.

- ✔ Loyal customers involve fewer business risks because you know their credit status, buying preferences and purchasing patterns.

- ✔ Loyal customers respond to customer service that costs far less than the cost involved to recruit a new customer.

- ✔ Loyal customers are the best source of qualified referrals to your business.

- ✔ Loyal customers lead to a loyal staff (and vice versa), because the long-term relationships create a pleasant environment in which to work and do business.

Making Customers for Life

Small businesses have an advantage when it comes to making customers for life.

In most small businesses, the person who facilitates the sale continues to have customer contact after the fact. As a result, the style and service mode that attracted the customer in the first place continues unaltered, and the customer's buying decision is reaffirmed during every future contact.

On the contrary, large businesses are usually organized in departments: The marketing group is in charge of getting customers. Then, once the customers are on board, their contacts switch to people in the purchasing, distribution, delivery, and other departments. The *marketing* mindset changes to an *operational* mindset, and too often the customer gets lost in the shuffle.

As small businesses begin to get larger, some begin to adopt structures that resemble those of their big-business role models — and suddenly their customer focus begins to change. Don't let this happen to you. Manage your business so that every person in your organization realizes the value of every customer — not only to your sales today, but also to your sales tomorrow and well into the future, when the customer's positive comments will lead others to your business. (See Chapter 18 for ideas on how to identify, serve, and win more business from your best customers.)

Valuing your customers

Imagine that each of your customers arrived wearing a price tag reading *Replacement Cost: $1,000.* Imagine that even your inquiries and responses to ads came equipped with signs saying *I cost $75.* Don't you think that everyone in your company would handle each contact with greater care if they realized what it cost to bring that person into your business — and what it will cost if you have to recruit a replacement?

Estimating the cost of a new customer

To roughly estimate the cost of bringing a new customer into your business, apply the following formula:

Begin with the cost of last year's marketing program. Even a wild guess at what your company spent in advertising, sales, public relations, promotions, signage, brochures, and other communication vehicles will provide a good starting point.

Subtract marketing costs that were directed toward repeat or loyal customer marketing communications — for example, customer newsletters, customer promotions, and customer entertainment.

Divide by the number of new customers you attracted last year.

The result is a rough approximation of what it costs to develop a new customer for your business.

Share your findings with others in your company so that they are aware of the valuable commodity with which they are dealing each time they have customer contact.

Once you know the cost of getting a customer, you'll have an indicator of how much expense you can justify to keep that customer on board.

If your calculations show that getting a new customer costs you $300, you'll know not to risk losing that person's business over a $50 dispute. Whether it means accepting a questionable return, or writing off a contested charge, or indulging a customer with extra service or an unexpected gift, the investment will likely cost less than the expense and effort required to replace that customer with a new recruit.

Customer economics

Whether a customer buys from you once or a hundred times, your initial marketing investment is the same. What changes is your *ROI* or return on investment — demonstrated in the following formula — which goes up dramatically when the consumer becomes a long-term customer, allowing you to offset the cost of customer acquisition with revenue from multiple sales:

ROI for a One-Time Customer = Profit from 1st and Only Sale

ROI for a Long-Term Customer = Profit from 1st Sale + Profit from 2nd Sale + Profit from 3rd Sale + Profit from 4th Sale + Profit from 5th Sale + Profits from all future sales over coming weeks and years

Expanding your share of your customer's billfold

When you increase your *market share* (see Chapter 4), you win a greater portion of all the sales of products like yours that are purchased in your market area. This requires an *offensive marketing* approach that seeks to win business from competitors.

When you increase your *share of customer,* you capture a greater number of purchases from existing customers, employing a *defensive marketing* approach that fortifies and builds upon your valuable existing relationships.

The most efficient way to put money on your bottom line is to increase business with existing customers.

Here's how:

- ✔ Think of the initial sale as the first step toward winning the customer's business for life — or at least for as long as that person remains in the market for the kind of products you offer.

- ✔ Develop relationships. Let customers tell you what they want. Let them do most of the talking. Hear what they're saying and work hard not to jump in with reasons why their ideas won't work. Realize that if you can't address your customers' needs, someone else will. Their words are the path to their billfolds — and to your success.

✔ Help customers understand your full product range. Use customer communications, promotions, and packaged offers to make it easy for customers to make additional purchases from your business.

✔ Increase the relationship between your business and your customers by developing loyalty programs (see the section at the end of this chapter) to reward customers for increased business.

✔ Offer products your customers want to buy, provide them in the way that customers want to receive them, emphasize value rather than price, and convert each customer into a friend of your business.

Capturing additional sales

Make a list of all the products and services your business offers and use it to analyze how much of your full product line your customers currently buy.

Act upon your findings following these steps:

✔ **Determine which products your customers are buying from your competitors rather than from your business.** This finding will help you evaluate reasons behind this uncaptured business. Does your customer not know that you offer this product? Does your customer believe that your competitor offers better value for this product? Would this product gain appeal if it were packaged with a primary product that your customer *is* buying from your business?

✔ **Discover which products your customers aren't buying from you *or anyone else.*** This information may help you decide whether to drop certain products from your line or whether these products merit reintroduction via a new marketing investment. You may choose to let a lagging product fade out on its own, but only if it isn't costing you an unwarranted investment in space or staff attention.

✔ **Learn the combinations of products your customers tend to buy.** If your best customers consistently purchase a certain combination of products from you, use this information to create added-value product packages that bundle the offerings along with a bonus product or a beneficial price. By doing so, you will be giving your best customers additional value, and you'll also be using the purchasing patterns of your loyalists to attract the interest of others like them.

✔ **Develop ways to lock in sales of products your customers buy on a regular basis.** Try to make buyers *customers for life* by seeking to automate the purchases they make from you on a frequent basis.

  • Offer an annual contract at a preferred rate. Your customer will benefit from preferential pricing while you benefit from assured business.

- Sell a service contract at the time of equipment purchase, or bundle the price of the contract right into the purchase price. Doing so helps ensure that your customer's purchase gets consistent service while also tying the customer to your business through frequent contact and a positive ongoing relationship.

- Set up the next appointment before the customer leaves the current appointment. Promise a reminder 48 hours before the next meeting to ensure your own repeat business.

- See whether there is an equivalent to the good old milk delivery service for your business, allowing you to automatically deliver products on a regular schedule rather than waiting for the customer to initiate the purchase. Can you think of some way to establish a standing agreement for product delivery to circumvent the need for the customer to place an order prior to each purchase?

- Think of ways that you can establish an *on approval* agreement with your best customers — where you deliver new offerings on the condition that customers can return them (or you will pick them up) if they aren't wanted or needed.

As an example, interior designers are perfect *on agreement* suppliers. They charge a set fee for decorating services and install their recommendations — with price tags intact. The clients then buy and keep the whole works or call for pickup of the items they don't want.

What Customers Want

Simply put, customers want their needs to be met and their expectations to be exceeded.

- ✔ They want value that exceeds the price paid.
- ✔ They want clarity in the messages they receive.
- ✔ They want their concerns addressed with sensitivity and efficiency.
- ✔ They want their situation to be understood.
- ✔ They want to be greeted and served promptly.
- ✔ They want to feel important and valued.

When asked to rank the factors that contribute to their satisfaction, customers list such attributes as responsiveness, competence, convenience, and reliability. But guess which attribute tops the list? More than anything else, customers want good communication.

Benchmarking customer satisfaction levels

Table 19-1 helps you analyze areas where customers might praise or fault your business. Use it to assess your business from your customer's viewpoint. Then look for up to five services you could offer to make your customers feel more appreciated by your business.

Table 19-1	Customer Satisfaction Analysis
Customer Satisfaction Factor	**How We Rate on a 1–10 Scale**
Communication	
Clear, friendly communication from informed, courteous staff	
Error-free correspondence, estimates, invoices	
Prompt follow-up	
Open to ideas, concerns, and complaints	
Attention by owners/managers	
Responsiveness	
Customized solutions for customer wants/needs	
Flexible to special requests	
Effective, prompt response to ideas and problems	
Answers phones, mail, and e-mail promptly	
Greets customers upon arrival	
No unnecessary management layers	
Competence	
Expertise in customer's field of interest	
Experience with customer's problems	
Delivers high value	
Convenience	
Convenient hours, toll-free phone line, good Web access	
Good location, parking, access, services	

(continued)

Table 19-1 (continued)

Customer Satisfaction Factor	How We Rate on a 1–10 Scale
Convenient payment/delivery options	
Enjoyable, attractive atmosphere	
Reliability	
Meets deadlines/exceeds promises	
Delivers accurate, quality products	
Stays within estimated costs	
Attention by owners/principals	
Good reputation/highly recommended	

Using the cash register as a customer satisfaction monitor

Customers vote with their billfolds and your cash register is their ballot box. If your sales-per-customer and repeat business rates are increasing, you're doing something right. If they're declining, it's time to go into repair mode.

Monitor the size of your sales transactions. Is the dollar volume of your average sale going up or down? If you're a retailer, you can get this data from the cash register tape. If you're a service business, your invoices will tell the story.

Your business is on the right track if it has

- A growing number of new customers coming through the door.
- A declining number of customers defecting after one or two purchases.
- An increase in the expenditure per sales transaction.

Good marketers consider the customer their boss. As you monitor customer satisfaction, ask yourself, *Is my boss giving me a raise?*

Building Loyalty

Service builds loyalty.

To walk into a business and be greeted by name is a customer luxury.

To check into a hotel and be welcomed like a valued frequent guest is a pleasure.

To be walked to your favorite table in a restaurant, to have your voice recognized in a phone call to a small business, to have a record of your recent purchases on file for easy reference — these are the kinds of conveniences and service indicators that move satisfied customers into the loyal customer category.

Imagine this hotel check-in scenario:

The clerk enters your name in the computer, looks up and says, *Welcome back! It's been nearly three months since your last stay, so you haven't seen our remodeled restaurant. Let us know if we can make a reservation for you, and here's a card for a complimentary glass of wine with dinner. For now, let me get you registered. Last time you preferred a nonsmoking room on the tenth floor. Do you have a different preference for this stay?*

Now compare it with this approach: *Good afternoon. Do you have a reservation? Under what name? Could you spell that again? Have you stayed with us before?*

To develop loyalty, never make a frequent guest feel like a first-time guest and aim to make even a first-time guest feel like a long-time friend. See Chapter 18 for customer service guidelines and tips.

Closing the quality gap

A *quality gap* occurs when there is a difference between a customer's service expectation and the perceived level of service received.

The quality gap exists entirely in the mind of the customer. Whether service is satisfactory depends completely on your customer's opinion. The litmus test is simply whether the perception of service exceeded or fell short of what was expected.

To eliminate the possibility of a quality gap — and to build customer loyalty — train your customers to have high service expectations. Then exceed them with each customer encounter.

Customer loyalty prescriptions

Sort your customers into the following three categories and then use Table 19-2 as you work to move as many as possible to the invaluable *loyal customer* rank:

- ✔ **Satisfied customers** find their relationship with your business acceptable. They have no complaints about the promptness with which they are served, the accuracy of their transactions, the responsiveness of your service, or the effectiveness and friendliness of your staff. But neither are they amazed by their dealings with your business, and for that reason they are susceptible to better offers from competitors.

- ✔ **Dissatisfied customers** believe that their value and service expectations were not met. Perhaps they received outright poor service. More often they received mediocre service, based on how they were greeted, the time it took to help them, the way their complaints were handled, or the quality of the service or product they received.

  Once dissatisfied, they will make an immediate or gradual departure from your business. Most pay their final bill politely and say thank you on the way out the door, and 94 out of 100 leave without a word of complaint to your business. But they won't remain silent. They'll personally share their dissatisfaction with anywhere from 5 to 20 other people, and thousands more if they use the reach of the Internet as they air their discontent.

- ✔ **Loyal customers** are the only customers who are safe from defection. They reduce the cost side of your profit and loss statement while benefiting the revenue side by costing less and spending more than others who buy from your business.

Use Table 19-2 as you work to move customers into the loyal customer category.

Table 19-2	Customer Loyalty Prescriptions	
Customer Type	*Customer Mindset*	*Service Prescription*
Dissatisfied Customer	Service expectations have not been met.	Establish rapport. Learn and address concerns. The damage may be done, but try anyway.

Customer Type	Customer Mindset	Service Prescription
Satisfied Customer	Satisfied customers are vulnerable customers. They find your service acceptable but they aren't overwhelmed. They will leave for a better price, offer, convenience, or recognition.	Treat them like VIPs. If they sense indifference, they'll slip out the door. Demonstrate appreciation. Do them favors. Offer added value. Bend your rules. Anticipate their needs. Win their trust.
Loyal Customer	Loyal customers are safe from defection so long as their service expectations are met, and their expectations are sky-high.	Treat them like your most valuable assets. Follow the prescription for converting "Satisfied Customers" but double the dosage. Caution: Don't take them for granted. Don't burden them with your problems or test their patience while you court new customers.

Using loyalty programs

Loyalty programs inspire customers to increase use of a company's products or services by rewarding repeat purchases with discounts or added-value offers.

Playing the 80/20 customer odds

The 80/20 rule maintains that 20 percent of your consumers will account for 80 percent of your sales. Conversely, 80 percent of your problems will come from 20 percent of your customers. The concept actually has a name. It's called Pareto's Law, named after the economist who developed the theory, which is formally known as the *law of misdistribution*.

The problem: You want to acquire and cultivate customers in the trouble-free, highly profitable 20 percent group, but if you're not careful, the problematic 20 percent will consume your time instead.

The solution: Listen to discontented customers and do what you can to right the wrongs they cite. But don't allow your energy to be consumed by those who may never be entirely happy with you or your business — or any other business, for that matter. Instead, tip the marketing odds in favor of your business by focusing on your most content and profitable customers. Plan your marketing program to cater to their wants and needs, telegraph their satisfactions to your market, and let them serve like a magnet to attract more people just like them to your business.

The concept of loyalty programs took hold in the 1970s when airlines launched the first frequent flyer reward programs. Over the past decade, as businesses have put ever-greater emphasis on keeping current customers, loyalty programs have grown to the point that today the majority of consumers participate in at least one program, and businesses everywhere are working to figure out how to add a loyalty program to their marketing efforts.

Before starting your own program, first choose one of the following loyalty program goals:

✔ To maintain customer spending habits in an effort to reverse the natural decline in buying activity that otherwise tends to occur over time.

✔ To increase sales by enhancing a feeling of inclusion and loyalty to your business.

✔ To show customer appreciation by providing rewards for past purchases, which tends to inspire additional buying activity.

✔ To collect information on customer buying patterns and preferences. Be cautious, though: Customers can feel duped if your program looks more like an effort to conduct research than to extend rewards.

The next step is to design your program, using one of the following loyalty program formats:

✔ **Buy-ahead discounts.** This kind of program aims to lock in loyalty at the time of a first purchase with a card that entitles the buyer to an immediate bonus along with discounts on future purchases.

Benefit: The business receives up-front revenue and customer commitment due to the lure of the ongoing discount and the constant reminder provided by the membership card. The customer receives valuable rewards extended only to those participating in the program.

Downside: Because they require a purchase, customers view buy-ahead discounts more as product promotions than customer rewards.

✔ **Purchase-level rewards or discounts.** These programs offer customers a free gift or discount when they pass a certain spending level. For instance, a clothing retailer might offer customers a discount when sales in a single year reach $500. Or a hotel might offer a fifth night free.

Benefit: The program inspires customers to consolidate their purchases at a single business to become eligible for the purchase-level bonus.

Downside: The program sometimes requires a fair amount of small print to explain what kinds of purchases apply, what spending level needs to be reached, what time period is involved, and what discount applies. Its appeal relies upon the simplicity with which it can be explained and the significance of the spending-level reward.

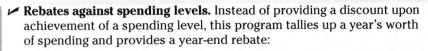

✔ **Rebates against spending levels.** Instead of providing a discount upon achievement of a spending level, this program tallies up a year's worth of spending and provides a year-end rebate:

Benefit: Urges buyer to rack up purchases for end-of-year payoff.

Downside: Success relies on the size of the rebate. Also, because the customer has to wait so long for payoff, it inspires only the most cost-sensitive consumer, who is likely not the buyer in whom you want to invest your marketing effort.

✔ **Upgrades and special treatments.** This program relies on the value of surprise rewards. Imagine driving into a car wash, pulling out your bill-fold, and having the attendant say, *Our license plate reader tells us this is your tenth trip through our car wash, and we want to make this one on us, along with a complimentary wax and hand-dry finish.*

Benefit: The spontaneous nature of the reward combines customer recognition and customer service, a surefire loyalty-development formula.

Downside: Customers will begin to anticipate and expect this kind of acknowledgement, so be prepared for ongoing commitment to customer recognition to keep your best customers inspired by demonstration of appreciation.

Avoid programs that look more like promotions than rewards or that provide incentives with too many strings attached.

For example, a $10 certificate good *through the end of this month on any in-stock, regularly priced item of $24.99 or more* looks more like a come-on than a gift.

In customer service and in customer loyalty programs, give customers what they want, deliver consistently, show true appreciation, and exceed expectations that only your business can meet. See Chapter 18 for tips.

Part VI
The Part of Tens

The 5th Wave   By Rich Tennant

In this part . . .

The marketing world operates on a fast clock, and this part keeps pace with rapid-fire advice and ten-step answers to commonly faced marketing issues.

If you want an at-a-glance list of ten ideas to embrace and avoid as a marketer, or ten thoughts to consider before choosing or changing a business name, or ten steps to follow when writing a marketing plan (in a hurry!), Part VI is your place.

These three quick final chapters are followed by an Appendix listing great places to turn for yet more information as you build your marketing program.

Here's to your marketing solutions — and to your marketing success!

Chapter 20

Ten Questions to Ask Before You Choose a Name

In This Chapter
- ▶ Figuring out what kind of name you want
- ▶ Looking at a name from every angle
- ▶ Determining whether the name you want is available

*Y*our name is the key to your brand image in your customer's mind. Chosen well, it will unlock an image that is unique, memorable, appropriate, likeable, and capable of advancing a promise for your business.

Here are ten questions to ask before committing to or changing your business name.

What Kind of Name Do You Want?

Most business names fit into one of the following categories:

- ✓ **The owner's name:** If Jim Smith is opening an accounting firm, he can name it Jim Smith Accounting. The name is easy to choose, easy to register, and sure to put forth the promise that Jim Smith is proud of this business and willing to give it his own name. On the downside, the name is hard to pass along if Jim decides he wants to sell his practice.

- ✓ **A geographic name:** If a new financial institution calls itself Central Coast Bank, the name has local market appeal but it restricts the institution from expanding outside the Central Coast area.

- ✓ **An alphabet name:** With a name like ABC Paving, you can assure yourself first place in the Yellow Pages — if the name is available. Be aware, however, that alphabet soup names are generic and don't advance a personality or promise.

✔ **A descriptive name:** This type of name tells what you do and how you do it. A consulting firm specializing in business turnarounds might call itself U-Turn Strategies to convey its offerings and promise to clients.

✔ **A borrowed interest name:** This type of name bears no direct relationship to the company or product. Borrowed interest names require heavy marketing to link the name to a business image, but done right they can work marketing magic. Just look at Apple, Nike, or Infinity.

✔ **A fabricated name:** You can create a name from an acronym, from words or syllables linked to form a new word, or by stringing together letters that result in a pleasant sound with no dictionary meaning, for example Verizon, Kodak, or the Toyota Ciera.

A fabricated name is likely to be available and protectable, and because the word doesn't yet exist, the Internet domain name probably hasn't yet been taken.

What Do You Want the Name to Convey?

Choose a name that depicts or supports your desired business image and position (see Chapter 7).

Attributes you may want your name to convey include service, speed, quality, skill, expertise, convenience, efficiency, creativity, professionalism, and unique knowledge.

Avoid words like *quality, creative,* or *premier,* even if they define your offering well. Fair or not, there's an inverse relationship between companies that claim that they're the best and consumers who believe that they are.

Is the Name You Want Available?

The law will stop you from using a name that is too close to an existing business name or trademark, so before falling in love with a name, see whether it's available. If it is, move quickly to protect it for your use.

✔ **Screen the name.** The U.S. Patent and Trademark Office has an online database of registered and pending trademarks. Go to www.uspto.gov to conduct an online search to see whether the name you want is available.

✔ **See whether the name is available as a domain name.** Search for the name using at least three major search engines to see whether it is already part of a domain name. Or conduct a free search at www.networksolutions.com, following the instructions for registering a domain name.

> ✔ **Protect the name if it's available.** Register the name with your state's Secretary of State office. If you plan to do business across state or international borders, also consider a trademark to help prevent others from promoting a similar name, logo, or distinctive aspect of your business.
>
> Contact an attorney who specializes in trademark protection or visit the U.S. Patent and Trademark Office at www.uspto.gov.

Is It Easy to Spell?

The best names have four to eight letters, look good in writing, and are spelled just like they sound.

Avoid unusual spaces, hyphens, or symbols, aiming instead for a straightforward presentation that consumers are almost certain to spell correctly based on guesswork alone. Be aware that names that begin with *The* or *A* are confusing to find in the Yellow Pages.

And try to steer clear of clever alternate spellings (for example, *Compleat* for *Complete*) unless you have the ad dollars to teach the market how you spell the name.

Is It Easy to Say?

Show your name to people and ask them to read it. Do they pronounce it correctly? Is it phonetically pleasing? Do you think it will work well in normal business conversation?

As a test, imagine a receptionist answering the phone using the name. *(Good morning, this is Greatname Consulting. May I help you?)*

Be sure that the name sounds good when it is said out loud.

Is It Original?

Look up the name in your local phone book and in the phone book for the biggest city in your state to see how many other companies have sound-alike names.

Aim for an original name that stands apart from the pack.

Avoid names tied to dominant local geographic features, as they tend to get lost in a line-up of similarly named businesses. For example, in a mountainous area, you'll find names like Mountain View, Mountain Comfort, Mountain Country, Mountain Cycle, Mountain Pine, Mountain Shadow, and a mountain of other similar and easy-to-confuse names.

Is It Universal?

The Internet gives every company access to a worldwide market, so think globally as you settle on a business name. Look for a name that has a positive connotation in a range of major languages — and especially in the languages of those you feel may represent future markets for your business.

Is It Memorable?

Look for a name that reflects a distinct aspect of your company.

Businesses named after their founders are easy to remember because they link to the face of the owner, which triggers recollection of the name. Similarly, businesses named after a physical characteristic (Pebble Beach, for example) are memorable because the unique attribute creates such a strong impression.

Strong logos that reinforce the name also add to consumer recall of names.

Can You Live and Grow with This Name?

You're going to live with this name a long time, so the most important question of all may be *Do you like it?* Ponder this question alone. Names are like ads in that they don't get better as they undergo consideration by a committee. It's your business. Be sure that you like the name and that you're comfortable saying it, and you'll be proud repeating it countless times over years to come.

And that leads to the next most important question: Will the name adapt to your future?

Be careful about names that tie you to a specific geographic area or product offering, and especially be careful about names that include faddish buzzwords that can get stuck in time.

Are You Ready to Commit to the Name?

Once you settle on a name and determine that people can spell it, say it, remember it, and relate well to it (even in other cultures), you're ready to take the following steps:

1. **Register the name in your state, file for a trademark if you choose to, and secure the domain name if you can.**

2. **Create a professional logo to serve as the face of your name.**

3. **Make a list of every place that your name and logo will appear (see the "Impression Points" in Chapter 6) to use as you plan your name introduction.**

4. **Look for new ways to advance your name — on uniforms, apparel, signage, and other items that increase name awareness.**

If you're changing your name, budget to replace all items that carry your old identity. Also, plan to fund new communications to inform your customers, prospects, suppliers, colleagues, and friends about the reasons behind your new name.

Don't be two-faced by trying to use up your old materials while also introducing the new ones. Make a clean break.

Chapter 21

Ten Ideas to Embrace and Ten to Avoid

In This Chapter

▶ What the best marketers don't do

▶ What the best marketers do better than everyone else

Remember the old line about how half of all ad dollars are wasted but no one knows which half? The truth is, the best marketers do know.

The following two lists highlight what great marketers try awfully hard to avoid — and what they work awfully hard to do instead.

Ten Worst Marketing Ideas

The following ten marketing landmines masquerade as quick fixes. When the business chips are down, each of these worst ideas pops up to look like a good solution. Don't be fooled. Make sure every new idea soars above every single idea on this list.

1. Fight bad business with good advertising.

Here's the scenario: Business is down, so the owner points fingers at the economy and the competition and decides to run ads to overcome the problem. But the economy and the competition likely aren't the culprits. Business is down because customers have defected — and new prospects haven't been converted — because the company's product or service is lacking.

Running ads before improving the offering will only put a spotlight on the problem. In the words of advertising legend Bill Bernbach, "Nothing kills a bad product like a good ad." Instead, fix the product, polish the service, then run the ad.

2. Run kitchen sink ads.

A kitchen sink ad is like a kitchen sink argument in that every point — every feature, every idea, every department's viewpoint — is tossed into the mix in an effort to get *more bang for the buck* (a truly awful phrase that deserves its own place on the list of worst ideas). The result is a jam-packed ad featuring a long list of product bells and whistles but no clear focus and no attention-grabbing consumer benefit to seize and hold the prospect's mind.

Take aim instead: Know your best prospect and what need that person seeks to address (see Chapter 2). Then stop that person with a headline that highlights the promise of your most compelling benefit, backed by copy that proves your claim with facts (see Chapter 8).

3. Portray the customer as a fool.

Trying to be funny or grabbing attention by showing the customer as an inept bumbler wandering through life in search of your solution is hardly the way to win customers and influence buying decisions.

Form a sincere relationship with your prospect instead of poking fun at the very person you're trying to influence.

4. Save the best for last.

It happens in presentations, sales letters, and ads. Businesses wait to divulge the greatest benefits of their product until the last minute, thinking that prospects will be sitting on the edges of chairs in rapt anticipation.

Not so. If your opening doesn't grab them, they won't wait around. Four out of five people read only the headline (see Chapter 11), they listen to only the first few seconds of a radio ad, and if the first impression of a personal presentation is weak, they tune out for the rest. Eliminate slow starts and lead with your strengths.

5. Change your logo often and dramatically.

And while you're at it, change your Web site constantly. And your advertising tagline, too. It sounds ridiculous, but it's what happens when businesses let media departments, freelance artists, employees, and others create materials without the strong parameters of image guidelines to ensure a consistent company image (see Chapter 6).

If you want prospects to trust that yours is a strong, steady business (and you do!), show them a strong, steady business image.

6. Build it and trust they will come.

Sorry, but consumers aren't just sitting around waiting for the next new business, new Web site, new branch outlet, or new event to come into existence. They need to be told, reminded, inspired, and given reasons and incentives to take new buying actions. When you build it, build a plan to market it.

7. Move fast: If you snooze you might lose.

This is irresistible bait for businesses that operate without a marketing plan (see Chapter 22). They don't know their own objectives and strategies, and so any tactic sounds like a fine idea.

As a result, when a proposal comes in from an ad salesperson, an Internet business opportunity promoter, or even from a company that wants to merge or partner, the business owner is all ears, fearful that this might be an opportunity too good to pass on. Often, the idea comes with a quick deadline or the threat of involving a competitor instead, leading straight to a hasty decision.

Remember what they say about the correlation between haste and waste.

8. Think people will care that you're *under new management.*

Or think that they'll care that *We've doubled our floor space, We've added a new drive-up window,* or any other self-congratulatory announcement that produces similarly low market enthusiasm. To move the spotlight off yourself, add a customer benefit. Turn *We're celebrating our fifth anniversary* into *We're celebrating our fifth anniversary with five free events you won't want to miss.*

Remember, prospects care most about what's in it for them.

9. Believe there's a pie in the online sky.

Contrary to rampant belief, the opportunities of the cyber world aren't just ripe for the picking. The chance of opening a Web site and instantly winning business from distant new prospects is as likely as opening a toll-free line and immediately having it ring off the hook with orders.

To win your slice of online opportunity, invest time and money to drive people to your site (see Chapter 16).

10. Believe your customer is captive.

Reality is, your customers know they have other options.

If they're standing in front of you, and you turn your attention to answer a phone, they notice. If you offer new customers a better deal than current customers enjoy, they notice. If you spend more time and money courting new prospects than rewarding business from current clientele, they most certainly notice and in time will begin to disengage from your business as a result.

Realize that customer loyalty is the key to profitability, and that earning it is a never-ending process (see Chapters 18 and 19).

Ten Best Marketing Ideas

One marketing idea rises above all the others: *Write, commit to, and invest wisely in a marketing plan for your business.* That's the focus of this whole book and it's the topic of Chapter 22, which shrinks the task of writing your plan down to ten steps that fit even the busiest small business owner's calendar. Then as you implement your marketing program, join the best marketers by embracing the following ten ideas:

1. Know your elevator speech.

Elevator speeches grew out of the 1990s, when venture capitalists listened to full presentations only from entrepreneurs who could first provide a great 20-second answer (about the length of a typical elevator ride) to the question, *What does your business do?*

A good elevator speech is concise, well delivered, and capable of inspiring interest and generating questions — all while conveying what you do, whom you serve, and the unique benefits or solutions you offer.

Strike openings like *I sell life insurance, I run a social service agency,* or *I'm a consultant.* None of those inspires questions or leads to a conversation. Instead, differentiate yourself and communicate the unique benefits you provide.

For example, *After years as a university admissions director, I now help about 50 students a year to narrow college selections and complete their applications, coaching them as they write their essays and complete their financial aid forms.*

Businesses with the sharpest elevator speeches hone the sharpest marketing plans. Write yours today.

2. Make a great product before you make a great ad.

Be prepared before you promote. Be sure your product is ready for prime time before you announce its availability. Be sure you have an adequate inventory to fulfill the interest your marketing will generate. Be sure your distribution and sales channels are in place. Be sure your staff is knowledgeable about your product and about the ads you're running. And be sure that your business is prepared to provide enthusiastic service that exceeds what customers might encounter at any competing business.

3. Sweat the big stuff.

Make a great first impression.

Put at least as much effort into your ad headline as into your body copy. Devote at least as much energy to your introduction as you do to the entire rest of your sales presentation. Invest in your business lobby, the home page of your Web site, the cover of your brochure, the first sentence of a phone call, and every other first impression you're lucky enough to make for your business.

People decide to tune in based on early snap judgments. If you don't grab them with a strong opening, they won't be around to hear the details.

4. Sweat the little stuff.

Details tip the balance between good and great businesses. Answer your phones with a real live voice on the second ring, and your business will rise above the others. Promise same-day delivery and meet the promise consistently, and you'll create a league of your own. Come in under budget. Anticipate customer needs. Respond to nonverbal customer concerns.

Write prompt, personal thank-you notes. Follow up on suggestions. Become the most reliable business your customer deals with — then beat your own standard of excellence — and you'll set your customer's expectations higher than competitors can reach.

5. Say what you mean.

Believe in your product. Believe in your price, your quality, your service, and your value. Know everything there is to know about your product. Know why your product and your customer are a perfect fit. Know why your solution is better than any other option on the market. Know why people should place faith in your offering.

Then reduce what you know — and what you believe — to a few major points and powerful benefits that will make your prospect a believer, too.

6. Make new customers but cherish the old.

Develop new customers, of course, but develop profitability by concentrating efforts on your established customers. It costs five times more to get a new customer than it does to keep a current one, and a *totally satisfied* customer is six times more apt to become a repeat buyer. Those facts make existing customers your most lucrative marketing goldmine.

Capture the opportunity and leverage the power of your customer base following the advice in Chapters 18 and 19.

7. Like your customers.

Everyday shopping experiences validate the fact that people buy from people they like, and from people who seem to genuinely like them in return.

Treat every customer as an individual. Eliminate one-size-fits-all sales pitches. Listen to your customer's needs and tailor your offerings in response. Make eye contact. Build rapport. Send personally worded follow-up messages. Deliver value and continually enhance the customized service you train your customer to expect.

8. Increase value before lowering prices.

When customers see a price tag, they start a mental balancing act. In a split second they perform some pretty elaborate mental calculations to determine whether the product under consideration is worth the price being asked. They weigh the price against their assessment of the quality, features, convenience, reliability, trustworthiness, guarantee of excellence, and ongoing service they believe they can count on as part of the deal.

Price becomes a bone of contention when the customer feels it exceeds the value of the product under consideration. In that case, a marketer has two options: Ask for less money, or offer more value. Because prices can only go so low, and value can increase without limit, the best marketers know that enhancing value is the best first plan of attack.

See Chapter 3 for more information.

9. Break down barriers.

Eliminate unnecessary expenses, unnecessary waits, unnecessary frustration, and unnecessary inconvenience.

Eliminate management layers that contribute costs without value. Eliminate service snags that cost time and try patience. Eliminate the reasons behind recurring problems. Eliminate inconveniences that stand between you and your customer. If your phone system is annoying, replace it. If your Web site is slow or crashes frequently, rebuild it.

If getting to your business is inconvenient, take away the obstacles or find a way to bring your business to your customer via mail, e-mail, e-commerce, or personal delivery. Eliminate anything that erodes the value for which your customer is willing to pay a premium.

10. Get continuously better at what you do best.

People demand fair price, product quality, and prompt service.

They consider a company a contender only if it offers all three, and they make a company their first choice only if it excels at the attribute they value most highly. But here's the kicker: Customers expect a company to get continuously better at what they count on it to do best. This makes lowest price a pretty hard position to protect.

But if your business stands for the best quality, or the best service, you can — and must — find ways to improve on that point of distinction year after year after year.

When you do, your customers will reward you with positive word-of-mouth, new business referrals, repeat purchases, and — the most valuable marketing asset — their loyalty to your business.

Chapter 22

Ten Steps to a Great Marketing Plan

In This Chapter

▶ Tailoring a plan for your small business

▶ Using the plan to reach your goals

Contrary to popular misconception, *marketing plans* aren't just for the big guys. When small business owners hear the term, they tend to envision a leather-bound tome weighing down a polished bookshelf in some corporate VP's high-rise corner office.

In reality, you can write a marketing plan for your small business on a couple of sheets of paper that will turn your marketing effort into a planned investment rather than a hopeful risk. The following ten steps tell you how.

Step 1: State Your Business Purpose

Start with a one-sentence summary of your business purpose (see Chapter 7). For example, the purpose statement for *Small Business Marketing For Dummies* could be this:

To empower small businesses and entrepreneurs by providing big-time marketing advice scaled to fit the clocks, calendars, budgets, and pressing realities of the small business world.

Step 2: Define Your Market Situation

Describe the changes, problems, and opportunities that your business will face over the coming marketing plan period. In analyzing your situation, consider the following factors:

- ✓ **Your customers:** Are they undergoing changes that will affect their buying decisions? (See Chapter 2 for help defining your customers and their needs.)

- ✓ **Your competition:** How much direct and indirect competition do you face? Are new businesses entering your market arena to compete for your customers' buying decisions? Are competing companies making moves that threaten your business? Or are long-time competitors closing down and leaving a hole that you might move to fill?

  (See Chapter 4 for help assessing your competitive situation.)

- ✓ **The market environment:** Do you foresee economic changes that will affect your business? What about physical changes such as a building renovation that will affect buying patterns, or roadwork that will alter access to your business? Will your business be affected by special regional or industry events that will boost business if you promote around them? If your business is weather reliant, are forecasts in your favor? Factor these conditions into your situation analysis.

Step 3: Set Goals and Objectives

Marketing becomes a far more manageable task once you establish the goal you're trying to achieve. It might be that you want to win three new business clients. Or maybe you want to increase revenues by 10 percent. Arriving at your destination starts with naming where you want to go. After that, you can put your efforts in perspective and get moving toward success.

Your *goal* defines *what* you want your marketing plan to achieve. Your *objectives* define *how* you will achieve your goal.

Put your goal and objectives in writing and then stick with them for the duration of the market plan period. Each time a marketing opportunity arises, ask yourself, *Will this opportunity help us meet our goal? Does this opportunity support one or more of our objectives?* If the answer to either question is no, quickly pass on the opportunity.

Chapter 5 provides step-by-step advice for setting goals and objectives, which are the foundation of the marketing program.

Step 4: Define Your Market

Define your market in terms of *geographics* (where your customers and prospects live), *demographics* (who your customers are in factual terms such as age, gender, religion, ethnicity, marital status, income level, and household size), and *psychographics* (how your customers live including their attitudes, behavioral patterns, beliefs, and values). See Chapter 2 for assistance. By defining your market and knowing your customer profile, you can

- ✔ Develop marketing tactics that appeal to your target market.
- ✔ Create advertising messages that align with the unique interests and emotions of existing and prospective customers.
- ✔ Select effective communication vehicles.
- ✔ Weigh media sales pitches based on the ability of proposed advertising packages to reach those who match your customer profile — accepting opportunities with confidence *or* rejecting them quickly if they don't provide a cost-effective way to reach your clearly defined target market.

Step 5: Advance Your Position, Brand, and Creative Strategy

Your marketing plan should state your company's position and brand statements, along with the creative strategy you will follow to ensure that all marketing efforts implemented over the marketing plan period will advance a single, unified image for your company. Here are some definitions to help you with this step:

- ✔ Your *brand* is the set of characteristics, attributes, and implied promises that people remember and trust to be true about your business.
- ✔ Your *position* is the available and meaningful niche that your business — and *only* your business — can fill in your target consumer's mind.
- ✔ Your *creative strategy* is the formula you will follow to uphold your brand and position in all your marketing communications.

See Chapter 7 for information, examples, and step-by-step advice for creating your brand, positioning, and creative strategy statements.

Step 6: Set Your Marketing Strategies

The next component in your marketing plan details the strategies you will follow, including the strategies for each of the following:

- ✔ **Product strategies:** How will you use your products to develop customers and sales? Will you be introducing new products or revising existing products over the marketing period? Will you shift emphasis to a certain product or package of products?

See Chapter 3 for information on analyzing your product line, enhancing the appeal of existing products, and developing new products.

✔ **Distribution strategies:** Will you be altering the means by which you get your product to your customer? Will you be partnering with other businesses or opening additional outlets for off-premises sales? Will your Web site play an expanded role in getting your message or product to customers?

Chapter 2 includes a section on how to analyze distribution channels, along with advice on how to respond if a distribution channel begins to taper off in volume.

✔ **Pricing strategies:** Are you considering new payment options, a new frequent buyer pricing schedule, quantity discounts, rebates, or other pricing offers? Maybe you have a service business and this is the year you need to amend your rate structure.

Chapter 3 includes pricing facts to consider, along with advice for building a pricing strategy capable of bringing in new business rather than simply cutting prices on purchases by existing customers — and eroding your bottom line as a result.

✔ **Promotion strategies:** This part of your marketing plan describes how you will support your marketing strategies through advertising, public relations, and promotions.

For example, if your product strategy calls for a new product introduction, your promotion strategy needs to reflect that effort through a new product promotion campaign.

Once your strategies are set, you can spend time implementing an orchestrated and well-planned marketing program rather than frantically reacting to far-flung ideas all year long.

Step 7: Outline Your Tactics

The next section of your marketing plan details the tactics you will employ to implement your strategies. For example, if one of your strategies is to introduce a new product, the sequence of tactics may look like this:

✔ Review and select an ad agency; develop and produce ads.

✔ Develop a direct mail program and direct mail list.

✔ Develop a product brochure.

✔ Develop a publicity plan.

- ✔ Develop a Web page.

- ✔ Place ads in industry magazines.

- ✔ Send a direct mailer.

- ✔ Generate industry and regional-market publicity.

- ✔ Train your staff.

- ✔ Unveil product at a special event.

Parts III and IV of this book describe the marketing tools that you can use in your tactical plan, and Part V helps you make decisions about your Web site and online sales capability.

Step 8: Establish Your Budget

Your plan needs to define what your marketing program will cost. Avoid simply pulling out last year's budget and adding x percent for inflation. Opt instead for what is called a *zero-based* budget, which means starting with nothing and adding in costs to cover development of each element in your plan. Include costs for ad creation, media placements, direct mail, Web site design, trade show fees, displays, new packaging, and any other tactics included in your plan.

If you think you will need the professional assistance of freelancers or an agency, or if you will require additional staffing to implement your plan, now is the time to incorporate those costs into your budget request. Then add a contingency of up to 10 percent to cover unanticipated costs. No one ever built a successful business by marketing with leftover dollars. Plan your marketing budget as an integral part of your marketing plan, get it approved as part of the plan, and invest the money wisely.

Step 9: Blueprint Your Action Plan

This part of your plan brings all your strategies and tactics together into an action plan. One easy way to prepare this blueprint is to create an action agenda in calendar form. Make a page for each month of the year. Create four columns down each page — one each for the specified action, the budget for that action, the deadline, and the responsible party for each step along the way. If it's on the calendar, and someone is responsible to meet a deadline, chances are better than good that it will actually happen.

Step 10: Think Long Term

In the final section of your marketing plan, include a list of market development opportunities that you will research over the coming year for possible action in future marketing plan periods.

Some ideas can't be (or shouldn't be) rushed into. Spend some time as you produce *this* year's marketing plan to think of what ideas you want to research for possible implementation over the course of *next* year's plan.

Your long-term planning might focus on the development of one or several of the following areas:

- ✔ New or expanded business locations to serve more consumers
- ✔ New geographic market areas outside you current market area
- ✔ New customers different than those represented by your current customer profile
- ✔ New products or product packages that will inspire additional purchases
- ✔ New pricing strategies
- ✔ New distribution channels
- ✔ New customer service programs
- ✔ Mergers, business acquisitions, recruitment of key executives, and formation of new business alliances

Choose one to three opportunities to explore and commit to producing an analysis before development of next year's marketing plan begins.

One Final Step: Use Your Plan

This step is the easiest to state and the most important.

Use your plan.

Share it with key associates. Provide it when you give background information to your ad agency. And use it to keep yourself on track as you manage your business to marketing success.

Appendix

Where to Find More Information

* *

*T*he resources available to marketers are far-reaching and continually updated. To simplify your search, start with these information-rich Web sites, periodicals, and books.

Small Business Web Sites

The Kauffman Foundation's Entreworld: www.entreworld.org This site offers an entrepreneur's search engine and areas full of links to information for starting and growing your business.

SCORE: www.score.org The Web site of the Service Corps of Retired Executives includes an area titled *Business Toolbox* with links to hundreds of Web sites, along with business and financial-planning templates, online workshops and quizzes, and even a tip of the day.

Small Business Administration: www.sba.gov Visit the SBA site and click on "Starting Your Business" or "Managing Your Business" for advice and information including links to dozens of useful sites.

About Small Business: www.about.com Click on *Business* and then on *Small Business* to reach links to how-to articles and resources for managing and marketing.

Advertising and Marketing Web Sites

Advertising World: http://advertising.utexas.edu/world/ This University of Texas site rightly bills itself as the "ultimate marketing communications directory." Click on your interest area to access a world of related resources.

Know This: www.knowthis.com A virtual library with links to sites providing information ranging from advertising and marketing basics to advice for writing and implementing marketing plans.

Marketer's Portal: www.marketersportal.com This resource links to 5,000 sites. Click on *Useful Sites* to access resources for advertising, creating, and promoting Web sites, Internet marketing, and media research.

Internet Marketing Web Sites

Network Solutions: www.networksolutions.com Site-building advice, e-business resources, and a no-obligation domain name search function.

Search Engine Watch: www.searchenginewatch.com Click on *Search engine submission tips* for information about getting your site recognized and to learn current tips for optimizing your site for crawlers.

Wilson Internet Services Web Marketing Today: www.wilsonweb.com This site is all about doing business online. The free weekly newsletter covers e-mail, e-commerce, site design and promotion, affiliate marketing, and more.

The Newsstand

Business 2.0: Insights and advice about business, technology, and innovation in today's business world. To view the current issue and search an archive of articles, visit the magazine's Web site (www.business2.com).

Entrepreneur: Offering business advice for growing companies in print or online (www.entrepreneur.com), where you can click to access business management and marketing advice or to view articles from the current issue.

Fast Company: Information on recruiting, managing, and fueling business and careers. The Web site (www.fastcompany.com) offers access to back issues and archives.

Inc.: "The magazine for growing companies" offers information in print and online (www.inc.com), where in addition to reading recent issues, you can access business advice, guides, and polls.

The Wall Street Journal: Subscribe for breaking, financial, and business news, or read headlines online (http://public.wsj.com), where you can also access free small business resources and tools (www.startupjournal.com).

Advertising Periodicals

Advertising Age: A weekly magazine covering advertising and industry trends, news, and insights.

AdWeek: Weekly news on the advertising community.

Communication Arts: This highly regarded creative resource, available in many libraries, will inspire you with top-quality reproductions of advertising and marketing materials.

"For Dummies" Books for Small Business Marketers

***Building Your Business With Google For Dummies* by Brad Hill:** Climb higher on the Google index and explore Google advertising opportunities.

***Customer Service For Dummies* by Karen Leland and Keith Bailey:** This book holds the keys to quality service and success.

***Home-Based Business For Dummies,* 2nd Edition, by Paul and Sarah Edwards and Peter Economy:** Everything from when and whether to leave your day job to how to find and deal with insurance, competitors, and lawyers.

***Sales Closing For Dummies* by Tom Hopkins:** Hands-on tools to execute the critical part of the sales negotiation — the close.

***Sales Prospecting For Dummies* by Tom Hopkins:** Full of insights about prospecting — the first step of a successful sales effort.

***Small Business For Dummies,* 2nd Edition, by Eric Tyson and Jim Schell:** The resource for those starting or growing a small business.

Marketing Classics

***Guerilla Marketing* by Jay Conrad Levinson:** Secrets for making big profits from your small business (Houghton Mifflin).

***How to Win Customers and Keep Them for Life* by Michael LeBoeuf:** An action-ready blueprint for achieving the winner's edge (Berkley).

Positioning: The Battle for Your Mind **by Al Ries and Jack Trout:** How to be seen and heard in the overcrowded marketplace (McGraw-Hill).

Selling the Invisible **by Harry Beckwith:** A field guide to modern marketing (Warner Books).

The One-to-One Future **by Don Peppers and Martha Rogers, PhD:** Building relationships one customer at a time (Doubleday).

The 22 Immutable Laws of Branding **by Al Ries and Laura Ries:** How to build a product or service into a world-class brand (HarperCollins).

Why We Buy **by Paco Underhill:** Shopping science (Simon & Schuster).

The Library Reference Area

Bacon's Media Directories: The *Newspaper/Magazine Directory* lists media descriptions and editorial contacts at U.S., Canadian, Mexican, and Caribbean newspapers; 15,000 magazines and newsletters; community, ethnic, college, and university publications; and news services. The *Radio/TV/Cable Directory* lists U.S. and Canadian stations, broadcast syndicators, and news bureaus. The *Internet Media Directory* lists nearly 7,000 Web site listings, organized by media type, geography, and subject matter.

ESRI Community Sourcebooks (formerly CACI Marketing Systems): These references help you forecast demand for your products, define changes in your market area, analyze your trade area, and target your marketing efforts by providing population, demographic data, income, and other consumer information for every U.S. ZIP code, Direct Marketing Area (DMA), and Metropolitan Statistical Area (MSA).

Standard Rate and Data Service (SRDS) Media Source books: SRDS assists media buyers by publishing standardized advertising rates, media contact information, and links to online media kits, Web sites, and audit statements. Available source books include the *Business Publication Advertising Source,* the *Consumer and Magazine Advertising Source,* the *Newspaper Advertising Source,* the *Out-of-Home Advertising Source,* the *TV and Cable Source,* the *Radio Advertising Source,* and the *Interactive Advertising Source,* which provides planning information for online advertising vehicles.

The Lifestyle Market Analyst: Published by SRDS and Equifax, this guide provides demographic and lifestyle data organized by geographic market area, lifestyle preferences, and consumer profiles.

Index

• *S* •

BUSINESS, CAREERS & PERSONAL FINANCE

0-7645-5307-0

0-7645-5331-3 *†

Also available:
- Accounting For Dummies †
  0-7645-5314-3
- Business Plans Kit For Dummies †
  0-7645-5365-8
- Cover Letters For Dummies
  0-7645-5224-4
- Frugal Living For Dummies
  0-7645-5403-4
- Leadership For Dummies
  0-7645-5176-0
- Managing For Dummies
  0-7645-1771-6

- Marketing For Dummies
  0-7645-5600-2
- Personal Finance For Dummies *
  0-7645-2590-5
- Project Management For Dummies
  0-7645-5283-X
- Resumes For Dummies †
  0-7645-5471-9
- Selling For Dummies
  0-7645-5363-1
- Small Business Kit For Dummies *†
  0-7645-5093-4

HOME & BUSINESS COMPUTER BASICS

0-7645-4074-2

0-7645-3758-X

Also available:
- ACT! 6 For Dummies
  0-7645-2645-6
- iLife '04 All-in-One Desk Reference
  For Dummies
  0-7645-7347-0
- iPAQ For Dummies
  0-7645-6769-1
- Mac OS X Panther Timesaving
  Techniques For Dummies
  0-7645-5812-9
- Macs For Dummies
  0-7645-5656-8

- Microsoft Money 2004 For Dummies
  0-7645-4195-1
- Office 2003 All-in-One Desk Reference
  For Dummies
  0-7645-3883-7
- Outlook 2003 For Dummies
  0-7645-3759-8
- PCs For Dummies
  0-7645-4074-2
- TiVo For Dummies
  0-7645-6923-6
- Upgrading and Fixing PCs For Dummies
  0-7645-1665-5
- Windows XP Timesaving Techniques
  For Dummies
  0-7645-3748-2

FOOD, HOME, GARDEN, HOBBIES, MUSIC & PETS

0-7645-5295-3

0-7645-5232-5

Also available:
- Bass Guitar For Dummies
  0-7645-2487-9
- Diabetes Cookbook For Dummies
  0-7645-5230-9
- Gardening For Dummies *
  0-7645-5130-2
- Guitar For Dummies
  0-7645-5106-X
- Holiday Decorating For Dummies
  0-7645-2570-0
- Home Improvement All-in-One
  For Dummies
  0-7645-5680-0

- Knitting For Dummies
  0-7645-5395-X
- Piano For Dummies
  0-7645-5105-1
- Puppies For Dummies
  0-7645-5255-4
- Scrapbooking For Dummies
  0-7645-7208-3
- Senior Dogs For Dummies
  0-7645-5818-8
- Singing For Dummies
  0-7645-2475-5
- 30-Minute Meals For Dummies
  0-7645-2589-1

INTERNET & DIGITAL MEDIA

0-7645-1664-7

0-7645-6924-4

Also available:
- 2005 Online Shopping Directory
  For Dummies
  0-7645-7495-7
- CD & DVD Recording For Dummies
  0-7645-5956-7
- eBay For Dummies
  0-7645-5654-1
- Fighting Spam For Dummies
  0-7645-5965-6
- Genealogy Online For Dummies
  0-7645-5964-8
- Google For Dummies
  0-7645-4420-9

- Home Recording For Musicians
  For Dummies
  0-7645-1634-5
- The Internet For Dummies
  0-7645-4173-0
- iPod & iTunes For Dummies
  0-7645-7772-7
- Preventing Identity Theft For Dummies
  0-7645-7336-5
- Pro Tools All-in-One Desk Reference
  For Dummies
  0-7645-5714-9
- Roxio Easy Media Creator For Dummies
  0-7645-7131-1

* Separate Canadian edition also available
† Separate U.K. edition also available

Available wherever books are sold. For more information or to order direct: U.S. customers visit www.dummies.com or call 1-877-762-2974.
U.K. customers visit www.wileyeurope.com or call 0800 243407. Canadian customers visit www.wiley.ca or call 1-800-567-4797.

SPORTS, FITNESS, PARENTING, RELIGION & SPIRITUALITY

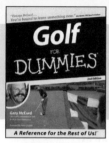

0-7645-5146-9

0-7645-5418-2

Also available:
- Adoption For Dummies
  0-7645-5488-3
- Basketball For Dummies
  0-7645-5248-1
- The Bible For Dummies
  0-7645-5296-1
- Buddhism For Dummies
  0-7645-5359-3
- Catholicism For Dummies
  0-7645-5391-7
- Hockey For Dummies
  0-7645-5228-7

- Judaism For Dummies
  0-7645-5299-6
- Martial Arts For Dummies
  0-7645-5358-5
- Pilates For Dummies
  0-7645-5397-6
- Religion For Dummies
  0-7645-5264-3
- Teaching Kids to Read For Dummies
  0-7645-4043-2
- Weight Training For Dummies
  0-7645-5168-X
- Yoga For Dummies
  0-7645-5117-5

TRAVEL

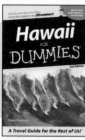 

0-7645-5438-7

0-7645-5453-0

Also available:
- Alaska For Dummies
  0-7645-1761-9
- Arizona For Dummies
  0-7645-6938-4
- Cancún and the Yucatán For Dummies
  0-7645-2437-2
- Cruise Vacations For Dummies
  0-7645-6941-4
- Europe For Dummies
  0-7645-5456-5
- Ireland For Dummies
  0-7645-5455-7

- Las Vegas For Dummies
  0-7645-5448-4
- London For Dummies
  0-7645-4277-X
- New York City For Dummies
  0-7645-6945-7
- Paris For Dummies
  0-7645-5494-8
- RV Vacations For Dummies
  0-7645-5443-3
- Walt Disney World & Orlando For Dummies
  0-7645-6943-0

GRAPHICS, DESIGN & WEB DEVELOPMENT

0-7645-4345-8

0-7645-5589-8

Also available:
- Adobe Acrobat 6 PDF For Dummies
  0-7645-3760-1
- Building a Web Site For Dummies
  0-7645-7144-3
- Dreamweaver MX 2004 For Dummies
  0-7645-4342-3
- FrontPage 2003 For Dummies
  0-7645-3882-9
- HTML 4 For Dummies
  0-7645-1995-6
- Illustrator CS For Dummies
  0-7645-4084-X

- Macromedia Flash MX 2004 For Dummies
  0-7645-4358-X
- Photoshop 7 All-in-One Desk
  Reference For Dummies
  0-7645-1667-1
- Photoshop CS Timesaving Techniques
  For Dummies
  0-7645-6782-9
- PHP 5 For Dummies
  0-7645-4166-8
- PowerPoint 2003 For Dummies
  0-7645-3908-6
- QuarkXPress 6 For Dummies
  0-7645-2593-X

NETWORKING, SECURITY, PROGRAMMING & DATABASES

0-7645-6852-3

0-7645-5784-X

Also available:
- A+ Certification For Dummies
  0-7645-4187-0
- Access 2003 All-in-One Desk
  Reference For Dummies
  0-7645-3988-4
- Beginning Programming For Dummies
  0-7645-4997-9
- C For Dummies
  0-7645-7068-4
- Firewalls For Dummies
  0-7645-4048-3
- Home Networking For Dummies
  0-7645-42796

- Network Security For Dummies
  0-7645-1679-5
- Networking For Dummies
  0-7645-1677-9
- TCP/IP For Dummies
  0-7645-1760-0
- VBA For Dummies
  0-7645-3989-2
- Wireless All In-One Desk Reference
  For Dummies
  0-7645-7496-5
- Wireless Home Networking For Dummies
  0-7645-3910-8

Diabetes
FOR DUMMIES

0-7645-6820-5 *†

Low-Carb Dieting
FOR DUMMIES

0-7645-2566-2

Also available:

Alzheimer's For Dummies
0-7645-3899-3
Asthma For Dummies
0-7645-4233-8
Controlling Cholesterol For Dummies
0-7645-5440-9
Depression For Dummies
0-7645-3900-0
Dieting For Dummies
0-7645-4149-8
Fertility For Dummies
0-7645-2549-2

Fibromyalgia For Dummies
0-7645-5441-7
Improving Your Memory For Dummies
0-7645-5435-2
Pregnancy For Dummies †
0-7645-4483-7
Quitting Smoking For Dummies
0-7645-2629-4
Relationships For Dummies
0-7645-5384-4
Thyroid For Dummies
0-7645-5385-2

Spanish
FOR DUMMIES

0-7645-5194-9

The Origins of Tolkien's
Middle-earth
FOR DUMMIES

0-7645-4186-2

Also available:

Algebra For Dummies
0-7645-5325-9
British History For Dummies
0-7645-7021-8
Calculus For Dummies
0-7645-2498-4
English Grammar For Dummies
0-7645-5322-4
Forensics For Dummies
0-7645-5580-4
The GMAT For Dummies
0-7645-5251-1
Inglés Para Dummies
0-7645-5427-1

Italian For Dummies
0-7645-5196-5
Latin For Dummies
0-7645-5431-X
Lewis & Clark For Dummies
0-7645-2545-X
Research Papers For Dummies
0-7645-5426-3
The SAT I For Dummies
0-7645-7193-1
Science Fair Projects For Dummies
0-7645-5460-3
U.S. History For Dummies
0-7645-5249-X

Get smart @ dummies.com®

- **Find a full list of Dummies titles**
- **Look into loads of FREE on-site articles**
- **Sign up for FREE eTips e-mailed to you weekly**
- **See what other products carry the Dummies name**
- **Shop directly from the Dummies bookstore**
- **Enter to win new prizes every month!**

Separate Canadian edition also available
Separate U.K. edition also available

Available wherever books are sold. For more information or to order direct: U.S. customers visit www.dummies.com or call 1-877-762-2974.
K. customers visit www.wileyeurope.com or call 0800 243407. Canadian customers visit www.wiley.ca or call 1-800-567-4797.

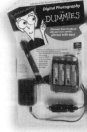

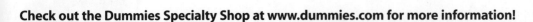